THE
BREAD OF LIFE
CATHOLIC
BIBLE STUDY

Cycle C

THE
BREAD OF LIFE
CATHOLIC
BIBLE STUDY

Cycle C

DEACON KEN AND MARIE FINN

Queenship

QUEENSHIP PUBLISHING COMPANY
P.O. Box 42028
Santa Barbara, CA 93140-2028
Phone: (800) 647-9882 FAX: (805) 569-3274

I have concluded that the materials presented in
this work are free of doctrinal or moral errors.

Bernadeane Carr, STL
Censor Librorum
7 July 1992

In accord with 1983 CIC 827 § 3, permission to
publish this work is hereby granted.

+ Robert E. Brom
Bishop of San Diego
15 July 1992

Published by:
    Queenship Publishing
    P.O. Box 42028
    Santa Barbara, CA 93140-2028
    Phone: (800) 647-9882 FAX: (805) 569-3274

Library of Congress No: 94-66593

ISBN 0-882972-32-5 (Volume C)

ACKNOWLEDGMENTS

Our special thanks to all those who have helped Marie and me in the writing of this bible study.

To the many translators, Josefina, Rosa, Javier, MaryLou, Stella, Carmen, Luis & Magdelina, Maria, Larry & Myrna, Frances, we say thank you. To all the Word Processor operators, Jean, Grace, Debbie, Nicole, Paul, Jerry, Deacon Tom, Bob, Joe, Steve, we say thank you. To Marianne and Paul, for their work on the cover, we say thank you. To all those who helped with the mailing, Ray & MaryJane, Marlene, Bob & Rosemary, Rick & Leonore, Greg & Laura, Eunice, Eloise, Marlene, Glen, Geri, Julie, and the students from St. Mary's and St. Timothy's, we say thank you. To all the proofreaders, Nap, Alice, Marlene, Ernie, Roberto, Martha, Diane, Geraldine, Cathy, Helen, Larry, Phyllis, the women of St. Mary's and St. Timothy's Bible Study, we say thank you. To all the board members and advisors of St. Dismas Guild, Bob, Greg, Carol, Terry, Fred, Ed, we say thank you. To our Pastors, Fr. Fred & Fr. Ramon, we say thank you. To our children and their spouses, Mom, sisters & brothers, we say thank you for all your love and support. To all those we have not named that have donated or contributed, time, talent, or treasure, we say thank you. To the Holy Spirit for using all of us to bring His Holy Word to the many who are longing to know Our Heavenly Father and His Son Jesus, and have fellowship with Him, we say thank you.

Dedicated to the memory of

Grace Dinger

Whose death from cancer took place during the final days of writing this book. Grace's life was a total commitment to the word of God.

"THERE ARE DIFFERENT GIFTS BUT THE SAME SPIRIT; THERE ARE DIFFERENT MINISTRIES BUT THE SAME LORD; THERE ARE DIFFERENT WORKS BUT THE SAME GOD WHO ACCOMPLISHES ALL OF THEM IN EVERYONE." 1 CORINTHIANS 12:4-6

INTRODUCTION

In this work are excerpts from the documents of Vatican II, one of which is a Decree on the Apostolate of Lay People. That document was written by some 2500 bishops in 1965. The council of bishops have challenged the Christian laity by encouraging them in their role of becoming disciples of Jesus Christ.

The church was founded to spread the Kingdom of Christ over all the earth for the glory of God the Father to make men partakers in redemption and salvation, and through them to establish the rich relationship of the entire world to Christ.

Christ sent by the Father, is the source of the Church's whole apostolate; "Whoever dwells in me and I in him bears much fruit, for separated from me you can do nothing (John 15:5)". Only the light of faith and the meditation on the Word of God can enable us to find everywhere and always the God "In whom we live and exist" (Acts 17:28). The Church's mission is concerned with the salvation of men; and men win salvation through the grace of Christ and faith in him. The apostolate of the Church therefore, and of each of its members, aims primarily at announcing to the world by word and action the message of Christ and communicating to it the grace of Christ. The principal means of bringing this about is the ministry of the Word and of the sacraments.

There is a famine today that is raging across this great land of ours. There is a deep hunger and thirst for the healing Word of the lord Jesus Christ. Many people in our society are looking for false gods to heal their wounded lives. Many of our people are looking for status, power, success, wealth, good jobs, and they look to their peers for recognition and approval. When this fails many try to find the solution in drugs, alcohol, sex, money, good works, philosophies, morality, even political systems. None have worked, nor will they ever work. Our society can not live together in love and peace until there is a spiritual change which only God's Word can produce.

Today much of mankind is still reluctant to admit that the only way that man can get back to God is through his son Jesus Christ. All of the many varied hurting experiences of the people in the world can only be changed when we begin to acknowledge that the world itself cannot satisfy our deeply personal needs. We need to come to the realization that man indeed does live by everything that proceeds out of the mouth of God (Deuteronomy 8:3).

Jesus has come into our world to end the famine that ravages the human heart. Therefore with humility, boldness, and energy, we must personally hear the Word, pray the Word, study the Word, proclaim the Word, and live the Word of the Lord Jesus Christ.

Guidelines for those leading
the Bread of Life Catholic Bible Study.

The opening prayer may be spontaneous or planned. Include John 14:26, which is, "The Paraclete, the Holy Spirit whom the Father will send in my name, will instruct you in everything, and remind you of all that I told you."

Reread the application from the previous week. Ask each person in turn how they fulfilled the application. Begin by sharing your own application.

Write answers to the application and the questions, including the personal questions. Keep the answers brief. If answers are not written down, pass to the next person.

Answers written in the quiet of our own home give the Holy Spirit an opportunity to speak to us directly and reveal His truths to us. We are more open to hearing and responding to the Holy Spirit. We build community when we share in the group what He has revealed to us.

First Day – Read the two questions and answer them yourself. Then have each person (only those who have written down their answers) respond to the questions.

Second Day – Read the first reading, have each person answer a question. Read the commentary for that day. (You could have those comfortable at reading take a paragraph at a time.) Note: The personal questions should be written down.

Third and Fourth Day – Same as above

Fifth Day – Read the psalm and ask the two questions (giving your answer). Have those who have written down their answers share.

Read the application, then remind everyone to do the lesson for the following week.

The closing prayer can be spontaneous or planned. Follow the lead of the Holy Spirit.

Schedule

BEFORE YOU BEGIN

Before you begin reading and studying God's Holy Word, always pray and ask God to speak to you through his Holy Spirit.

God's Word tells us "The Paraclete, the Holy Spirit whom the Father will send in my name, will instruct you in everything and remind you of all that I told you." (John 14:26)

It is imperative that you both understand and believe that scripture. The Holy Spirit is your teacher. There is one teacher, one Father, one God. For you to grow and become more like Jesus every day of your life.... you must be in submission to his teaching. His teaching can come to you in different ways.

1. By a revelation directly to you from God. In your quiet time alone with God in prayer many times God will speak to you. Sometimes we don't hear him because we are so busy talking and asking him for things. "Be still and know that I am God".

2. Through the Scriptures. God speaks to us and shows us how to live our lives according to his plan in his Holy Word.

3. Through the Church. (Church meaning the people of God) Every time the priest, deacon, or readers proclaim the Word of God there is a message for you personally.

As you take time each day to do this study in preparation for the celebration of Mass on Sunday the Lord is able to teach you and help you in dealing with your everyday relationships with the people you come in contact with. The key to this study is in training you to listen to what God is saying to you. When the priest or deacon give their homily at Mass and you listen carefully to what God is saying to you as he speaks through them, you will each day become more alert to his teaching through others. As you obey and follow his way in your life you will find a transformation taking place within you and you will find the joy and peace of knowing your God by loving others.

Our prayer for you is that you come to know the loving, just God that we have come to know through his Word and find the joy and peace that is yours in him.

In Jesus' name,

Deacon Ken & Marie

Deacon Ken & Marie Finn

FIRST SUNDAY IN ADVENT - CYCLE C

BEFORE YOU BEGIN:

Pray and ask God to speak to you through His Holy Spirit. "THE PARACLETE, THE HOLY SPIRIT WHOM THE FATHER WILL SEND IN MY NAME, WILL INSTRUCT YOU IN EVERYTHING, AND REMIND YOU OF ALL THAT I TOLD YOU." (JOHN 14:26)

FIRST DAY   **Reread last week's readings.**

1. What was a helpful or new thought from the readings or from the homily you heard on Sunday?

2. From what you learned, what personal application did you choose to apply to your life this week?

SECOND DAY   **READ JEREMIAH 33:14-16**   **FIRST READING**

("The Lord our Justice.")

1. What does the Lord say is coming? Jeremiah 33:14

2. What promise has the Lord made, and how can we benefit from His promise? Deuteronomy 28:7-9

3. What will the Lord raise up for David, and what will he do? Jeremiah 33:15

4. As king, what will this righteous shoot do? Jeremiah 23:5-6

5. What did King Solomon, son and successor to King David, ask from the Lord, and what did he grant him? 1 Kings 3:9-12

6. Who was the righteous shoot of David for whom the Magi were looking, and what was the inscription over Jesus' head while he hung on the cross? Matthew 2:2 and 27:37

7. In those days, who will be safe and dwell secure? Jeremiah 33:16

8. What will the city be named? Jeremiah 33:16

9. How have we been made right with God or justified with God? Romans 3:21-26

10. How did David, Samuel and the prophets conquer kingdoms? Hebrews 11:33

Personal - In what way has God fulfilled his promise to you personally? Where do you find your security?

THIRD DAY	READ 1 THESSALONIANS 3:12-4:2	SECOND READING

("...may the Lord make you increase and
abound in love for one another.")

1. In what are you to abound and increase, and for whom? 1 Thessalonians 3:12

2. What will loving one another do to your heart? 1 Thess. 3:13

3. Why do you thank God always for one another? 2 Thessalonians 1:3

4. How will you become before God at the coming of our Lord Jesus Christ? 1 Thessalonians 3:13

5. Whom does Paul ask to make the brothers holy and blameless? 1 Thessalonians 5:23

6. How is Paul asking the brothers to conduct themselves? 1 Thessalonians 4:1

7. What were they to do with a brother who acted in a disorderly way, and how did Paul act? 2 Thess.3:6-7

8. What was given to the brothers, and who was it through? 1 Thessalonians 4:2

9. Who is able to instruct and admonish one another? Romans 15:14

10. What happens to a wise and just man who is instructed? Proverbs 9:9

Personal – How has your love increased for your spouse, children, friends, and neighbors during the past month? In what way do you see a difference in the way you love now compared to last year?

FOURTH DAY	READ LUKE 21:25-28, 34-36	GOSPEL

("Be vigilant at all times and pray that you have the
strength to escape the tribulations that are imminent.")

1. Where will there be signs, and why will nations be perplexed? Luke 21:25

2. What will happen to the sun, moon, stars and powers of the heavens? Matthew 24:29

3. What will happen to people in anticipation of what is to come upon the world? Luke 21:26

4. Who are you to fear? Luke 12:5

5. Who will people see coming on a cloud with power and great glory? Luke 21:27

6. When these signs begin to happen, how should you stand? Why should you stand

this way? Luke 21:28

7.   What will happen to God's chosen ones? Luke 18:7-8

Personal - If the heavens shook today, would you die of fear or would you stand erect looking up to see him coming on the cloud?

8.   Of what should you be wary, and what will happen to everyone who lives on the earth? Luke 21:34-35

9.   What are you to be at all times, and for what are you to pray? Luke 21:36

10.   What did Jesus tell his disciples while he was in the Garden of Gethsemane? Matthew 26:41

Personal - What have you been doing in anticipation of his coming again? Share this scripture with a family member or a friend.

FIFTH DAY   **READ PSALM 25:4-5,8-10, 14**

("He guides the humble to justice,")

Read and meditate on Psalm 25:4-5,8-10, 14.

What is the Lord saying to you personally through the Psalm?

How can you apply this to your life?

SIXTH DAY   **READ ALL OF THE COMMENTARY**

JEREMIAH 33:14-16

This passage tells about God's plan to restore Jerusalem, not because the people cried, but because it was part of his ultimate plan. The disaster brought to the Jews by the Babylonians did not change God's purpose for his people. Although Jerusalem would be destroyed, it would eventually be restored, because God's justice is always tempered by his mercy. The emphasis is on the promise of a worldwide reign on earth by a Messiah. The immediate historical context is not what this reading is about. It is about God's control of history; he can act anytime he chooses. We must never forget that God will act in his time (Hebrews 12:26, 27).

Today's reading refers to both the first and second comings of Christ. When this long-awaited Messiah would come, he would set up his reign in the hearts of the believers. At his second coming he will execute justice and righteousness throughout the whole earth. What a tremendous prophecy this was for the people. They knew that no matter what horror was done to them their Messiah was coming to bring them freedom. Today, all over the world, there is tyranny, oppression, hunger and violence. In the deepest darkness of all of this pain is the "Good News." The Good News is a message of hope. It is the light of the world that has pierced and defeated the darkness of death. Today, our world is caught up in its own self-prophecy and refuses by its action to say, "The Lord is our righteousness."

The promise of eternal life and joy is far more meaningful for us because the Messiah has come and his name is Jesus Christ, Our Lord and Savior. He is the Good News.

1 THESSALONIANS 3:12-4:2

In today's passage we are treated to a special glimpse of the apostle Paul's mind, because for him everything was of God. He prays to God to show him the way to Thessalonica. He turns to God for guidance in the ordinary day-to-day problems.

One of the great and incredibly common mistakes of life is to turn to God only in the over-powering emergencies and shattering crises. How many times have you or someone you know called on Christ in an emergency? Like a good fireman, he comes and puts out the fire. You say a few, quick "thank yous" and send him back to his fire station to await yet another call from you.

Paul is talking about prayer being an active type of relationship. When two people are in love, they want to share all their successes as well as all their sorrows. Christ becomes the person with whom we share our minds, hearts and souls; and we do this in prayer. Prayer is two people in love telling each other how much they love each other. This love that we have for Jesus will overflow to others. This is how people judge us, not by what we say, but by how much we love others. Being polite and courteous is not enough, we need to show our love to others, especially the unlovable.

Our love should be continually growing, and if it seems your love for others has remained unchanged for some time, get on your knees and ask him to fill you with his Holy Spirit (Ephesians 5:18), and then you will be able to love even the unlovable. This passage ends with a call to please God with our daily living. The standards of the world want to entice us and kill us. The standard of God wants to free us, to save us, to love us, and to let us become capable of loving others. Which standard will we choose?

LUKE 21:25-28, 34-36

We are confronted with a very piercing question in today's Gospel. If the heavens shook and opened up, would we die of fear or would we stand erect, looking up to see him coming on the clouds? To the believer, this calls for some serious thought; to the unbeliever, this is foolishness to even talk about the subject. Jesus told his disciples to be on guard and pray. The picture of the coming persecutions and natural disasters is gloomy, but ultimately they are cause not for worry, but for great joy. He knew that when believers see these events happening, they will know that the return of their Messiah is near. They can look forward to his reign of justice and peace.

Today we are experiencing natural disasters like earthquakes, forest fires, famine, and drought. Rather than being terrified by what is happening in our world, we should be confident and prayerful awaiting Christ's return. Jesus told his disciples to keep a constant watch for his return. Are you keeping a faithful watch with the lifestyle you are living? The followers of Jesus Christ live in anticipation of his return, and they are very much on guard against the temptation of the world.

Although nearly two thousand years have passed since he spoke these words, their truth remains: He is coming again, and we need to watch and be ready. This means working faithfully at the tasks God has given us, and not wishing we were someone else. If you were the only person in the world, Christ would have gone on that cross anyway, simply because he loves us enough to die for us, so that we can be with him when he comes back again.

Application

The first reading tells us that the light is coming to destroy the darkness. In the second reading we see that prayer is alive and active because it is a dialogue between two people. The Gospel calls us to be on guard and to pray about everything.

This week, show your family, school or work associates what you are doing in anticipation of Jesus' return. Your actions can be shown in taking time alone in prayer with the Lord, by reading scripture with your family, by doing bible study on your lunch hour and by loving others even when you do not feel loving. Remember, love is not a feeling; love is a decision. Get active in prayer, reading God's Holy Word, in God's church and fellowship with the believing community.

SECOND SUNDAY IN ADVENT - CYCLE C

BEFORE YOU BEGIN:

Pray and ask God to speak to you through His Holy Spirit. "THE PARACLETE, THE HOLY SPIRIT WHOM THE FATHER WILL SEND IN MY NAME, WILL INSTRUCT YOU IN EVERYTHING, AND REMIND YOU OF ALL THAT I TOLD YOU." (JOHN 14:26)

FIRST DAY   **Reread last week's readings.**

1. What was a helpful or new thought from the readings or from the homily you heard on Sunday?

2. From what you learned, what personal application did you choose to apply to your life this week?

SECOND DAY   **READ BARUCH 5:1-9**   **FIRST READING**

("For God will show all the earth your splendor.")

1. What is Jerusalem to take off, and what is it to put on? Baruch 5:1

2. What shall no longer enter Jerusalem? Isaiah 52:1

3. In what shall Jerusalem be wrapped, what shall it have on its head, and what does that display? Baruch 5:2

4. What was engraved on a seal that was tied over the miter? Exodus 39:30-31

5. Why do we rejoice heartily in the Lord? Isaiah 61:10

6. What will God show all the earth, and what will we be named by God forever? Baruch 5:3-4

7. Who will Jerusalem see to the east, how were they gathered together from the east and the west, and about what will they rejoice? Baruch 5:5

8. Who led your children away, and who will bring them back? Baruch 5:6

9. What has God commanded so that Israel may advance secure in the glory of God? Baruch 5:7

10. What has happened to Israel at God's command, and how is He leading Israel? Baruch 5:8-9

Personal – What are the enemies that have led the children away in this day? How do you see God bringing them back? How has this affected your family?

5

| THIRD DAY | READ PHILIPPIANS 1:4-6, 8-11 | SECOND READING |

("...how I long for all of you
with the affection of Christ Jesus.")

1. How are Paul and Timothy praying for the Philippians, and for what reason? Philippians 1:4-5

2. What did the Philippians do at the beginning of the Gospel when Paul left Macedonia? Philippians 4:15

3. About what are they confident? Philippians 1:6

4. Who is Paul's witness, and how does he long for the brothers? Philippians 1:8

Personal – Who do you long for with the affection of Christ?

5. What is Paul's prayer for the people of Philippi? Philippians 1:9

6. What do you become filled with through all spiritual wisdom and understanding? Colossians 1:9

7. What must you discern so that you may be pure and blameless for the day of Christ? Philippians 1:10

8. From what are you instructed in order to know his will, and what is important? Romans 2:18

9. What are you filled with that comes through Jesus Christ, and for what reason? Philippians 1:11

10. How is the Father glorified? John 15:8

Personal – Give specific examples of how you have glorified the Father.

| FOURTH DAY | READ LUKE 3:1-6 GOSPEL |

("...proclaiming a baptism of repentance
for the forgiveness of sins.")

1. During whose reign and who was the governor when the Word of God came to John? Luke 3:1-2

2. Whose son was John, and where did the Word of God come to him? Luke 3:2

3. What did John do throughout the whole region of the Jordan? Luke 3:3; see also Matthew 3:1-2 and Mark 1:4

4.   What is evidence of repentance? Luke 3:8

5.   What leads us to repentance? Romans 2:4

6.   What does godly sorrow produce, and what does worldly sorrow produce? 2 Corinthians 7:10

7.   What is a voice crying out in the desert? Luke 3:4

8.   What will happen to the valleys, mountains, roads and rough ways? Luke 3:5

9.   What will happen to all flesh? Luke 3:6

10. What has the Lord made known in fulfillment of what was written by the prophecy of Isaiah, and what has he revealed to the nations? Psalm 98:2

Personal – How has the Lord revealed to you personally that you have been saved from your sins? How have you come into godly sorrow or repentance for your sins?

FIFTH DAY   **READ PSALM 126:1-6**

("The Lord has done great things for us.")

Read and meditate on Psalm 126:1-6.

What is the Lord saying to you personally through the Psalm?

How can you apply this to your life?

SIXTH DAY   **READ ALL OF THE COMMENTARY**

BARUCH 5:1-9

Baruch was the well known secretary of Jeremiah, and in today's reading he tells how God will lead a "new exodus" at the end of time, from east to west, to the ideal city of Jerusalem. He is telling the people who have been through exile, captivity, and total destruction that salvation is God's gift and God's holy work. He goes on to encourage them to accept this gift because if they do not they will become spiritual refugees.

Accepting the gift of salvation from God involves a conversion that turns all men toward their homeland. Today's message is a message of consolation and hope. It is a call to come out of mourning and to trust in the Lord. It is a call to put on the cloak of justice and walk in the glory of the eternal name. It is a call to rise from the dirt and to shake yourself clean.

The people were being encouraged to stand on the heights or the shoulders of those who went before them into exile and keep their faith alive by staying very close to God's Holy Word. They knew that no matter how difficult the times would get, their God would never forget them or abandon them.

God is leading all of his people who are being oppressed. The people in today's reading knew that, and in today's world that same God makes the same promise to his children of today. Jesus Christ is the light that has broken the darkness, and we follow him in his justice and mercy and finally in his glory.

PHILIPPIANS 1:4-6, 8-11

This reading clearly emphasizes that, for the Christian, evangelism is not a duty, it is a joy. This letter to the Philippians has been called an epistle of joy. It is with joy that Paul prays for his friends. The joy of Christian prayer is bringing those we love to the mercy seat of God. There is the joy that Jesus is preached in all parts of the world today. If Christianity does not make a man happy, then it will not make him anything at all. There is the joy of suffering for Christ in that it is a chance to demonstrate our trust in him and know that in our weakness is his strength. There is the joy of Christian hospitality. It is a great thing to have a door (your heart) from which the stranger and the one in trouble know that they will never be turned away.

Paul is seeing the life of every Christian as a sacrifice ready to be offered to Jesus Christ. We are called to make our bodies a living sacrifice acceptable to God (Romans 12:1). The task of the Christian then is to make his life fit to offer to Jesus Christ. Only the power of the Holy Spirit can empower us to do that. Paul tells us that we are also partners in grace. We are to share our common debt to God for always bestowing on us his healing, saving grace.

It was Paul's prayer for his people that their love would grow and grow. To love is to know and to know is to learn. When we learn, we discover truth and truth is Jesus Christ, yesterday, today and forever.

LUKE 3:1-6

Today's Gospel sees it fitting to announce that in the loneliness of a terrible desert, the "Good News" of salvation was available for all those who repent. We see that Pilate, Herod and Caiphas were the most powerful leaders in Palestine. But they were upstaged by a desert prophet from Judea. God chose to speak through this loner, John the Baptist, who has gone down in history as greater than any of the rulers of his day.

Even today we often judge by our culture's standards, - power, beauty, wealth, education - as in John's time, and miss the really special people through whom God works. Greatness is not measured by what we have, but by what we do for God. We can be like John the Baptist and give ourself entirely to God so his power can work through us. Mother Teresa has a saying that is very appropriate to our world today, "Unless life is lived for others, it is not worthwhile."

John the Baptist's whole life was lived to tell others that the time to repent has come to all. We must realize that repentance has two sides - turning away from sin and turning to God. Repentance does not mean "I am sorry;" it means "change." To be forgiven we must repent. We just can not say we believe and then live any way we want to live, nor can we simply live a good moral life without reference to Christ. Forgiveness from sin is the message of repentance. Determine to rid your life of any sins God points out to you, and put your trust in him. You will be living for others because knowing you are saved makes your life worthwhile.

Application

The first reading shows that those who refuse God's gift of salvation become spiritual refugees. The second reading reveals joy as the infallible sign of the presence of God. The Gospel reveals that God calls on ordinary people to do extraordinary things.

This week, show your family that Advent is a time of changing, watching and preparation. Let the message of John the Baptist touch your heart and "Repent of your sins." Right now, ask the Holy Spirit to reveal to you what needs to change in you. Write down what it is, and if it is several areas, take one at a time. Share your journey with a non-judgmental person. You are that ordinary person whom God has chosen to do extraordinary things. Pray, thank, and accept from God the miracle that is going to take place in your life this Advent season.

THIRD SUNDAY IN ADVENT - CYCLE C

BEFORE YOU BEGIN:

Pray and ask God to speak to you through His Holy Spirit. "THE PARACLETE, THE HOLY SPIRIT WHOM THE FATHER WILL SEND IN MY NAME, WILL INSTRUCT YOU IN EVERYTHING, AND REMIND YOU OF ALL THAT I TOLD YOU." (JOHN 14:26)

FIRST DAY   **Reread last week's readings.**

1. What was a helpful or new thought from the readings or from the homily you heard on Sunday?

2. From what you learned, what personal application did you choose to apply to your life this week?

SECOND DAY   **READ ZEPHANIAH 3:14-18**   **FIRST READING**

("He will rejoice over you with gladness.")

1. What are we to do with all of our heart? Zephaniah 3:14

2. Why is Israel to rejoice and shout for joy? Zechariah 9:9

3. What has the Lord removed, and of what is there no further need? Zephaniah 3:15

4. On the day of the Lord what shall be said? Zephaniah 3:16

5. What did Jesus say to his disciples? Matthew 14:27

6. What does perfect love do? 1 John 4:18

7. What is the Lord, our God, called? What will he do to you, and what will he do because of you? Zephaniah 3:17

8. What will people no longer call you, and what does the Lord call you? Isaiah 62:4-5

9. What will the Lord remove from among you? Zephaniah 3:18

Personal - How have you been renewed in God's love? How does the joy show in you since the personal realization that Jesus has come into your heart? Give examples, as in Psalm 12.

THIRD DAY	READ PHILIPPIANS 4:4-7	SECOND READING

("Rejoice in the Lord always,
I shall say it again: rejoice!")

1. What are we to do always? Philippians 4:4

2. Why do we rejoice in the Lord? Psalm 85:7

3. What should be made known to all, and who is near? Philippians 4:5

4. What is love? 1 Corinthians 13:4-7

5. What was God, our Savior, to us when he appeared, and what did his mercy do for us? Titus 3:4-6

6. Kindness is a fruit of whom? Galatians 5:22

7. What are we not to have, and what are we to do in everything? Philippians 4:6

8. What does anxiety do to us, and what does a kindly word do? Proverbs 12:25

9. What will guard our hearts and minds in Christ? Philippians 4:7

10. What did Jesus say he was leaving his followers? (Note: This is also a fruit of the Holy Spirit, Galatians 5:22) John 14:25-27

Personal - What acts of kindness have you shown towards your spouse, children, parents, friends, co-workers, and neighbors?

FOURTH DAY	READ LUKE 3:10-18	GOSPEL

("He will baptize you in the Holy Spirit and in fire.")

1. To whom were the crowds talking, and what did they ask him? Luke 3:10, also see Luke 3:2

2. What was John's reply to the crowd, who else came to him, and for what reason? Luke 3:11-12

3. What did John tell the tax collectors? Luke 3:13

4. What did Jesus tell his disciples his Father was pleased to give them, what should they do, and what did he say about the heart? Luke 12:32-34

5. What did the soldiers ask John, and what three things did he tell them to do? Luke 3:14

6. What were the people beginning to think about John? Luke 3:15

7. What did John say to the priests and Levites when they asked him who he was? John 1:19-20, 23

8. When John answered the people, with what did he say he was baptizing them? Who did he say was coming, and of what was John not even worthy? Luke 3:16

9. With what did John say the "one who was coming" was going to baptize them? What did he say about the winnowing fan? Luke 3:16-17

10. What does the Holy Spirit give us? Acts 1:8

11. What did John preach to the people? Luke 3:18

Personal – In what way have you shared your clothing and food with someone who has none? Examine your conscience: Do I have excessive clothing cluttering my closet? Do I spend a lot of money on food? Have I extorted anyone? Have I accused anyone falsely? Have I been dissatisfied with my wages?
Seek the Sacrament of Reconciliation this week.

FIFTH DAY   **READ ISAIAH 12:2-6**

("God indeed is my savior; I am confident and unafraid.")

Read and meditate on Isaiah 12:2-6.

What is the Lord saying to you personally through this reading?

How can you apply this to your life?

SIXTH DAY   **READ ALL OF THE COMMENTARY**

ZEPHANIAH 3:14-18

In this reading the church joyfully anticipates the Messiah's coming through the words of the prophet Zephaniah. The prophet's exuberant message anticipates a revelation that cannot be contained: The Lord is in our midst and his presence gives us joy. Zephaniah points out that great gladness results when we allow God to be with us. We sin when we try to find happiness in ways that bring a cutting off of ourselves from fellowship with God, the only person who can make us truly joyful.

There is an old saying that joy is the infallible sign of the presence of God. One can be very hot and thirsty and be very happy to receive a cold glass of water. The person may be in complete turmoil, but for a few moments he is happy. Because joy is the presence of the Lord, a person may have his own personal life under attack through sickness, accident, death of a loved one, or even a divorce, and still be joyful and at peace.

To experience God in our midst goes far beyond any technical explanation. We are told that the Holy Spirit is upon us; he has appointed us to preach Good News to the poor; He has sent us to heal the broken hearted. This joy of knowing that he is in our midst, knowing that his Spirit is upon us comes when we faithfully follow him and obey his Word. This is the anticipation of joy that Zephaniah tells his people about and it applies, especially today, to you, wherever you are. If you want to be joyful, draw close to the source of joy by obeying God. Then listen as God rejoices over you in song.

PHILIPPIANS 4:4-7

How powerful and yet how wonderfully strange that a man in prison would be telling a church to be joyful. But Paul's attitude teaches us a very important lesson: Our inner attitudes do not have to reflect our outward circumstances. Paul is saying that we may not be able to control the circumstances, but we always can control our response to those circumstances.

Paul takes up the joyful anthem; the Lord himself is near, dismiss all anxiety from your minds. Paul was full of joy because he knew that no matter what happened to him, the Holy Spirit was within him and he had nothing to fear (1 John 4:4). Paul is urging the Philippians to be joyful, and he is speaking to you; maybe you need to hear this.

It is easy to get discouraged about unpleasant circumstances or to take unimportant events too seriously. If we have not experienced joy lately, we may not be looking at life from the right point of view. Never having to worry about anything is not an escape from responsibility. We all have worries in work, in our homes, schools and with our families.

Do you want to worry less? Paul is saying that we need to turn our worries into prayers. Then pray much more. Whenever you start to worry, stop and pray. The peace that you receive is God's peace, and his peace is different from the world's peace (John 14:27). This peace is not in positive thinking, in absence of conflict, or in good feelings. This is a real peace, and it comes from knowing that God is in control of our life. This means our destiny is set, our victory over sin is certain, and this is a peace that surpasses all understanding.

LUKE 3:10-18

The message of John the Baptist broke upon the people like a giant clap of thunder. He did not tickle the people's ears. He was not cute or an entertainer. His message was not good news, it was news of terror. John had lived in the wilderness and sometimes fire would break out. The animals would come out of their nicks and crannies, scurrying in terror from the menacing flames. It was to them that John likened the people who came to be baptized. The Jews thought that God would judge other nations with one standard, and the Jews with another and that as sons of Abraham they were exempt. John told them that racial privilege meant nothing, that life, not lineage, was God's standard of judgment.

John's message took root in unexpected places, among the poor, the criminals, and the soldiers. They were painfully aware of their needs. Many people then, as well as today, failed to see that respectability is not always connected with right living. John states that respectability can hinder right living if it keeps us from seeing our need for God.

If you had to choose between them, would you protect your character even if it ruined your reputation? John warns of impending judgment by comparing those who refuse to work for God to chaff, the useless outer husk of the grain. In contrast, he compares those who repent and reform their lives to the nourishing grain itself. Those who refuse to believe in God will be discarded because they have no value in furthering God's work. Those who repent and believe hold great value in God's eyes because they are beginning a new life of service for him.

Application

The first reading tells us that the Lord is in our midst. The second reading reveals that peace is not worrying, but praying, about everything. The Gospel calls us to more than respectability; it calls us to right living.

This week, let your witness to right living have a strong measure of joy. Start with yourself and take a spiritual, emotional and physical inventory of yourself. Be honest, specific and joyful. Take any area of you that needs correcting and pray constantly every day for just that one area of brokenness.

You do not need to tell yourself how bad you are; you need to tell yourself how blessed you are to have someone forgive and love you. Jesus loves you so much he died for you. So look at an area of yourself that you can change this week. Share this change with a loved one, a friend, or maybe a clergyman.

FOURTH SUNDAY IN ADVENT - CYCLE C

BEFORE YOU BEGIN:

Pray and ask God to speak to you through His Holy Spirit. "THE PARACLETE, THE HOLY SPIRIT WHOM THE FATHER WILL SEND IN MY NAME, WILL INSTRUCT YOU IN EVERYTHING, AND REMIND YOU OF ALL THAT I TOLD YOU." (JOHN 14:26)

FIRST DAY   **Reread last week's readings.**

1.   What was a helpful or new thought from the readings or from the homily you heard on Sunday?

2.   From what you learned, what personal application did you choose to apply to your life this week?

SECOND DAY   **READ MICAH 5:1-4**   **FIRST READING**

*("He shall stand firm and shepherd his flock
by the strength of the Lord.")*

1.   What is too small to be among the clans of Judah? Who is to come forth from there, and where is his origin? Micah 5:1

2.   Who was a son of an Ephrathite named Jesse, and where was he from? 1 Samuel 17:12

3.   What will the Lord do until the time she is to give birth, and what shall happen to the rest of the brethren? Micah 5:2

4.   What does scripture say about the Messiah? John 7:42

5.   Where was Jesus born, and whom shall he shepherd? Matthew 2:1, 6

6.   How shall he stand and shepherd his flock, with Whose power or strength, and by Whose majestic name will he do it? Micah 5:3

7.   What will happen to his flock and for what reason? Micah 5:3

8.   What shall he be? Micah 5:4

9.   Because of the blood of Christ, what is he to us, and what did he break down? Ephesians 2:13-14

10. If Assyria invades their country, what will the people do? Micah 5:4-5

Personal - Who is ruler or has authority over you, and where do they get their strength? Over whom do you rule, and where do you get your strength?

THE BREAD OF LIFE CATHOLIC BIBLE STUDY

THIRD DAY **READ HEBREWS 10:5-10** **SECOND READING**

("Behold, I come to do your will, O God.")

1. What was not desired, and what was prepared on his coming into the world? Hebrews 10:5

2. What was sought not, and what was given? Psalm 40:7

3. In what did the Lord take no delight? Hebrews 10:6

4. What is written of Jesus in the scroll? Hebrews 10:7

5. What was the prayer of Jesus at the Mount of Olives? Luke 22:42

6. What was Jesus' food? John 4:34

7. With what are sacrifices and offerings in accord? Hebrews 10:8

8. What does Jesus say, and what has he done with the first to establish the second? Hebrews 10:9

9. What was the new Law he established over which he was sorrowful? Matthew 26:38-39

10. How have we been consecrated once and for all? Hebrews 10:10

11. From what does his death cleanse us? Hebrews 9:14

Personal - Whose "will" do you follow on a daily basis? How often does it occur to you to ask for his will to be done? How often do you die to yourself to do the will of the Father on a daily basis?

FOURTH DAY **READ LUKE 1:39-45** **GOSPEL**

("Blessed are you who believed that what was spoken to you by the Lord would be fulfilled.")

1. Who traveled to the hill country to a town of Judah? Whose house did she enter, and whom did she greet? Luke 1:39-40

2. What was Zechariah, where was his wife from, and what kind of people were they? Luke 1:5-6

3. What was Zechariah told by the angel, and what did the child in her womb do when Mary greeted her? Luke 1:13, 41

4. With what was Elizabeth filled? Luke 1:41

5. With what was John filled, even from his mother's womb? Luke 1:15

6.   To whom does the Father give the Holy Spirit? Luke 11:13

7.   What did Elizabeth cry out in a loud voice? Luke 1:42-44

8.   Who is the woman to be praised, and what will give her the praise?
     Proverbs 31:30-31

9.   What did Mary do to become blessed? Luke 1:45

10. Who did Jesus say is blessed? John 20:29

11. What confined all things under the power of sin, how was the promise given, and to
     whom was it given? Galatians 3:22

Personal - When were you filled with the Holy Spirit or became aware of his presence within you? Can those around you call you blessed, and if so, why? What effect has Mary's response had on your life?

FIFTH DAY   **READ PSALM 80:2-3, 15-16, 18-19**

("Rouse your power, and come to save us.")

Read and meditate on Psalm 80:2-3, 15-16, 18-19.

What is the Lord saying to you personally through the Psalm?

How can you apply this to your life?

SIXTH DAY   **READ ALL OF THE COMMENTARY**

MICAH 5:1-4

The prophet, Micah, assures a small, obscure town in Judea that it will be the birth place of the Messiah. Jerusalem's leaders were obsessed with wealth and position. Micah not only prophesied that Jerusalem with its wealth and power would be besieged and destroyed, but that its king could not save it. In startling contrast, Bethlehem, a tiny town, would be the birth place of the only king who could save all of his people. The Messiah would be born as a baby in Bethlehem (Luke 2:4-6) and eventually would reign as the eternal king. The king that was defeated was Zedekiah, and he was the last of the kings in David's line to sit on the throne in Jerusalem. Micah prophesied that the next king in David's line would be the Messiah, and his kingdom would never end. The Messiah, although eternal, entered human history as the man, Jesus of Nazareth.

Today's reading provides us with a very clear Old Testament prophecy of Christ's coming. Micah tells us that the Messiah will be our peace (5:4). Jesus tells us that he is leaving us with a gift, a gift of peace of mind and heart, and the gift is not fragile like the peace of the world (John 14:27). So do not be afraid, fear is useless. What is needed is trust (Mark 5:36). Christ's peace gives us assurance even though wars continue. We need to have no more fear of judgment, no more conflict and guilt. This is what the peace of Christ really means. You can dismiss anxiety, worry about nothing, pray about everything, and you will receive the peace (Phil. 4:6-7) of the "Messiah" which surpasses all understanding.

HEBREWS 10:5-10

Today's reading shows us that our link with God is not animal sacrifice. We are bound to God through a person and that person is Jesus Christ. We have in him a Savior, who shows us what our love must be like through his example. Animal blood could not take away sin; it could only take it out of sight until Jesus came to deal with it permanently.

The people in Old Testament times were forgiven of their sins, just as they are forgiven today, through God's grace which they accepted through faith. The costly sacrifice of a valued animal's life impressed upon the sinner the seriousness of his sin before God. Because Jesus shed his own blood for us, his sacrifice is far greater than an Old Testament offering. Christ came to offer for us his body upon the cross as a sacrifice completely acceptable to God.

Looking at the incredible gift that he has given us, we should be overwhelmed with a joyful desire to obey him. Today we see so many people trying to fill emptiness in their lives with drugs, alcohol, and immorality and becoming more empty. The only way one can become full and alive is to first become really clean and free. If your life is empty and confused, then fall on your knees and accept the incredible gift of forgiveness and salvation that was won for you through the death and resurrection of Jesus Christ. He tells us in verse 9 of today's reading that he has come to do the will of his Father, and that is, that we all be united with him through Jesus. He is the Way (John 14:6), and only he can set you free (John 8:32).

LUKE 1:39-45

The miracle of love is in its sense of expectancy. Love is far more than a feeling, it is a decision that says "Yes." Mary has just received the incredible news that she has been chosen to be the Mother of God. She tells the angel that she is the Lord's servant, and she will do whatever is in accordance with his Word. She then waits, with the knowledge and expectation that she will bear the fruit the prophets had predicted.

Mary was to be the Mother of the God of her fathers, and all would call her blessed. And yet, in her waiting, she attends to her surroundings. Her cousin, Elizabeth, who was much older, was also expecting a child. Mary goes out to attend to her, and in her love she gives a signal of the love she bears with her. Elizabeth recognizes Mary's desire to serve her, and in that service is the core of love called humility. Elizabeth tells Mary that blessed is her fruit, and Mary's child became the instrument of salvation for the whole world.

This time of Advent, a time of waiting for the new coming of Christ in our own lives, is a time for us to be like Mary. We can share Mary's blessing. Through us Christ can become real for others. Out there, right where you are, there is an Elizabeth who needs your visit. As you wait, like Mary waited, go out of yourself to others as she did. Who is your Elizabeth? Someone hungry, lonesome, angry or neglected? That person awaits your visit. You may not have to go any further than across the street, or just across the kitchen table. As we wait for the Christmas celebration, the promise of the prophets will once again be fulfilled. What will it bring you?

Application

The first reading shows that God chose ordinary things and ordinary people to produce extraordinary results. The second reading tells us that salvation is a person and his name is Jesus Christ. The Gospel reveals that waiting is a decision to serve while waiting.

This week, let the humility of Mary be your model. You might look at the times you have to wait during the week, such as in traffic, in cafeteria lines at work, or waiting to see a teacher in school. The example that you show by your actions can be very powerful. Mary was very humble even though she knew that what had happened to her was very special. Give your family and friends a tremendous gift this Christmas time. Give them the gift of your humility, and Christ will come alive through you, and you will be blessed.

HOLY FAMILY SUNDAY - CYCLE C

BEFORE YOU BEGIN:

Pray and ask God to speak to you through His Holy Spirit. "THE PARACLETE, THE HOLY SPIRIT WHOM THE FATHER WILL SEND IN MY NAME, WILL INSTRUCT YOU IN EVERYTHING, AND REMIND YOU OF ALL THAT I TOLD YOU." (JOHN 14:26)

FIRST DAY   **Reread last week's readings.**

1.   What was a helpful or new thought from the readings or from the homily you heard on Sunday?

2.   From what you learned, what personal application did you choose to apply to your life this week?

SECOND DAY   **READ SIRACH 3:2-6, 12-14**   **FIRST READING**

("He who honors his father atones for sins.")

1.   Where does the Lord place a father over his children, and what does he confirm over sons? Sirach 3:2

2.   What happens to one who honors his father? Sirach 3:3

3.   What do we store up when we revere our mother? Sirach 3:4

4.   By what is the man gladdened who honors his father, and what happens when he prays? Sirach 3:5

5.   What will happen to him who reveres his father? Sirach 3:6, Exodus 20:12

6.   What is he doing who brings comfort to his mother? Sir. 3:6

7.   What are we to do, and what are we not to do when our father gets old? Sirach 3:12

8.   To whom are we to listen, for what reason, and whom are we not to despise? Proverbs 23:22

9.   How are we to treat our father, even if his mind fails? Sirach 3:13

10.   What will not be forgotten, and as what will it serve? Sirach 3:14

Personal - In what ways do you listen to and honor both your earthly father and your heavenly Father? In what ways has your earthly father become a burden to you in his old age? Compare your relationship with your heavenly Father and your earthly father. Repent where it is necessary.

THIRD DAY   **READ COLOSSIANS 3:12-21 SECOND READING**

("You children, obey your parents in everything,
for this is pleasing to the Lord.")

1.   With what five things are we to clothe ourselves, and for what reason? Colossians 3:12-13

2.   What are these five qualities called, according to Galatians 5:22?

3.   What are we to do with one another, and what are we to do over any grievance we may have for another? Colossians 3:13

4.   Why are we to forgive? Colossians 3:13

5.   What did Jesus say as he was dying on the cross, and to whom was he speaking? Luke 23:34

6.   In the Lord's Prayer, what are we saying and what is the Father saying? Matthew 6:12-15

Personal – How have you sinned and received the forgiveness of God? In what way is that reflected by your forgiveness of others when they have hurt you?

7.   What virtue do we put on over all the rest? Colossians 3:14

8.   What must reign in our hearts, of what are we members, to what are we called, and to what must we dedicate ourselves? Colossians 3:15

9.   What must dwell in us, how are we to treat one another, and how are we to sing gratefully to God? Colossians 3:16

10. Whatever we do, in speech or action, in whose name are we to do it, and to whom are we to give thanks? Colossians 3:17

11. How are husbands to act toward their wives, and how are wives to act toward their husbands? Colossians 3:18-19

12. How are children to act toward their parents, and how are fathers to act toward their children? Colossians 3:20-21

Personal – What do you think causes the most break-ups in the family today? How do you think this can be remedied? In what ways are you obeying or disobeying what God says in Colossians 3:18-21. Reflect on this, and make changes where necessary. Remember, we receive grace from the sacrament of reconciliation.

FOURTH DAY   LUKE 2:41-52   GOSPEL

("Did you not know that I must be in my Father's house?")

1. Where did Mary and Joseph go each year, and what did they do when Jesus was 12 years old? Luke 2:41-42

2. When Mary and Joseph were returning home, what did they not know? Luke 2:43

3. Where did they think Jesus was, what did they do, and where did they go when they did not find him? Luke 2:44-45

4. What is not the will of your heavenly Father? Matthew 18:14

5. Where did they find Jesus, what was he doing, and what was the reaction of all who heard him? Luke 2:46-47

6. Who instructs us in everything? John 14:26

Personal - What have you learned the last time you sat and listened to your teacher?

7. What was the reaction of Jesus' parents when they saw him, and what did his mother say to him? Luke 2:48

8. What did Jesus say to his parents, and what was their understanding of it? Luke 2:49-50

9. What did Jesus do, what was he to his parents, and what did his mother do? Luke 2:51

10. Who are we to obey, and who does this please? Colossians 3:20

Personal - How have you advanced in wisdom and knowledge of God's will for you in your personal life?

FIFTH DAY   READ PSALM 128:1-5

("Happy are those who fear the Lord and walk in his ways.")

Read and meditate on Psalm 128:1-5.

What is the Lord saying to you personally through the Psalm?

How can you apply this to your life?

SIXTH DAY   **READ ALL OF THE COMMENTARY**

SIRACH 3:2-6, 12-14

Sirach was a pious and learned Jew who lived in the second century B.C. He wrote a collection of sayings to help others live their lives in accordance with God's Holy Word. In today's passage he speaks of family. He shows us that the family unit has been honored as the foundation of the human race.

The foundation of the family was traditionally the father and he had the place of honor. The father was given the right to be respected and obeyed by his family. We see the mother also shares the authority with the father in the home. The authority of both parents in accordance with God's Word is to be respected by the children.

This passage really applies very strongly to today's families because the family structure is under a severe attack by Satan. Children who respect their parents are not only doing God's will, but also are storing up spiritual rewards for themselves. Over the centuries it has been shown that children who respect their parents generally have children who will respect their parents.

We see that prayer is very important for a family's growth and that all prayer is answered. The call to love, honor, and respect your parents carries with it the reward of your children's care for you in your old age with love and respect, a long life thus becomes a sign of God's blessing for those who follow his commands.

Children are called to give their aging parents loving care. The child who has learned to respect his parents is respecting God. No matter how feeble, mentally or physically, one's parents may become, it is the children's responsibility to care for them. This is not some social health care program's slogan; this is in accordance with God's Holy Word. God wants love, kindness, respect, honor, sacrifice, comfort, safety, etc.

COLOSSIANS 3:12-21

Paul wrote this letter while imprisoned in Rome. He was told by a follower, named Epaphras, that recent converts to the Christian faith were being disturbed by false teachers. Paul's letter spells out some very practical rules for the Christians; to clothe themselves with compassion, kindness, lowliness, meekness and patience. Paul is telling them that these virtues must be secure in their hearts in order for the community to live out the Christian vision.

Forgiveness is one of the main virtues of a Christian. This is what separates us from the non-believers. God wiped out all our sins in Baptism and is constantly waiting to wash away the sins of a repentant sinner in the Sacrament of Reconciliation. We also must imitate God and be willing to forgive a repentant brother or sister. Paul again shows Christ as the head of the body and the source of unity, harmony and peace. We hear that it is not enough to know the doctrines of Christ, but we must live Christ's life, and our lives must be witnesses of good and bearing fruit.

Today, as then, we are called to help each member of the family of God. Paul deals with the family by telling the husband to "love your wife," and wives to be subject to the spiritual authority of the husband. Children are called to obey their parents. This may sound common today, but in Paul's time, wives had few rights and were often considered to be the property of the husband. Paul's call to "love your wife" brings her into equality and a full sharing in the authority of the family. Paul also tells fathers not to provoke their children. The authority of a father comes from God, and this authority is to lead, to love, and to serve his family. A loving father leads his children by serving them in the name of the Lord. A loving father puts on the mind of Christ (Philippians 2:2-5).

LUKE 2:41-52

According to God's law, every male was required to go to Jerusalem three times a year for the great festivals of Unleavened Bread, Weeks, and Shelters (Deut. 16:16). In the spring the Passover was celebrated, followed immediately by the week-long feast of Unleavened Bread. Jesus has just reached the age of adulthood, so he did not spend a lot of time with his parents during the festival. The people traveled in caravans to the city and it was common for the women and children to travel at the front. A twelve year old boy could have been in either group, and probably Mary and Joseph assumed Jesus was with the other.

The caravan, however, left Jerusalem without Jesus, who was absorbed in his discussion with the religious leaders. He would have been eager to listen and ask probing questions. It was not his youth, but the depth of his thoughts that amazed the teachers. Mary searched frantically, and when she finally found him, she knew she had to let go of her child and let him become a man.

For parents, it is both sweet and painful to see our children as adults. But when the time comes to step back and let go, we must do so in spite of the hurt. Then our children can take flight and soar to the heights God intended for them.

This was the first hint that Jesus realized he was God's Son. But even though he knew his real Father, he did not reject his earthly parents. God's people do not reject family relationships or family responsibilities. If Jesus Christ obeyed his parents, how much more we should honor our parents.

Application

The first reading emphasizes that the family unit has been honored as the foundation of the human race. The second reading shows false teachers are destructive to families and society. The Gospel reveals Jesus' responsibility of obedience to his parents.

Today, let your suffering be for the Lord and for someone else in your family. Maybe you can offer your pain for someone who is on drugs or alcohol. Pick a family member, a friends, or a co-worker, and pray for that person all week. Let your soul be pierced so that the heart of others will be laid bare and they will turn to God.

EPIPHANY OF THE LORD - CYCLE C

BEFORE YOU BEGIN:

Pray and ask God to speak to you through His Holy Spirit. "THE PARACLETE, THE HOLY SPIRIT WHOM THE FATHER WILL SEND IN MY NAME, WILL INSTRUCT YOU IN EVERYTHING, AND REMIND YOU OF ALL THAT I TOLD YOU." (JOHN 14:26)

FIRST DAY   **Reread last week's readings.**

1.   What was a helpful or new thought from the readings or from the homily you heard on Sunday?

2.   From what you learned, what personal application did you choose to apply to your life this week?

SECOND DAY   **READ ISAIAH 60:1-6**   **FIRST READING**

("But upon you the Lord shines.")

1.   To what are the Israelites being called, whose light has come, and what shines upon the Israelites? Isaiah 60:1

2.   How did the glory of the Lord appear, in the following scriptures?
Exodus 16:7, 10 Exodus 24:16, 17 Leviticus 9:6, 23, 24 Ezekiel 3:12-13 Luke 2:9

Personal - In your life, in what way has "the glory of the Lord" appeared to you?

3.   What covers the earth and the unbelievers? Isaiah 60:2

4.   Upon whom does the Lord shine, and what appears over them? Isaiah 60:2

5.   Fill in the blank: Nations shall walk by your _____ and kings by your shining radiance. Isaiah 60:3

6.   Who is the light? John 8:12

7.   Why must we raise our eyes, and who comes to the light? Isaiah 60:4

8.   Who shall be radiant, whose heart shall overflow, and what will happen to the sea and the nations? Isaiah 60:5

9.   What will the camels do, and from where will they come? Isaiah 60:6

10.   What shall they bear, and what will they be proclaiming? Isaiah 60:6

Personal - In what way is the light of Christ shining through you in your family, your work, and your environment? Are people drawn to you because they see that light within you?

THIRD DAY   **READ EPHESIANS 3:2-3, 5-6**   **SECOND READING**

("In Christ Jesus the Gentiles are now co-heirs with the Jews.")

1.   Who heard of the ministry which God gave Paul, and for whose regard? Ephesians 3:2, Ephesians 2:11

2.   What was revealed? Ephesians 3:3

3.   What was unknown to men in former ages? Ephesians 3:4-5

4.   Who has revealed this mystery, and to whom was this mystery revealed? Ephesians 3:5

5.   Read the following scriptures: John 14:26, Acts 11:12, 1 Corinthians 2:13

Personal - Do you listen each day for the Holy Spirit's instructions for you? What has he taught you as you have been reading his Word? Remember to pray before you read God's Word, asking the Holy Spirit to teach you and give you wisdom, knowledge, and obedience to follow his plan for your life.

6.   Who were some of the holy apostles and prophets? Isaiah 1:1-2, Jeremiah 1:1-2, John 1:35-50, Romans 1:1

7.   What is the mystery revealed? Ephesians. 3:6-8

8.   How do the Gentiles and the Jews become co-heirs? Eph. 3:6

9.   Whom has God commissioned to preach the gospel? Ephesians 3:6 Matthew 28:18-20

Personal - In what way have you ever felt called to teach or share God's Word with others? A good beginning is to share with your spouse, children or a close friend how the Lord has touched you in his Word or from the homily on Sunday.

FOURTH DAY   **READ MATTHEW 2:1-12**   **GOSPEL**

("They prostrated themselves and did him homage.")

1.   Where was Jesus born, who was king at that time, and who arrived from the east? Matthew 2:1

2.   Read the following scriptures: Daniel 2:27 and Daniel 4:4. According to these verses, are those who read the stars able to know God's plan for their lives?

3.   Who is the only sign we follow? Isaiah 7:14 Luke 11:30

4.   For whom were the astrologers searching, and what did they observe? Matthew 2:2

5.   How did King Herod react, and who reacted along with him? Matthew 2:3

6.   Whom did King Herod summon, and what did he inquire of them? Matthew 2:4

7.   What did the chief priest and scribes tell Herod, and to what prophet were they referring? Matthew 2:5, Micah 1:1,3, 5:1

8.   What is the ruler to do? Matthew 2:6

9.   Read the following and write out your favorite verse: John 10:11, John 10:14, John 10:16, Acts 20:28, 1 Peter 2:25, 1 Peter 5:3-4, Revelation 7:17

        _____

        _____

Personal – Share the scripture you chose and tell how it has affected your life.

10.   What did King Herod find out from the astrologers? Matt. 2:7

11.   Where did he send them, and what were his instructions to them? Matthew 2:8

12.   What was the astrologer's reaction to the star as they followed it? Matthew 2:10

Personal – Have you had any insight to God's light in his Word? What is your reaction to this?

13.   When the astrologers found the child with his mother, Mary, what did they do? Is this in fulfillment of the Old Testament prophesy? Matthew 2:11, Isaiah 60:5-6.

Personal – Have you bowed before the Lord? Have you prostrated yourself in homage before our Holy God? In his Presence in the Eucharist, have you knelt to do him homage, or do you do it just out of habit? Reflect on this.

FIFTH DAY   **READ PSALM 72:1-13**

("For he shall rescue the poor man when he cries out.")

Read and meditate on Psalm 72:1-13.

What is the Lord saying to you personally through the Psalm?

How can you apply this to your daily spiritual life?

SIXTH DAY   READ ALL OF THE COMMENTARY

ISAIAH 60:1-6

This week's reading from Isaiah comes from a section sometimes called Third Isaiah (Chapters 56-66), and is generally considered to be written by an unknown poet. The time frame of this passage is about 520 B.C. and the writer prophesies the role of the temple and offers to open its doors to all other nations. The invitation was given to the whole world to join the ranks of Israel as the Lord's chosen people.

The passage is calling on the people to rise up in the splendor and radiance of the Lord (verse 1). It tells them that the glory of the Lord shines in them and through them (verse 3). It urges them to be confident in that love and they will become leaders of all nations and many from all nations will be drawn to them (verses 4-5).

Today we are being called to rise up and become symbols of light and hope. We are called to be a light to a world that is covered with much darkness. We can be a light to the world only as long as we ourselves walk in the light of Christ. Each one of us is called by the Psalmist (Psalm 119:105) to be a light unto each other's path. We are being called today, as in the time of Isaiah, to let the glory of God's light shine through each one of us.

EPHESIANS 3:2-3,5-6

Paul wrote this letter while in prison awaiting trial before Nero. He reflects on his mission to the Gentiles (those who do not believe in the Jewish faith), and he speaks about his own conversion as being a great mystery of Christ.

Paul was on a journey to Damascus to persecute disciples of the Lord when suddenly a light flashed around him that seemed to come from heaven. He was challenged by the Lord to stop persecuting him and to come follow him. Paul did and his whole life changed. He uses that conversion experience to bring others to the Lord (Acts 9:3-9). He claimed his place as an apostle because he was an eyewitness to the Lord during his "metanoia" or conversion experience.

Paul gained a deeper understanding of God's plan of salvation through Christ. He reveals to us in this letter that into his life had come the great secret of God. That secret was that the love and mercy and grace of God were meant not for the Jews alone, but for all mankind. When Paul met Christ on the road to Damascus there was a sudden flash of revelation that affected his whole life. That "metanoia" is open to all of us, and we are being called to bring to the world that same message. It was to the Gentiles that God sent Paul, to open their eyes that they might turn from darkness to light. We hear Paul stating very boldly that God's love and mercy are given to all, Jews and Gentiles alike.

MATTHEW 2:1-12

We celebrate the feast of Epiphany, which means the visitation of the seekers, or as they are often called, the Magi, and Christ's manifestation of his glory to them. It was in Bethlehem, a little town six miles south of Jerusalem, that Jesus was born.

The name Bethlehem means "house of bread," and the manger in which Jesus slept was used to feed the animals. It is significant that Jesus was born in a place called "house of bread," as he chose to feed us with his Word and in his Presence in the Eucharist. He calls himself "Living Bread," in John 6:35-66, and we share his living bread in our liturgies in accordance with scripture (Luke 22:14-20), in churches throughout the world. Bethlehem was where Jacob buried Rachel (Genesis 48:7) and it was there that Ruth married Boaz (Ruth 4:11-13). This city was the home of David (1 Sam. 16:1, 17:12, 20:6) and it was in Bethlehem that the Jews expected God's Anointed One to come into the world (Micah 5:1-2). When Jesus was born, there came to Bethlehem astrologers from the east to do him homage. The Magi were holy and wise men and were skilled in philosophy, medicine, natural sciences, soothsaying, and interpretation of dreams. Many later became members of a tribe of pagan priests in Persia and functioned almost exactly like the Levite priests in Israel.

About the same time that Jesus was born, the Roman poet, Virgil, was praising through his writings and poems the "savior of the world," the emperor, Augustus Caesar of Rome. So it was to a waiting world that Jesus came and the astrologers from lands far away gathered at his cradle. It was the first sign and symbol of the world's conquest by Jesus Christ.

Today many of the learned men and women are coming to praise the King of Kings, Jesus; but many are not. What about you? Is Jesus your King and are you bringing him your presence as a gift? We need to reflect on the gift given to all who believe in the Christ Child of Bethlehem. The gift is being co-heirs of his kingdom, members of the one body and sharers of the promise. Have we made someone feel like an unwanted stranger? Have we dared label anyone a foreigner, alien, outsider, or pagan? Have we welcomed all to our "manger scene?" Is the light in our hearts drawing others to him, as the star did in Bethlehem? The manifestation of the star's brilliance spoke to the Magi of the entry of a King into the world. The glory of God's love for all is called to be manifested in us through the power of the Holy Spirit and in the saving name of Jesus Christ.

Application

The first reading tells us to look at the glory of God being unfolded before us. The second reading describes God's secret plan. The gospel reveals the joy and anticipation of following the star.

This week, like the wise men or Magi, let us bring Jesus our gift. Yours might be a gift of joy or love, peace or patience, etc. Then you need to share this gift with someone in your family or work place. The wise men came in humility and left encouraged and full of hope. We can expect no less, when we bring Jesus our gift.

BAPTISM OF THE LORD - CYCLE C

BEFORE YOU BEGIN:

Pray and ask God to speak to you through His Holy Spirit. "THE PARACLETE, THE HOLY SPIRIT WHOM THE FATHER WILL SEND IN MY NAME, WILL INSTRUCT YOU IN EVERYTHING, AND REMIND YOU OF ALL THAT I TOLD YOU." (JOHN 14:26)

FIRST DAY   **Reread last week's readings.**

1.   What was a helpful or new thought from the readings or from the homily you heard on Sunday?

2.   From what you learned, what personal application did you choose to apply to your life this week?

SECOND DAY   **READ ISAIAH 42:1-4, 6-7**   **FIRST READING**

("Here is my servant whom I uphold.")

1.   Fill in the blanks in the following scripture: "Here is my _____ whom I uphold, my _____ _____ with whom I am pleased, upon whom I have put my _____; he shall bring forth _____ to the nations" Isaiah 42:1

2.   To whom do the following scriptures refer? Luke 1:38, 48 _____, John 12:26 _____, Acts 3:13 _____, Acts 4:29-30 _____.

Personal - Do you see yourself as a servant of the Lord Jesus Christ in your home or at work? Share how you are a servant of Christ.

3.   Who are the chosen ones? Read the following scriptures:
1 Chronicles 16:13 _____, Tobit 13:11 _____,
Psalm 89:3-4_____, Psalm 106:23 _____,
Ephesians 1:3-5 _____.

Personal - Do you feel you are among the chosen ones of God?

4.   In the following scriptures, who are receiving the Spirit or have the Spirit of God working through them? 2 Samuel 23:1-2 _____,
Matthew 3:16 _____, John 20:19-22 _____,
Acts 8:14-19_____.

Personal - Do you have the power of the Holy Spirit working in your life? If not, read Matthew 7:7-8 and see what you must do to receive this power.

5. In the following scriptures, who brings forth justice to the nations?
Deuteronomy 10:17-18 _____,
Psalm 9:8-9 _____, Acts 17:31 _____.

6. In what way was this prophecy in Isaiah 42:1-4 fulfilled?
Matthew 12:16-21

7. Whom has God grasped by the hand, formed, and set as a covenant of the people?
Isaiah 42:6

8. Whom has he made a light to the nations, and what are we to do? Isaiah 42:6-7

Personal - Are you a light to others? Do those in your family, your work and your environment see the love of Christ shining out of you? If you are yielding to the Spirit of God dwelling in you others will see the light.

THIRD DAY   **READ ACTS 10:34-38**   **SECOND READING**

("I begin to see how true it is that God shows no partiality.")

1. Who was addressing the people, and what did he say? Acts 10:34

2. In the following scriptures, what does God's Word say about showing partiality?
Leviticus 19:15 _____,
2 Chronicles 19:7 _____,
Wisdom 6:7 _____.

3. What must we do to become acceptable to God? Acts 10:35

4. What does it mean to fear God? Daniel 6:27, Isaiah 8:13 and Malachi 2:5

5. Through whom is the good news proclaimed, and who is the Lord of all? Acts 10:36

6. What was reported all over Judea about Jesus, and where did it begin? Acts 10:37-38

7. What was the baptism John preached? Matthew 3:11 Acts 19:4

8. Who anointed Jesus, and with what? Acts 10:38

9. Did God intend for us to be anointed with the Holy Spirit?
John 14:14-17

10. What is one of the functions of the Holy Spirit?
John 14:25-26

11. What did Jesus go about doing, and who was with him? Acts 10:38

Personal - When you receive the Holy Spirit, do you also receive the power to go about doing good works and healing as Jesus did? Is this evident in your life?

FOURTH DAY   **READ LUKE 3:15-16, 21-22**   **GOSPEL**

("…He will baptize you with the Holy Spirit and fire.")

1.   With what were the people filled, and what were they asking? Luke 3:15

2.   What did John tell the people? Acts 13:25

3.   With what did John say he was baptizing? With what two things did John say the One mightier than he would baptize? Luke 3:16

4.   What happened to the disciples on the day of Pentecost? Acts 2:3-4

5.   What does fire do? 1 Corinthians 3:13-16

Personal - How have you been baptized by fire?

6.   Who were baptized, and what were they doing? Luke 3:21

7.   What opened up, Who descended upon Jesus, and how was it done? Luke 3:21-22

8.   What did Jesus say we will receive when the Holy Spirit comes upon us? Acts 1:8

Personal - What is the evidence of the Holy Spirit in your life?

9.   What did the voice from heaven say when the Holy Spirit descended upon Jesus? Luke 3:22

10.   How is God pleased with us? Hebrews 13:16

Personal - What have you done that has pleased the Father this week?

FIFTH DAY   **READ PSALM 29:1-4, 9-11**

("The voice of the Lord is power;")

Read and meditate on Psalm 29:1-4, 9-11.

What is the Lord saying to you personally through the Psalm?

How can you apply this to your life?

SIXTH DAY   **READ ALL OF THE COMMENTARY**

ISAIAH 42:1-4, 6-7

This week's reading from Isaiah comes from a section sometimes called Second Isaiah (Chapters 40-55) and is generally considered to have been written by an unknown poet who prophesied near the end of the

Babylonian exile. In 520 B.C. the city of Jerusalem fell, the walls and palaces were destroyed and the sacred temple burned. King Zedikiah and the rest of the population were marched to Babylon in chains.

From these chapters come the great messianic oracles known as the Song of the Servant. In each song a different viewpoint of the mysterious "servant" is given. The destiny of suffering and glorification is fulfilled in the passion and glorification of Jesus Christ.

Isaiah is calling upon a figure, who represents Israel, and yet still addressed as "her." The "servant" is both a single individual and a nation as a collective individual. He talks about the qualities of the past, and he makes his "servant" very much a key figure of the future.

Isaiah points out that the servant's role is not limited to Israel, but would become universal. He saw his people in chains and exiled to Babylonia, which was one thousand miles away from Judah. The need for a messiah was of great importance, and the hope of being restored to their lost homeland was in great danger of being completely demolished. The "servant" is being described as different from other leaders, not relying on military might nor upon treaties with other nations. He will not be a victorious warrior nor king, nor like other prophets shouting out their warnings. What the servant is will speak much louder than his words. The servant will be empowered by the same "Spirit" that rushed upon David when he was anointed king by Samuel (1 Samuel 16:13). Isaiah exhorts the people to look to the servant as God's chosen one.

ACTS 10:34-38

In this passage, Peter is preaching to the crowd that God shows absolutely no partiality. We see this truth being reaffirmed constantly in the Old Testament. The Lord shows no partiality, nor does he fear the famous or powerful (Lev. 19:15 and Wis. 6:7). God will have no part of activity like that. Peter challenges his listeners to fear the Lord and act upright, which means to be in reverence and awe of the Lord and to follow his commandments. We are told that fear of the Lord is to hate evil (Prov. 8:13).

Peter tells the crowd that God has sent to all the people of Israel a Messiah, in Whom he baptizes people in the power of the Holy Spirit. He preached that Jesus is Lord of all, a message that still is being presented today to a waiting, hungry world. The Good News began when John baptized people in the name of repentance. Jesus was baptized by God in the power of the Holy Spirit. We have been anointed with the same power and Spirit as Jesus. Jesus went forth doing good works and healing the sick. Peter's message is very much alive today as we see in our newspapers and television how bribes, fear of the powerful, and partiality to favored people can be very destructive to our society. We are called to go forth in the power of the same Spirit and do good works and heal the sick in the name of Jesus (Acts 1:8). Jesus wants us to carry on through word and sacrament (Baptism and Confirmation), and to be witnesses to the world that he is alive here and now.

LUKE 3:15-16, 21-22

In today's Gospel we see a prophet bursting upon the scene, and the people becoming highly agitated. It was well known that there had not been a prophet in Israel for many years, and it was widely believed that when the Messiah would come, prophecy would reappear (Joel 3:1-2).

John looked and spoke like the prophets of old. His message was direct and hard. He told the people to share what they had with those who needed it, and whatever your job is, do it the best way you can. John had no time to comfort those who lived careless or selfish lives. He was calling the people to right living. He told them to turn from their sins to avoid punishment and then turn to God for his blessing. This is a message for all times and all places. John spoke with urgency because he was preparing the people for the coming Messiah. John's baptism with water symbolized the washing away of sins. Jesus' baptism by fire (Holy Spirit) includes the power needed to do God's will. The church received baptism of fire on Pentecost when the Holy Spirit in the form of tongues of fire came upon the believers. They were then empowered to proclaim Jesus' resurrection in many languages. The baptism of fire also symbolizes the power of the Holy Spirit in bringing God's judgment on those who refuse to repent.

Jesus in the true sense of humility chose not to be baptized in a big service in Jerusalem. He chose to be with simple people who were repenting. As Jesus prayed, God spoke to him and confirmed his decision to go forth in his ministry. God was breaking into human history through Jesus Christ. Jesus' mission on earth was to identify with our humanity and sin. He began his journey to Calvary for us on that very special day.

Application

The first reading reveals to us that the Messiah is to be a "servant." The second reading reveals that God has no favorites. In the Gospel, God speaks to us, even today, with his voice from heaven, "This is my beloved Son, listen to him."

This week be a servant to your family, a friend, or to someone in the community who is sick. Be available, be specific, be consistent, and be ready to see the joy of Christ in their eyes as you live what you believe. Let the joy of the Father be reflected in the way you love others. "You are his beloved child, and he is well pleased with you."

SECOND SUNDAY IN ORDINARY TIME - CYCLE C

BEFORE YOU BEGIN:

Pray and ask God to speak to you through His Holy Spirit. "THE PARACLETE, THE HOLY SPIRIT WHOM THE FATHER WILL SEND IN MY NAME, WILL INSTRUCT YOU IN EVERYTHING, AND REMIND YOU OF ALL THAT I TOLD YOU." (JOHN 14:26)

FIRST DAY	**Reread last week's readings.**

1. What was a helpful or new thought from the readings or from the homily you heard on Sunday?

2. From what you learned, what personal application did you choose to apply to your life this week?

SECOND DAY	READ ISAIAH 62:1-5	FIRST READING

("But you shall be called 'My Delight,'")

1. For whose sake will there be no silence until what happens? Isaiah 62:1

2. Whom shall the Lord rescue, where will the remnant be, and who dwells there? Joel 3:5 and Joel 4:21

3. What will nations see, by what shall you be called, and who will pronounce it? Isaiah 62:2

4. What does the Spirit say to the churches? Revelation 2:17 and 3:12

5. What shall you be in the hand of the Lord? Isaiah 62:3

6. If you fall, what sustains you? Psalm 37:24

7. What will men no longer call you or your land? Isaiah 62:4

8. Where has the Lord written your name? Isaiah 49:14-16

9. What shall you and your land be called, and what does the Lord do for you and your land? Isaiah 62:4

10. Who is your husband, and what is he called? Isaiah 54:5

11. Who shall marry you, and who shall rejoice in you? Isaiah 62:5

Personal - What has been your response to being "His Delight" or being so precious to the Lord? Spend some time alone and meditate on these five verses of Isaiah 62.

THIRD DAY   **READ 1 CORINTHIANS 12:4-11**   **SECOND READING**

*("To each individual the manifestation of the Spirit
is given for some benefit.")*

1.   Of what is there a variety, but the same Spirit? 1 Corinthians 12:4

2.   Our gifts differ because of what? Romans 12:6

3.   In what are there differences, but the same God Who produces all of them? 1
     Corinthians 12:5-6

4.   What have some in the church been designated to be? 1 Corinthians 12:28

5.   Who gives us the desire to work, and for what purpose? Philippians 2:13

6.   What is given to an individual for some benefit? 1 Corinthians 12:7

7.   What are the gifts given by the Spirit? 1 Cor. 12:8-10

8.   What shall we seek, and for what reason? 1 Cor. 14:12

9.   Who produces all the gifts, and how does he distribute them? 1 Corinthians 12:11

10. How is grace given to us, and what is said about Jesus? Ephesians 4:7-8

Personal – What gifts has the Lord given you, and how has the church been built up because of your gift?
Seek after gifts that will build up the church.

FOURTH DAY   **READ JOHN 2:1-12**   **GOSPEL**

("Do whatever he tells you.")

1.   What was happening in Cana of Galilee, and who was there? John 2:1-2

2.   When the wine ran short, what did the mother of Jesus say to Him? How did he
     address her, and what did he say to her? John 2:3-4

3.   What did Jesus' mother say to the servants? John 2:5

Personal – How have you followed Mary's instructions to the servants today?

4.   How many stone water jars were there, how much did they hold, and what did Jesus
     tell them to do? John 2:6-7

5.   What did Jesus tell them to draw, and where were they to take it? John 2:8

6.   What did the headwaiter taste, who knew where it came from, and whom did he
     call? John 2:9

7.   What did the headwaiter say to the bridegroom? John 2:10

8.   Of what was this the beginning, what did it reveal, and who began to believe in him? John 2:11

9.   Where did Jesus perform his second sign, and what did he say to the people? John 4:46, 48, and 54.

10. What signs accompany those who believe? Mark 16:17-18

11. After the changing of the water to wine, where did Jesus and the others go? John 2:12

Personal – What signs can you see in your everyday life that reveal the presence of God's Spirit?

FIFTH DAY   **READ PSALM 96:1-3, 7-10**

*("Sing to the Lord; bless his name;
announce his salvation,")*

Read and meditate on Psalm 96:1-3, 7-10.

What is the Lord saying to you personally through the Psalm?

How can you apply this to your life?

SIXTH DAY   **READ ALL OF THE COMMENTARY**

ISAIAH 62:1-5

In today's reading we see Isaiah in earnest prayer for not only Jerusalem, but for all of God's people. He prays for the time of future deliverance, when all people will live with God in perfect peace. God offers us not only hope in the future, but help in our present needs. Isaiah's zeal for his country and his desire to see the works of salvation completed caused him to pray without ceasing, hoping that Israel would be saved.

Isaiah prays that the name of Jerusalem will bring upon itself the full protection of God and will be called a city in which God takes delight. He prays that never again shall his people have to go through such suffering. We would do well today to have some of Isaiah's zeal to see God's will done. We are told in scripture not to worry about anything; instead pray about everything. Tell God your needs and do not forget to thank him for his answers (Philippians 4:6). Isaiah has shown us that when we put our trust in God through prayer, he listens and answers.

St. Paul tells us to turn our hopes and even our worries into prayers. Do you want to worry less and to be at peace? Then pray more. Whenever you start to worry, stop and pray. Isaiah found God's peace, not in positive thinking, but in knowing that God was in control and that prayers of praise would be heard very clearly by God. We can pray just like Isaiah, and find peace, too.

1 CORINTHIANS 12:4-11

Spiritual gifts are special abilities given to each person by the Holy Spirit. These gifts may bring diversity, but they constantly orient us to unity. They enable us to minister to the needs of the believers. There are many spiritual gifts and one gift is not superior to another. All of the spiritual gifts come from the Holy Spirit and their purpose is to build up Christ's body, the church.

Paul was concerned about the friction going on in the Corinthian church because, instead of building and unifying the church, spiritual gifts were splitting it. The spiritual gift is given for the benefit of the community and not for the individual. All Christians have faith; some, however, have the spiritual gift of faith which is an unusual measure of trust in the Holy Spirit's power. Paul encourages us to remember that whatever spiritual gift we have been given, it is to be used to uplift the community. The power of the Holy Spirit is upon all of us, and we all have been given a spiritual gift.

The gifts are manifested in our life as we daily receive the grace from God through our prayer life, reading of scripture, sacraments, and fellowship with other believers. St. Peter tells us everyone has some abilities; find yours and use them. All of our abilities should be dedicated to others. None are for our own exclusive enjoyment.

JOHN 2:1-12

Today's Gospel shows us that whatever Jesus touched was changed. He changed the water into wine, and he changed sinners into saints. The weddings in Jesus' day were celebrations that lasted for a full seven days. Banquets were prepared for many guests, and the week was spent celebrating the new life of the married couple. Many times the whole village was invited, and because it was an insult to refuse an invitation, most people came. To run out of wine was an embarrassment and broke the strong unwritten laws of hospitality of the area.

Jesus was called upon by his mother to protect the honor of a good local family. Jesus was on a mission to save the world, and yet he took time to attend a wedding and take part in its festivities. Jesus knew that being part of people's lives was very much a part of his mission to Calvary. He valued these wedding festivities because they involved people, and he came to be with the people. Mary did not understand Jesus' reply, but she trusted in him completely and knew he would do what was needed.

Our call to ministry or our mission to bring God's word to others can often be accomplished in joyous times of celebration with others. We need to bring balance into our lives and we do that by bringing Jesus into times of pleasure as well as times of work. Today we who believe in Jesus, but run into situations we cannot understand, must continue to trust that he will work in the best way.

Application

This week's first reading tells us that God gives us, not only a new name, but also a new life. The second reading explains how each individual gift of the Holy Spirit is for the benefit of the community. The Gospel shows what Jesus touches, he changes...be it water or hearts.

This week, let your gifts of the Holy Spirit be manifested in the community. Pray with your family, school or work associates. Let your gifts uplift those around you. A gift of healing can be a simple hug or making someone a meal. A gift of teaching or preaching may be reading scripture to someone who can not read or it may be teaching a scripture class to the community. The gift of hospitality might be driving someone to church or to the store. The gifts are many, but they come from the one Spirit. The Holy Spirit resides in your temple (1 Corinthians 6:19).

THIRD SUNDAY IN ORDINARY TIME - CYCLE C

BEFORE YOU BEGIN:

Pray and ask God to speak to you through His Holy Spirit. "THE PARACLETE, THE HOLY SPIRIT WHOM THE FATHER WILL SEND IN MY NAME, WILL INSTRUCT YOU IN EVERYTHING, AND REMIND YOU OF ALL THAT I TOLD YOU." (JOHN 14:26)

FIRST DAY   **Reread last week's readings.**

1. What was a helpful or new thought from the readings or from the homily you heard on Sunday?

2. From what you learned, what personal application did you choose to apply to your life this week?

SECOND DAY   **READ NEHEMIAH 8:2-6, 8-10**   **FIRST READING**

("Ezra read plainly from the book of the law of God,...")

1. What did Ezra, the priest, bring before the assembly, and who composed the assembly? Nehemiah 8:2

2. What did Ezra do? When did he do it, and what did the people do? Nehemiah 8:3

3. As Mary sat at the feet of Jesus listening to his words, what did Jesus tell her sister Martha? Luke 10:39, 41-42

Personal - How much time do you take to listen to God speaking to you through his Word?

4. On what did Ezra stand? What did he do with the scroll, and what did the people do? Nehemiah 8:4-5

5. Whom did Ezra bless, and what did all the people say and do? Nehemiah 8:6

6. What was Paul's wish in his letter to Timothy? 1 Timothy 2:8

7. How did Ezra read from the book, and in what was he well versed? Nehemiah 8:8 and also see Ezra 7:6

Personal - When the readings are read from the Bible at mass on Sunday, who is speaking to you and how attentive are you?

8. Why do we want to be instructed in the statutes of the Lord? Psalm 119:33-34

9. Who was instructing the people, what did they say to them, and what were the people doing? Nehemiah 8:9

10. What were the people told to do, what did they say the day was to the Lord, and what must be their strength? Nehemiah 8:10

Personal - In what way have you found strength by rejoicing in what the Lord has done for you?

THIRD DAY	READ 1 CORINTHIANS 12:12-14, 27	SECOND READING

("Now you are Christ's body and, individually, members of it.")

1. Though it has many parts, what is a body? What do these parts make? 1 Corinthians 12:12

2. In whom are we one body? Romans 12:5

3. How were we baptized into one body, and of what were we given to drink? 1 Corinthians 12:13

4. Between what is there no difference? What are we in Christ Jesus? Galatians 3:28

5. How have we come near to God in one body? Ephesians 2:13, 16, 18

6. Where is Christ, and what have the people done? Colossians 3:10-11

7. What is the body, and what is it not? 1 Corinthians 12:14

8. Who is the body of Christ? 1 Corinthians 12:27

9. Even though we have many parts in one body, how do the parts differ? Being one body in Christ, of whom are we members individually? Romans 12:4-5

10. How does the body grow, and in what does it build itself up? Ephesians 4:15-16

Personal - What is your function at home or church? How does it unite you into the one body of Christ?

FOURTH DAY	READ LUKE 1:1-4, 4:14-21	GOSPEL

("Today this Scripture passage is fulfilled in your hearing.")

1. What have many undertaken to do, some being eyewitnesses from the beginning? Of what were they ministers? Luke 1:1-2

2. How were the instructions given to the apostles? Acts 1:2-3

3. What did Luke decide to do, and for what reason? Luke 1:3-4

4. Why were these things written down? John 20:31

5.   How did Jesus return to Galilee? Where did news of him spread? What did he do in their synagogues? Luke 4:14-15

6.   What did Jesus do in Nazareth according to his custom? When handed the scroll to read, from what prophet did he read? Luke 4:16-17

7.   Who did he say was upon him? What has he done for him, and for what reason? Luke 4:18-19

8.   What does the One whom God sent speak? What has the Father given over to him? What will the one who believes in him have? John 3:34-36

9.   After Jesus sat down, what were all those in the synagogue doing? What did Jesus say to them? Luke 4:20-21

10. How can one fulfill the scriptures or the law? Romans 13:8, 10

Personal - What has been spoken to you personally through the scriptures, and how have you fulfilled what was said? How attentive are you to hearing and obeying God's Holy Word? Is there room for improvement? What can you do to improve your listening skills?

FIFTH DAY   **READ PSALM 19:8-10, 15**

("The ordinances of the Lord are true,
all of them just;...")

Read and meditate on Psalm 19:8-10, 15.

What is the Lord saying to you personally through the Psalm?

How can you apply this to your life?

SIXTH DAY   **READ ALL OF THE COMMENTARY**

NEHEMIAH 8:2-6, 8-10

Today's passage is about the reforming of God's people. We see Ezra as a strong religious leader and Nehemiah as a layman in a high government position, both working to restore more than just broken walls in Jerusalem. Nehemiah gathers the people to hear Ezra read God's law.

Ezra rolled out the scroll of Moses' law, stood on a wooden stage, and read from early morning until noon. He had selected people going among the crowd and explained the meaning of the passages that were being read. The people paid close attention and many were brought to tears and repented right there on the spot. They stood in the hot sun and continued to lift up their hands in praise.

Today, because the Bible is constantly available for many, it is often taken for granted. Many times we can become dulled to its words and immune to its teachings. Instead, we need to listen to God's Holy Word very carefully. Then we need to study the Word and ask the Holy Spirit to help us answer the question, "How does this apply to my life?"

Ezra told the people they should be filled with joy because they had the opportunity to listen and understand God's Word. He told them to celebrate and to give gifts to those in need. Today, when we celebrate and give to others, we are strengthened spiritually and filled with joy, and joy is the infallible sign of the presence of God.

1 CORINTHIANS 12:12-14, 27

In today's passage we see that it is not surprising that the Christian church at Corinth, to whom God gave a variety of gifts by his Holy Spirit, needed to be reminded that those seeking experiences for themselves were not in the best interest for the spiritual growth of the church. Christian unity does not imply uniformity.

The gifts come from a single source and are given for the good of the whole church. Every individual has a very important part to play in the life of the one body. This should prevent a universal scramble for the same gifts. The most important thing is not which gifts are most impressive, but which best serve to build up the church.

Paul makes an astounding statement when he says that by the one spirit we have all been baptized in such a way as to become one body, whether we be Jew or Gentile. He states that we have all been watered by the one Spirit. He is saying "you," yes, "you are the body of Christ." Christ is no longer physically in this world in the body; so if he wants something done within the world, he has to find a person to do it. We are called to be his hands to do his work, his feet to run his errands, and a voice to speak for him. The supreme glory of Christians is that they are part of the body of Christ on earth and that person is you.

LUKE 1:1-4, and 4:14-21

Luke was very much aware that there was a lot of interest in Jesus, and many people had written personal accounts of experiences with him. Luke set out to put these accounts into an historical, thorough, and complete form using all the available resources. Because it was important to Luke to know what was true, he relied heavily on eyewitness accounts.

Jesus arrived in Nazareth where he went into the synagogue and preached before an amazed audience. The synagogue was the real center of religious life in Palestine. There was only one temple and that was in Jerusalem. Wherever there were at least ten Jewish families, there must be a synagogue.

In every town and village it was in the synagogue that the people met to worship. There were three parts of a synagogue service. They were: (1) the worship part, (2) the reading of the scriptures, and (3) the teaching part.

Jesus' example makes most excuses for not attending church sound weak and self-serving. We all need to make regular worship a part of our lives. Even Jesus was not accepted as a prophet in his hometown. We have a similar attitude - an expert is anyone who carries a briefcase and comes from more than two hundred miles from home. Do not be surprised when your Christian life and faith are not easily understood or accepted by those who know you well, because Jesus was not accepted either.

Application

This week's first reading tells us that God's Word was proclaimed clearly and explained completely. The second reading shows that we are the body and Christ is our head. The Gospel reveals that a prophet is not recognized or accepted in his home town.

This week, ask the Holy Spirit to reveal your gifts. Then share them with your family, friends, and community. Remember, the Spirit of the Lord is upon you, and he has anointed you to teach your family about him. You can feed your family, friends, and community God's Holy Word.

Let the gift of healing be released in you by reaching out to someone who is hurting, sick or lonely. Do not be afraid to use your gifts. Just remember that you have been anointed by the Holy Spirit.

FOURTH SUNDAY IN ORDINARY TIME - CYCLE C

BEFORE YOU BEGIN:

Pray and ask God to speak to you through His Holy Spirit. "THE PARACLETE, THE HOLY SPIRIT WHOM THE FATHER WILL SEND IN MY NAME, WILL INSTRUCT YOU IN EVERYTHING, AND REMIND YOU OF ALL THAT I TOLD YOU." (JOHN 14:26)

FIRST DAY	**Reread last week's readings.**

1. What was a helpful or new thought from the readings or from the homily you heard on Sunday?

2. From what you learned, what personal application did you choose to apply to your life this week?

SECOND DAY	**READ JEREMIAH 1:4-5, 17-19**	**FIRST READING**

("...for I am with you to deliver you, says the Lord.")

1. To whom did the Word of the Lord come? Jeremiah 1:1, 2, 4

2. When did the Lord say he formed him, what did he do before he was born, and what did he appoint him? Jeremiah 1:5

3. Who are others that were called from their mother's womb? Isaiah 1:1, 49:1; Luke 1:13-15; Galatians 1:1, 15; Psalm 139: 13, 16

Personal - When do you think God called you to be his servant?

4. What was Jeremiah to stand up and tell the people, what was he not to be, and for what reason? Jeremiah 1:17

5. What does the Lord say he will never do, and what can we say with confidence? Hebrews 13:5-6

6. What has the Lord made Jeremiah, and who is it against? Jeremiah 1:18

7. Where do we draw our strength, and what are we to put on to become fortified? Ephesians 6:10-11

8. What will Judah's kings, princes, priests and people do, and what will happen? Jeremiah 1:19

9. What are we not to say, and what are we to do? Proverbs 20:22

10. What did Jesus tell Paul, and for what reason? Acts 26:17-18

Personal – For what reason has the Lord delivered you from the darkness of your sinful way to the light of Christ?

THIRD DAY	READ 1 CORINTHIANS 12:31-13:13	SECOND READING

("Love is patient, love is kind.")

1. For what are we to strive and what is to be shown? 1 Corinthians 12:31

2. If we speak in human and angelic tongues, but do not have love, what are we?
1 Corinthians 13:1

3. What can we have and gain without love, and what does that make us?
1 Corinthians 13:2-3

4. What two things does it say love is, what does it say it is not, and in what does love rejoice? 1 Corinthians 13:4-6

5. What does the one who loves fulfill? Romans 13:8

6. What does love cover? 1 Peter 4:8

7. What three things does love do? 1 Corinthians 13:7

8. What does love never do, what will end? 1 Cor. 13:8-10

9. What happened when you were a child and became a man? At present how do we see and know things, and how will it be then? 1 Corinthians 13:11-12

10. What remains, and what is the greatest? 1 Cor. 13:13

Personal – Within your family or those to whom you are closest during the day, how often do you show kindness and patience to them? If you brood over injuries and are prone to anger, you need to come into repentance. Spend more time alone with the Lord, so he can heal the hurts within you so you can be loving.

FOURTH DAY	READ LUKE 4:21-30	GOSPEL

("Amen I say to you, no prophet is accepted in his own native place.")

1. What did Jesus say after he read in the synagogue the passage from Isaiah? Luke 4:21

2. How did all speak of Jesus, and what did some ask? Luke 4:22

3. What did Jesus say, and where is no prophet accepted? Luke 4:23-24

4.   How was Jesus accepted by his own relatives? Mark 3:21

5.   What did Jesus say about the widows in Israel, the one widow in Zarephath in the land of Sidon, the lepers in Israel, and Naaman the Syrian? Luke 4:25-27

6.   With what were the people filled who heard Jesus in the synagogue? Luke 4:28

7.   To whom are we not to be a companion? Proverbs 22:24

8.   What does a fool do? Proverbs 29:11

9.   What did the people in the synagogue do to Jesus, and what did Jesus do? Luke 4:29-30

10.   What did the people try to do to Jesus, and what prevented this from happening? John 8:59

Personal – In what way have you not been accepted in your family, church or native place for your belief and for speaking about Jesus? In what way have you not accepted someone in your family, church or native place for their belief? What do you need to do to become one with other believers?

FIFTH DAY   **READ PSALM 71:1-6, 15-17**

("…from my mother's womb you are my strength.")

Read and meditate on Psalm 71:1-6, 15-17.

What is the Lord saying to you personally through the Psalm?

How can you apply this to your life?

SIXTH DAY   **READ ALL OF THE COMMENTARY**

JEREMIAH 1:4-5, 17-19

In today's reading we hear Jeremiah tell us that God knew us, long before we were born, or even conceived. He knew you, thought about you, and then planned for you. When you feel that your contribution in life is not worth very much, remember that God has always thought of you as being one of his most valuable creations and has had a specific purpose in mind for you. We need to always remember that there is no other like ourself, not now, not before or in the future. You are special because you are an original.

Each Christian has a specific purpose in life. Some are anointed by God or appointed by God for a special kind of work. Whatever work we are called to do should be done for the glory of God. If God has given you a special kind of job, accept it cheerfully and do it with excellence. If God has given you a job that is not very special in the eyes of the world, seek to fulfill the mission of all believers, which is to love, obey and serve God in all that you do or say.

Today many people struggle with new challenges because they lack self confidence. They feel they do not have the proper ability, training or experience. Jeremiah thought he was too young and inexperienced to be God's spokesman to the world. But God promised to be with him and God has made that same promise to you. He loved you so much he gave his only begotten Son to die on the cross for you. When Jesus left this world he told us that he would never leave us orphans. He told us that he would leave us his Spirit. Remember, if God gives you a job to do, he will provide all you need to do it.

1 CORINTHIANS 12:31-13:13

Paul describes, in this reading, the power that overcomes all obstacles — love. We are in an age when phony feelings and attitudes masquerade as love, but we need to measure our love by the standards that we have received in today's passage. What the world needs now is love, and Paul explains to the people of his time what real love is and the message is timeless.

We are told that love is more important than all the spiritual gifts exercised in the church today. There is no action of man that is good unless it is rooted in love. Great faith and miracle-working power produce very little without love. Love makes what we do and what we give have value. Many people may have different gifts, but the gift of love is available to everyone and is needed by everyone. Today's society has a tendency to confuse love with lust. Love is giving and lust is taking. God's love is directed outwardly toward others. Lust is directed inwardly and is utterly selfish. To be patient and kind is not natural, rather it is an integral part of the human struggle. It is only possible if God helps us supernaturally and we set aside our own desires and instincts, so we can give love while expecting nothing in return.

The closer we come to Jesus, the more love we will show others. We have been given these spiritual gifts by God to strengthen our fellow Christians who make up the body of Christ. One day we will be complete when we see Christ face to face, and we will no longer need the spiritual gifts. Someday we will be able to love God fully for all eternity and the best way to prepare for that kind of love is to love one another now, as he loves us.

LUKE 4:21-30

In experiencing the rejection and anger of his friends and neighbors, Jesus faced the cross at the beginning of his short public ministry. They were insulted and furious and they wanted to push him over a cliff and silence him completely.

The remarks by Jesus stung the people of Nazareth because Jesus was saying that non-believers were more interested in God's good news than they were. Jesus told them that they needed to enter into a deep state of repentance and even accused them of being as unbelieving as the people of the northern kingdom.

Today there are many so-called believers who become very angry and hostile when they are challenged about the way they are practicing their faith. In almost every country we see a breakdown in the family and traditional values. We hear from many religious leaders in different nations calling for a spiritual renewal. Before we can call for any kind of renewal, we have to call all believers into repentance. There can be no renewal unless there is first repentance. Jesus told them that in him everything is complete, and they did not believe him. In rising above their expectations, he began to reveal the mystery of the resurrection.

To know Christ is to know the truth, and knowledge of this truth is what this world desperately needs today. People all over the world are confused and lost. If we expect people to turn to God, we will have to let them see this truth in us. People that are confused need to see in us the love of Jesus. This is a love that reaches outwardly to the unloved, the unwashed, and the unwanted.

Application

The first reading shows that putting our trust in God will give us the strength to overcome our fears. The second reading revealed that the power of love overcomes all obstacles. The Gospel tells us this is the love that must be proclaimed outwardly even when it is not accepted.

This week, look at each member of your family with God's eyes and see their beauty and particular special gifts. With each family member or with a friend, take time to say, "What I like most about you is..." Then watch the power of love as that person becomes radiant in the glow of God's love through your love.

FIFTH SUNDAY IN ORDINARY TIME - CYCLE C

BEFORE YOU BEGIN:

Pray and ask God to speak to you through His Holy Spirit. "THE PARACLETE, THE HOLY SPIRIT WHOM THE FATHER WILL SEND IN MY NAME, WILL INSTRUCT YOU IN EVERYTHING, AND REMIND YOU OF ALL THAT I TOLD YOU." (JOHN 14:26)

FIRST DAY   **Reread last week's readings.**

1.   What was a helpful or new thought from the readings or from the homily you heard on Sunday?

2.   From what you learned, what personal application did you choose to apply to your life this week?

SECOND DAY   **READ ISAIAH 6:1-8**   **FIRST READING**

("All the earth is filled with his glory.")

1.   In the year King Uzziah died, what was seen? Isaiah 6:1

2.   What was seen stationed above the Lord, what did each of them have, and for what were they used? Isaiah 6:2

3.   What did the Seraphim cry to one another? Isaiah 6:3

4.   What is said about the Lord, of what is he worthy, and what did he create? Revelation 4:8, 11

5.   How have we seen God's glory? John 1:14 and John 2:11

6.   At the sound of the cry of the Seraphim, what happened to the door and the house? Isaiah 6:4

7.   What did the man of unclean lips say? Isaiah 6:5

8.   What did the Lord tell Moses when he asked to see his glory? Exodus 33:18-23

9.   What did the Seraphim do, what did he do with the ember, and what did it remove? Isaiah 6:6-7

10.   How do we get cleansed from sin? 1 John 1:7-10

11.   What did the voice of the Lord say, and what was the reply? Isaiah 6:8

Personal – Have you seen the glory of the Lord, and how has he shown himself to you? If you cannot say you have seen his glory, try to identify where the blockage might be. Ask him to reveal this to you.

THE BREAD OF LIFE CATHOLIC BIBLE STUDY

THIRD DAY   **READ 1 CORINTHIANS 15:1-11**   **SECOND READING**

*("But by the grace of God, I am what I am
and his grace to me has not been ineffective.")*

1.   Of what was Paul reminding the brothers? 1 Corinthians 15:1

2.   What is happening to you if you hold fast to the Word preached? 1 Corinthians 15:2, also Romans 1:16

3.   What did Paul pass on that he had also received? 1 Corinthians 15:3-4

4.   How did the gospel come to him? Galatians 1:11-12

5.   To whom did Jesus appear, who was the least of them, and why was he the least of them? 1 Corinthians 15:5-9

6.   How did Paul come to know Jesus personally? Acts 9:3-7

7.   How did Paul become who he is, and how did he respond? 1 Corinthians 15:10

8.   What does Christ Jesus come to give as an example for those who would come to believe in him? 1 Timothy 1:16

9.   What is done and what will you do? 1 Corinthians 15:11

10.   What are we being charged to do? 2 Timothy 4:1-2

Personal – What has the grace of God empowered you to do? How have those around you been affected by you?

FOURTH DAY   **READ LUKE 5:1-11**   **GOSPEL**

*("Do not be afraid; from now on you
will be catching men.")*

1.   What was the crowd doing, and where was Jesus standing? Luke 5:1

2.   What did Jesus see, where did he go, and what did he sit down and do? Luke 5:2-3

3.   After Jesus got through speaking, what did he tell Simon to do, and what was Peter's reply? Luke 5:4-5

4.   What is Jesus' command to you? John 15:12

Personal – Are you as quick as Simon was to God's command to you? How is that seen by those close to you?

5.   What happened when Simon did what Jesus commanded? And after signaling to their partners in the other boat to come help, what happened to the boats? Luke 5:6-7

6. What did Simon Peter do and say? Luke 5:8

7. How did Abraham see himself? Genesis 18:27

8. What was the reaction of Simon Peter and the others at the catch of fish? Luke 5:9

9. What did Jesus tell Simon not to be, and what did he tell him that he would be catching from now on? Luke 5:10

10. When the fishermen brought their boats to shore, what did they do? Luke 5:11

11. How are you made fishers of men? Matthew 4:19

Personal - Who are you following, and what has been the results?

FIFTH DAY   **READ PSALM 138:1-8**

("Great is the glory of the Lord.")

Read and meditate on Psalm 138:1-8.

What is the Lord saying to you personally through the Psalm?

How can you apply this to your life?

SIXTH DAY   **READ ALL OF THE COMMENTARY**

ISAIAH 6:1-8

In this reading we see Isaiah responding to a vision from God. Isaiah was called to be God's messenger to his people, and his message was going to be very unwelcome. He had to tell people who believed that they were the chosen nation and very much blessed, that God was going to destroy them because of their on-going disobedience. We see as Isaiah experienced the vision, a sense of God's greatness, mystery, and power.

Isaiah recognizes that he is sinful and confesses his sins before God. His picture of forgiveness reminds us that we, too, are forgiven, and we have the sacrament of reconciliation to bring us back into a right relationship with God. Today we can look back and see how many nations chose to be disobedient toward God and were destroyed as a consequence. When we recognize how great God really is, how sinful we are, and the extent of his forgiving nature, we will fall on our knees and praise him for his wonderful mercy.

Isaiah knew that there was no hope of measuring up to God's standard of holiness and yet God, through the burning coal, cleansed him. Isaiah responded by submitting himself entirely to God's service. He knew that the life he was being called to was very dangerous and difficult, and yet, he cries out, "Here I am Lord; I will go, send me."

Isaiah had to go through the painful process of cleansing before he could be ready to serve the Lord. You may be going through a time of painful cleansing right now. Like Isaiah, let the power and love of God completely engulf you, and let yourself be cleansed. Let the blood of Jesus Christ wash you free, and you will be able to say, "Here I am Lord, I will go Lord, I will hold your people in my heart," just like Isaiah did.

1 CORINTHIANS 15:1-11

In today's passage Paul reminds the people about the instruction that they have already received on the resurrection of Christ. Paul is saying that the Good News has not changed because the message is the truth. Paul was talking to unbelievers.

Today we still have churches where the people are moving in the direction of belief, and others filled with pretending impostors. Paul tells the people then and the people now that the Good News is that Jesus Christ died for our sins, he rose from the dead and sits in glory at the right hand of his heavenly Father. And when we believe and accept Christ, we too will die with him and rise with him and spend eternity with him. The real good news of this message was and is, that salvation is available to everyone because Christ's dying on the cross paid for our sins and makes us clean and acceptable to God. So, whatever your background has been, wherever a loved one of yours might be now, just fall on your knees and plead that the blood of Christ will wash you and your loved ones clean.

There will always be people who say Jesus did not rise from the dead. Paul faced this opposition even after pointing out that over 500 people saw Jesus after the resurrection. Jesus himself cooked and ate with the disciples on the shore of Lake Galilee after his resurrection (John 21:12). Today there are many doubters who have resorted to fiction, plays, books, and even movies to discredit the physical resurrection of Jesus Christ, but we do not need to be discouraged by doubters who really have not believed in the Good News, because to really believe in Christ calls for a commitment of our life, and in Jesus' name, we have made that commitment.

LUKE 5:1-11

Luke tells us that Jesus provides more than just a miraculous catch of fish. Imagine if you will, a group of tired fishermen who have been tending their nets unsuccessfully all night and into the dampness of early morning. As the fishermen were mending their nets, Jesus tells Simon, a professional fisherman, where to fish, and even where to drop their nets. Out of sheer curiosity and a little tinge of respect, Peter tells him that area did not look too good, but he would try it once more. Peter and the rest of the fishermen were awestruck at this miracle. Peter immediately recognized his own insignificance in comparison to Jesus' greatness. Peter knew about Jesus' healing power, but he was amazed that Jesus cared about his day-to-day routine and understood his needs.

God is interested, not only in saving us, but also in helping us in our daily lives. When we decide to follow God, two major preconditions appear. We must first recognize that our human nature is good but has been wounded by sin. Then we must recognize the futility of human effort by itself to overcome sin, just as these men had fished all night without success, but at the powerful command of Jesus, filled their nets. Jesus had established authority in the synagogue first by healing the sick and casting out demons. Now he established authority in their lives and on their level and helped them in their work. They then left their nets and followed him and became fishers of men (Luke 5:10-11).

For us to follow Jesus is more than acknowledging him as Savior. It means renouncing our sinful past completely and, in obedience and humility, devoting our lives and future to him.

Application

The first reading tells us that each one of us is called to say, "Here I am Lord, use me." The second reading reminds us that the central message of our faith is that Jesus' death and resurrection gave us salvation. In the Gospel we see Jesus make the fishermen real fishers-of-men.

This week, let the call to serve Christ be reflected in your daily routine of living. Take time to see where you can be a prophet in your family, school, or work area. Show your care and concern on the level of the person with whom you are attending or working. Remember, Jesus won them over with his personal care of their everyday needs. Isaiah said, "Here I am Lord, use me." Try saying this to a family member or someone with whom you have difficulty. Jesus will take you at your word, and the miracle will start with you.

SIXTH SUNDAY IN ORDINARY TIME - CYCLE C

BEFORE YOU BEGIN:

Pray and ask God to speak to you through His Holy Spirit. "THE PARACLETE, THE HOLY SPIRIT WHOM THE FATHER WILL SEND IN MY NAME, WILL INSTRUCT YOU IN EVERYTHING, AND REMIND YOU OF ALL THAT I TOLD YOU." (JOHN 14:26)

FIRST DAY   **Reread last week's readings.**

1. What was a helpful or new thought from the readings or from the homily you heard on Sunday?

2. From what you learned, what personal application did you choose to apply to your life this week?

SECOND DAY   **READ JEREMIAH 17:5-8**   **FIRST READING**

("Blessed is the man who trusts in the Lord.")

1. What does the Lord say about the man who trusts in human beings? Where does he seek his strength, and from whom does he turn his heart away? Jeremiah 17:5

2. Why do you not put your trust in man? Psalm 146:3

3. What is worthless? Psalm 108:13

4. Who else do we not trust? 2 Corinthians 1:9

5. What happens to the man who turns his heart away from the Lord? Jeremiah 17:5-6

6. What is the person who trusts in the Lord, whose hope is in the Lord? Jeremiah 17:7

7. What is Jeremiah telling Ebed-melech, the Cushite, will happen to him because he trusted the Lord? Jeremiah 39:18

8. What does he that trusts the Lord not fear, and what does he bear? Jeremiah 17:7-8

9. What makes you fruitful? Ezekiel 19:10

10. What will happen to those who believe and trust in Jesus? John 7:38-39

Personal – In whom do you put your trust for your shelter, food clothing, protection, guidance, etc.? How much control does your spouse, banker, or insurance agent have on your well-being or mood for the day?

THIRD DAY   **READ 1 CORINTHIANS 15:12, 16-20**   **SECOND READING**

("But now Christ has been raised from the dead,")

1.   As what was Christ being preached, and what were some saying?
     1 Corinthians 15:12

2.   What was Paul preaching to the brothers? 1 Corinthians 15:3-4

3.   If the dead are not raised, what is that saying about Christ? What happens to your
     faith, and what are you still in? 1 Corinthians 15:16-17

4.   Why was Jesus raised from the dead? Romans 4:23-25

5.   If you do not believe Christ was raised, what happens to those who have fallen
     asleep in Christ? 1 Cor. 15:18

6.   Who are the most unfortunate or pitiable people of all? 1 Corinthians 15:19

7.   Who is in you, and for what is this hope? Colossians 1:27

8.   What has Christ done, and what is he to those who have fallen asleep? 1
     Corinthians 15:20

9.   Who is the One who raised Jesus from the dead, where is he now, and what will he
     give you? Romans 8:11

10. Of what is Jesus the head, the beginning, and the first born of the dead? What does
     this make him? Colossians 1:18

Personal - What are you hoping for when you pass from this life to the next in Christ?

FOURTH DAY   **READ LUKE 6:17, 20-26**   **GOSPEL**

("Rejoice and leap for joy on that day!")

1.   When Jesus came and stood on level ground, who came to hear Him? Luke 6:17-18

2.   Toward whom did Jesus raise his eyes, and to who did he say the kingdom of God
     belonged? Luke 6:20

3.   Who became poor for our sake? 2 Corinthians 8:9

4.   Who will be satisfied and laughing? Luke 6:21

5.   If we come to the Lord, what will he do? Isaiah 55:1-2

6.   When people hate you, exclude and insult you, and denounce your name as evil
     because of Whom, what will you be? Luke 6:22

7.   What did Jesus tell his disciples, and what will those who kill you think they are doing? John 16:1-2

8.   What are you to do, where is your reward, and what did your ancestors do? Luke 6:23

9.   Who has received his consolation, and what will happen to those who are full and happy now? Luke 6:24-25

10.   About whom did your ancestors speak well? Luke 6:26

Personal - What has been your reaction to your own poverty and mistreatment here and now? Give an example of your rejoicing and leaping for joy on account of your love of Jesus and for being persecuted for that love.

FIFTH DAY   **READ PSALM 1:1-4, 6**

("For the Lord watches over the way of the just,")

Read and meditate on Psalm 1:1-4, 6.

What is the Lord saying to you personally through the Psalm?

How can you apply this to your life?

SIXTH DAY   **READ ALL OF THE COMMENTARY**

JEREMIAH 17:5-8

Jeremiah is describing two kinds of people in today's reading: the wicked and the righteous. The wicked trust false gods and military alliances instead of God and thus are barren and unfruitful. The people of Judah sought advice from everyone but God.

When we are driven by fear, we seem to look everywhere for advice and comfort, hoping to find an easy way out of our troubled situation. Instead, we should have gone to God first for direction. He will give us the help we need, but he prefers to be our source of everything throughout our lives. We can do this by reading his Word and actively seeking to do his will. We can maintain contact that gives us strength no matter what the problem.

In today's reading, God was not happy with his people because they sought power and protection from other nations. He warned that these alliances may seem inviting, but in the long run, they will turn out to be harmful.

We are not to turn for direction from those who are of the world and not of God. Ask God to help you choose what is the best and wisest action you should take. Trusting in the Lord is the first step of obedience in following the Lord. We always make another marvelous discovery of the depth of God's goodness and kindness when we step out and trust him.

Many people have grown up with a misunderstanding of God and right living. To live a lifestyle that is pleasing to God is found only by demonstrating a reverence for God and experiencing how good he actually is. You show reverence to God by showing deep respect and honor to one another. Jesus shows us how to reverence him when he tells us to love one another as he has loved us (John 15:12).

1 CORINTHIANS 15:12, 16-20

For Paul, the death and resurrection of Christ is the core of all Christian teaching. Paul states this very dramatically when he tells the Corinthian converts, "If Christ is not risen, our faith is in vain." The church at Corinth was in the heart of Greek culture and most Greeks did not believe that people's bodies would be resurrected after death. They saw life after death as something that happened only to the soul. At that time Greek philosophy states that only the soul was the real person, and it was imprisoned in a physical body. At death, there was no immortality for the body, but the soul entered an eternal state. In contrast, Scripture stated that the body and soul will be united after resurrection. Paul did not want the Christian converts to fall back into pagan ideas about what really happens to a believer after death.

Today there are false teachers proclaiming that the resurrection of Christ was not really physical, but spiritual. We know that by his resurrection is revealed as "the first fruits of those who have fallen asleep." Paul is telling the people that if Christianity has no eternal value, then what was the reason for going through the persecution and, in many cases, death?

The resurrection is the center of our Christian faith. Because Christ rose from the dead, we know that what he said was true — he is God. Because he rose, his death for our sins was validated, and we can be forgiven. Because he rose, he lives and makes intercession for us. Because he rose and defeated death, we who believe in him will rise also. Without the bodily resurrection of Christ, perseverance in faith, including the sacrifices involved in suffering and persecutions, is pointless and at best foolish.

LUKE 6:17, 20-26

In today's reading we see Luke giving an account on the beatitudes similar to Matthew's sermon (Matt. 5:1-12). Beatitude comes from a Latin word which means "blessing." The beatitudes describe what it means to be a real follower of Christ. They are also a standard of conduct, and a way in which we can live our lives in accordance with the teachings of Christ. They are referred by many as the Christian attitudes of being well, physically, emotionally, and spiritually.

There is tremendous conflict between the values of God's kingdom and the values of the world. The beatitudes show what Christians can expect from the world, and what God will give them. Like a very sharp knife, the beatitudes cut away false piety from true humility. They also very clearly show how the Old Testament expectations will be fulfilled in God's kingdom.

Jesus startled his listeners because each beatitude or blessing is in fact a challenge. The beatitudes are like flashes of lightning followed by a thunder of surprise and amazement. They take the accepted standards of the world and turn them upside down. The people whom Jesus called happy or blessed would be called wretches, misfits, or losers in today's world. Jesus reaches into the core of what he is teaching when he stated that if we set our heart and bend our energies to obtain things which the world values, we will get them, but that is all we will get.

Jesus puts the challenge to us very clearly. Will we take the easy way which yields immediate pleasure and profit, or will we take the hard way which yields immediate toil and sometimes much suffering? Will we concentrate on the world's rewards which are temporary or on God's blessings which will bring us eternal life?

Application

The first reading shows God, not man, as the source of all real power. The second reading says that because Christ rose from the dead, as a believer of him, so will we. In the Gospel we see that God's reward is forever, and the world's reward is temporary.

This week, let your attitude be an action of love, gentleness, and strength. Show your humility by putting family needs before your own needs. You can only demonstrate this kind of power if you are strong in your private time alone in prayer with the Lord. Read Scripture daily, and he will give you direction in your daily actions. Show the people at school or work that because you are loved, you are capable of loving others. Remember, blessed are they who love, for they are of God.

SEVENTH SUNDAY IN ORDINARY TIME - CYCLE C

BEFORE YOU BEGIN:

Pray and ask God to speak to you through His Holy Spirit. "THE PARACLETE, THE HOLY SPIRIT WHOM THE FATHER WILL SEND IN MY NAME, WILL INSTRUCT YOU IN EVERYTHING, AND REMIND YOU OF ALL THAT I TOLD YOU." (JOHN 14:26)

FIRST DAY   **Reread last week's readings.**

1. What was a helpful or new thought from the readings or from the homily you heard on Sunday?

2. From what you learned, what personal application did you choose to apply to your life this week?

SECOND DAY   **READ 1 SAMUEL 26:2, 7-9, 12-13, 22-23**   **FIRST READING**

*("The Lord will award each man for his
justice and faithfulness.")*

1. Why did Saul go to the desert of Ziph, and with whom did he go? 1 Samuel 26:2

2. When and where did David and Abishai go, who did they find sleeping, and how did they find him? 1 Samuel 26:7

3. Who surrounds you? Psalm 125:2

4. What did Abishai say to David? 1 Samuel 26:8

5. What came over Saul, and what did Saul do to David? 1 Samuel 18:10-11

6. What did David say to Abishai about the Lord's anointed? 1 Samuel 26:9

7. What does his anointing do for you? 1 John 2:27

8. What did David do, what did the Lord do to those sleeping, and where did David go? 1 Samuel 26:12-13

9. What did David say about the king's spear, and for what did he say the Lord will reward them? 1 Samuel 26:22-23

10. What does the Lord love, and what are the works of his hands? Psalm 33:5 and Psalm 111:7

Personal - How has the anointing that you received in baptism helped you in your times of temptation?

THIRD DAY   READ 1 CORINTHIANS 15:45-49   SECOND READING

("...we shall also bear the image of the heavenly one.")

1.   What is written about the first Adam and the last Adam? 1 Corinthians 15:45

2.   How did the first Adam become a living being, and who gives life to whomever he wishes? Genesis 2:7 and John 5:21

3.   What was not first? 1 Corinthians 15:46

4.   How is our body sown and raised? 1 Corinthians 15:44

5.   From where was the first man, and from where was the second? 1 Corinthians 15:47

6.   Who is the One who came down from heaven? John 3:13

7.   Who are the earthly and who are the heavenly? 1 Cor. 15:48

8.   What does the Lord Jesus do to our body? Philippians 3:19-21

9.   Just as we have borne the image of the earthly one, whose image shall we also bear? 1 Corinthians 15:49, Romans 8:29

10.   How do you bear the image of the heavenly one? Ephesians 5:1-2

Personal – In what way do you see yourself changed from an earthly being to a spiritual being? What characteristic changes took place in you?

FOURTH DAY   READ LUKE 6:27-38 GOSPEL

("Be merciful, just as your Father is merciful.")

1.   Who did Jesus say to love, and to whom did he say to be good? Luke 6:27

2.   For whom does Jesus say to bless and pray? Luke 6:28

3.   What was said before, and what is Jesus saying now? Matthew 5:43-44

4.   What are you to do when someone strikes you on the right cheek, takes your cloak, and asks for something? Luke 6:29-30

Personal – When someone has hurt you, what is your response?

5.   What are we to do to others, who do even sinners love, and do good to? Luke 6:31-33

6.   What were you called to inherit? 1 Peter 3:9

7. How should you lend money, what will be your reward, and what will you be called? Luke 6:34-35

8. Who is kind to the ungrateful and the wicked, and why should you be merciful? Luke 6:35-36

Personal - List how many things you gave away this past week for which you knew you would not be repaid?

9. What will happen if you stop judging and condemning, and if you forgive? Luke 6:37

10. What virtue triumphs over judgment? James 2:13

11. If you give, what will be given you, and what will be measured out to you? Luke 6:38

Personal - What are some of the gifts you have received for giving something away? In what way have you made judgments on others, and what do you need to do to repair the damage?

FIFTH DAY   **READ PSALM 103:1-4, 8, 10, 12-13**

*("He pardons all your iniquities,
he heals all your ills.")*

Read and meditate on Psalm 103:1-4, 8, 10, 12-13.

What is the Lord saying to you personally through the Psalm?

How can you apply this to your life?

SIXTH DAY   **READ ALL OF THE COMMENTARY**

1 SAMUEL 26:2, 7-9, 12-13, 22-23

Today's reading reveals the conscience of David. David knew that Saul was hunting him so that he could kill him. He caught King Saul by surprise and, even though David was a professional warrior, he knew that Saul was chosen by God, and David had no right to kill him.

David wrote Psalm 51, and in this psalm it gives us an insight into the depths of his character. He knew that God wants a contrite heart, and he knew that he would suffer miserable guilt if he killed Saul. David and his aide showed great courage, and David displayed the discipline of self-control that prevented his aide from killing King Saul. David's aide respected David's loyalty to authority and became one of David's most loyal and powerful warriors in his army. David was determined to follow God, and this carried over into his decision not to murder God's anointed king.

Today there is a drastic loss of respect for authority in our lands because there is a loss of reverence and fear of God himself. We see even today that the strongest moral decisions we make are the ones we make before temptation strikes. Who would you have been like in such a situation? Would you have been like David or David's men? When you decide to follow God you must realize that you cannot do wrongful things in order to execute justice. Even when your closest friends might encourage you to take a certain action that seems to be right, you must always remember to put God's commands first. David did not kill Saul because God had placed Saul in power, and David did not want to run ahead of God's timing. David left Saul's destiny in God's hands.

1 CORINTHIANS 15:45-49

In today's reading, Paul is talking not about verifiable matters of fact, but about matters of faith. Today we have believers who still ask, what kind of a body do people have when they rise again? Paul tells us that a seed is put into the ground, dies, and in due time rises again with a different kind of body. It is still the same seed, but it has gone through stages of development. In life there is development.

The first man was made from the dust of the earth (Genesis 2:7), but Jesus is the incarnation of the very Spirit of God. We share under the old way of life the sin of Adam, dying like him, and having a body like him. However, we share in the new life under Christ — his life and his being. We now have a physical body, but one day we shall have a spiritual body. Our present body is corruptible, and our future body will be incorruptible. Our present body is a natural body, and our future body will be a spiritual body. In the future the Holy Spirit will be able to fill us completely, and then we will be able to worship and love Almighty God completely, which for now can only be a vision and a dream enveloped in the mystery of faith.

When Christ rose from the dead, he entered into a new form of existence. Christ's new glorified human body suits his new glorified life. We see this as Adam's human body was suitable to his natural life. When we, who are believers of Jesus Christ, die, God will give us a new and glorified body suited to eternal life.

LUKE 6:27-38

Jesus makes known, very strongly in this reading, that love is a decision and not some sentimental sloppy emotion. He tells us that anyone can love someone who is easy to love or who in turn loves us back. He goes on to say that even pagans love their families and friends. He even states that anyone can love under those kinds of situations. Jesus ask for something more than a sentimental yes, he calls for a decision, a decision to love.

Jesus was well aware of the oppression of the Jewish people by the Romans. But he told the people to love their enemies. This kind of talk and teachings turned many people away from him. He was not talking about feelings, but about the use of our will. Jesus' teachings are about an act of love which is really an act of the will. We make a choice to love someone with our mind. We also make a choice to forgive someone with our mind.

The Greeks distinguished between three different types of love in the world at the time of Christ, and this still is true today. They are: 1, Eros - a natural love of man for a woman; 2, Philo - a love for relative or friend; and 3, Agape - a love that only builds up the other person with no expectation for any kind of response. This Agape-type of love is what Jesus was calling for as the type of love that he has extended to us.

Jesus died for all of us knowing quite well that many people could have cared less about him. He died for us knowing that many were sinning while he was dying for us and would be sinners long after he died. He knew first hand what it meant to love those who hate, persecute, and even put you to death. He asks us to do nothing that he has not done, and he tells us that he will give us the power to love like this through his Holy Spirit (Acts 1:8). His message today is for all the world just as it was then, and that message is to "Love one another as I have loved you." (John 13:34).

Application

The first reading tells us that the destiny of all people is in God's protective hands. The second reading explains how our present body is a natural body, and our future body will be a spiritual body. The Gospel reveals that love is a decision, not a feeling.

This week, take inventory of yourself, and see who is NOT getting your love. Look at members of your family, then your relatives, and then your work or school associates. Make a decision to love, and make a decision to forgive. You might begin this inventory and decision making by first getting down on your knees and confessing to God your own sins. Then listen to him as he discerns your inventory and puts it in proper order. Ask the Holy Spirit to clear all of the "stinking thinking" out of your head as you get ready to decide to love all, even your enemies.

EIGHTH SUNDAY IN ORDINARY TIME - CYCLE C

BEFORE YOU BEGIN:

Pray and ask God to speak to you through His Holy Spirit. "THE PARACLETE, THE HOLY SPIRIT WHOM THE FATHER WILL SEND IN MY NAME, WILL INSTRUCT YOU IN EVERYTHING, AND REMIND YOU OF ALL THAT I TOLD YOU." (JOHN 14:26)

FIRST DAY   **Reread last week's readings.**

1. What was a helpful or new thought from the readings or from the homily you heard on Sunday?

2. From what you learned, what personal application did you choose to apply to your life this week?

SECOND DAY READ SIRACH 27:4-7 FIRST READING

("...a man's speech discloses the bent of his mind.")

1. What happens when you shake a sieve, and when does a man's faults appear? Sirach 27:4

2. From what do we pray to be cleansed, and with what do we ask the Lord to find favor? Psalm 19:13, 15

3. As the test of what the potter molds is in the furnace, where is the test of the man? Sirach 27:5

4. Who has the king for his friend? Proverbs 22:11

5. What does the fruit of the tree show, and what does a man's speech disclose? Sirach 27:6

6. What is the fruit of the Holy Spirit? Galatians 5:22-23

7. How is a tree known, what does the mouth speak from, and what will happen on the day of judgment? Matthew 12:33-37

8. What should you not do before a man speaks, and for what reason? Sirach 27:7

9. What defiles a person? Matthew 15:11

10. How are you to set an example for those who believe? 1 Timothy 4:12

Personal – Look at yesterday and evaluate your speech. What effect did your speech have on those around you? How can you improve your speech?

THIRD DAY	READ 1 CORINTHIANS 15:54-58	SECOND READING

("The sting of death is sin, and the power of sin is the law.")

1. With what will this which is corruptible and mortal clothe itself?
   1 Corinthians 15:54

2. In what do the children share, and what did Jesus' death destroy? Hebrews 2:14-15

3. What words of scripture have come true? 1 Cor. 15:54-55

4. What is the sting of death, and what is the power of sin? 1 Corinthians 15:56

5. What does the law produce, and where there is no law what happens? Romans 4:15

6. How did you come to know sin, and how did you know what it means to covet?
   Romans 7:7

7. For what are we to be thankful to God? 1 Corinthians 15:57

8. Where does God always lead us, and what does he manifest through us?
   2 Corinthians 2:14

9. How should we be in our work for the Lord, and what are we to know?
   1 Corinthians 15:58

10. What will not happen to those blessed by the Lord? Isaiah 65:23

Personal – How have you experienced death and victory in your life? What does the phrase "to work for the Lord" mean to you?

FOURTH DAY	READ LUKE 6:39-45	GOSPEL

("..for from the fullness of the heart the mouth speaks.")

1. What did Jesus tell the people, what did he say about a blind person, and to whom
   is a disciple not superior? Luke 6:39-40

2. Who will a disciple be like when fully trained? Luke 6:40

3. What did Jesus say after he washed the feet of his disciples? John 13:15-16

4. What do you notice in your brother's eye, and what do you not notice in your eye?
   What can you not say to your brother? Luke 6:41-42

5. What did Jesus call them, and what did he tell them to do? Luke 6:42

6. What do the hypocrites do with their lips, and where are their hearts?
   Matthew 15:7-8

Personal – In what areas have you been correcting or trying to help others? Examine yourself in that same area and see whether you need to remove the plank from your eye.

7. What does a good tree not bear, and what does a rotten tree bear? Luke 6:43

8. How is every tree known, and what do people not do? Luke 6:44

9. What does a good person produce, and from where does it come? What does an evil person produce, and from where does it come? Luke 6:45

10. From what does the mouth speak? Luke 6:45

11. What are you to guard and for what reason? What are you to put away? Proverbs 4:23-24

Personal - Memorize Psalm 141:3. Use this psalm on a daily basis to see whether you have some great changes come from within your heart.

FIFTH DAY **READ PSALM 92:2-3, 13-14, 15-16**

("The just man shall flourish like the palm tree.")

Read and meditate on Psalm 92:2-3, 13-14, 15-16.

What is the Lord saying to you personally through the Psalm?

How can you apply this to your life?

SIXTH DAY **READ ALL OF THE COMMENTARY**

SIRACH 27:4-7

In today's reading we can see both the negative and positive power of the spoken word. Many times, Scripture has shown us how irresponsible words of speech have affected the spiritual lives of many. It is very important for us to always remember that what we say and what we do not say can have enormous power in many situations.

Proper speech is not only saying the right words at the right time, but controlling our desire to say what is not needed to be said and something we should not have said at all. Unfortunately, examples of wrongly using the tongue are several, such as gossiping, putting others down, bragging, manipulating, false teachings, exaggerating, complaining, flattering, and lying. Before we speak, we need to ask ourselves: is it true, is it necessary, and is it kind?

We show others what we are really made of and what is in our hearts by the way we speak. Scripture tells us that the damage the tongue can do to the human being is like comparing the tongue to a raging forest fire. The tongue's wickedness has its source in hell itself. Satan uses a person's speech to divide people and pit them against one another. A conversation that deals with joy and truth will be a conversation between joyful and truly free people. A person does not want to be flattered and does not need to be praised for his deeds either. A person wants to be respected and to be a product of a loving God, family and society. He can only be this when he asks what God wants of him, rather than what does God have for him.

Remember, a few words spoken in anger can destroy a relationship that took years to build. Remember, we are fighting in our own power and strength. The Holy Spirit will give us increasing power to monitor and control what we say. As Christians, we are not perfect; but we should never stop growing, and this means letting our speech disclose the love of God that overflows our hearts.

1 CORINTHIANS 15:54-58

In today's passage, Paul is developing the idea that a man always needs to be changed to enter into a higher level of life. He insists that before we can enter the kingdom of God we must be changed. To believe in Christ is to not fear any change, including the one that haunts most men - death. Most people fear death because it is unknown to them. But to man, it comes to many, many more from the sense of sin. The sense of sin comes from being under the law, and that is exactly why Jesus came.

Jesus came to tell us that God is not law, but love, and that the center of God's being is not legalism, but grace. When we die, we go out, not to a judge, but to a father who awaits his children coming home. Because of that, Jesus gave us the victory over death, and its fear is driven out in the wonder of God's love. True love drives out fear, because fear has to do with punishment (1 John 4:18). Death is no longer a source of fear, because Christ overcame it, and one day we will overcome it too.

Paul tells us that because of the resurrection we are to be ready and alert, and see that nothing we do is wasted. Sometimes we hesitate to step out and do something beautiful for God because we do not think it is important enough or because we probably will not see any results of our efforts. We need to remember that everything we do for God is important, and the effect will last into eternal life. Do the good that you have the opportunity to do, knowing that your work will have long-term results.

Paul has told us very strongly something that we all need to hear very much today. God has won his victory over death and sin because they were defeated by Christ. By his resurrection, Christ has shown us that death and sin are not the last word, but only lead to life. He reminded the Corinthians then, and he reminds us today, that our "labor is not in vain." (1 Corinthians 15:58).

LUKE 6:39-45

Today's Gospel speaks to us about criticizing others. All through the ages, no matter what type of situation may have been present, almost everyone would agree that if you are critical, rather than compassionate, you will also receive criticism. If you treat others generously, gracefully, and compassionately, these qualities will come back to you in full measure.

We are called to love others, not to judge them. Jesus is telling the people to make sure that they are following the right teachers and leaders. He tells them, and us, to look for leaders who will show us what faith is as well as teach us what faith is. Jesus strongly states that we should not be so intent on watching what the other person is doing wrong and overlook our own spiritual walk with God. He encourages us to look for guidance from those who love in accordance with his Holy Word and teachings of his church. Jesus does not mean we should ignore wrong doings, but we are not to become so critical of others that we begin to become one of God's frozen people instead of one of his chosen people.

We often rationalize our own sins by pointing out the same mistakes in others. We need to be able to address the term "hypocrite" and realize that the "hypocrite" is exactly the ones for whom Christ came and died. Many people do not go to church because that is where the hypocrites go on Sunday. Well, if that is where the hypocrites are, then you will certainly find Jesus there too. He came for the sick, and all sinners are sick. Jesus would be the first one to tell you that he wants his church to be a hospital for sinners and not just a haven for saints. Remember, it is not hypocrisy to be weak in faith, but it is hypocrisy to think that we are spiritually closer to God than someone else. What is in our hearts will come out in our speech and behavior.

Application

The first reading shows us that when our speech is motivated by God, it is full of mercy. The second reading reveals that God is not the law, but God is love. The Gospel tells us the church is a hospital for sinners, not just a haven for saints.

This week, let your heart be revealed to your family and friends by what you speak and how you act. A loving word by you can affirm, build up, strengthen and open a broken spirit in almost everyone. It is very important for you to listen to the people around you and ask the Lord to discern what you need to do to correct your decision. Let your family and friends really get what they see in you, and their vision be all that is of the Lord.

FIRST SUNDAY IN LENT - CYCLE C

BEFORE YOU BEGIN:

Pray and ask God to speak to you through His Holy Spirit. "THE PARACLETE, THE HOLY SPIRIT WHOM THE FATHER WILL SEND IN MY NAME, WILL INSTRUCT YOU IN EVERYTHING, AND REMIND YOU OF ALL THAT I TOLD YOU." (JOHN 14:26)

FIRST DAY   Reread last week's readings.

1.   What was a helpful or new thought from the readings or from the homily you heard on Sunday?

2.   From what you learned, what personal application did you choose to apply to your life this week?

SECOND DAY   READ DEUTERONOMY 26:4-10   **FIRST READING**

("He brought us out of Egypt with his strong hand and outstretched arm.")

1.   Who shall take the basket out of your hands, and what will he do with it? Deuteronomy 26:4

2.   In verse 5 of Deuteronomy 26, who is speaking? Deuteronomy 1:1

3.   Who is the wandering Aramean, and where did he go? Genesis 46:6

4.   How did the wandering Aramean live, and what did he become? Deuteronomy 26:5

5.   How did the Egyptians treat the Israelites, and to whom did they cry out? Deuteronomy 26:6-7

6.   What do the following verses say about oppression? A. Isaiah 53:8 B. Isaiah 58:9

Personal - In what way have you been maltreated and oppressed? How have you dealt with it?

7.   What two senses did the Lord use in Deuteronomy 26:7?

8.   In what way did the Lord answer their cry? Deuteronomy 26:8

9.   What was the land like to which the Lord brought them to? Deuteronomy 26:9

10.   What did Moses do in response to what the Lord did for him? Deuteronomy 26:10

11.   What should we do in response to what he has done for us? List the two things in verse 10 of Deuteronomy 26.

Personal - What has God personally done for you in the past? From what you have earned or produced financially, in what way have you responded to what God has done for you? Have you bowed down in thanksgiving and reverence to the Lord for all he has done for you?

THIRD DAY **READ ROMANS 10:8-13** **SECOND READING**

("Everyone who calls on the name of the Lord will be saved.")

1. What is near you, on your lips, and in your heart, and what does Paul say is preached? Romans 10:8

2. What or who is the Word? John 1:1, 14

3. With what do you confess, and what do you confess? Romans 10:9

4. Who gives you the ability to confess Jesus is Lord? 1 Corinthians 12:3

5. With what do you believe and what will happen to you if you do this? Romans 10:9

6. What leads to justification, and what leads to salvation? Romans 10:10

7. What does Scripture say in Romans 10:11, Romans 9:33, and Isaiah 28:16.

Personal - There are two requirements to being justified and saved. In what way have you fulfilled these requirements?

8. To whom is God rich in mercy? Romans 10:12

9. What must you do to receive God's mercy? Romans 10:12

10. Who will be saved? Romans 10:13, Acts 2:21

Personal - To whom and in what way have you spoken to others of what Jesus has done for you? Take a few minutes now and reflect on Jesus, who he is, and what he has done.

FOURTH DAY **READ LUKE 4:1-13 GOSPEL**

("You shall worship the Lord, your God, and him alone shall you serve.")

1. What was Jesus full of, and who conducted him into the desert? Luke 4:1

2. What had previously taken place in the Jordan River? Luke 3:21

3. How long was he in the desert, who tempted him, and what did he eat while there? Luke 4:2

4. What did the devil say to him? Luke 4:3

5. What one word in verse 3 denotes the devil's unbelief in him?

6. What was Jesus' response, and besides bread, what does Matthew 4:4 say man shall live on? Luke 4:4

7.   What did the devil show Jesus, and what did the devil say to him? Luke 4:5-6

8.   Deuteronomy 26:10 tells us to bow down in the presence of the Lord for all he has done for us. What is the devil saying in Luke 4:7?

9.   What was Jesus' reply to him? Luke 4:8

10. Then what did the devil do and say to Jesus, and what small word in verse 9 showed the devil's unbelief?

11. From what did the devil quote? Psalm 91:11

12. What did Jesus say to the devil, and when the devil had finished all the tempting, what did he do? Luke 4:12 and Deuteronomy 6:16

Personal – In which of the following ways have you been tempted by Satan: When you are hungry – When you feel inferior – When things are not going the way you would like them to go? In what practical way can you apply this lesson to your life this week? Share with someone.

FIFTH DAY   **READ PSALM 91:1-2, 10-15**

("My refuge and my fortress, my God
in whom I trust.")

Read and meditate on Psalm 91:1-2, 10-15.

What is the Lord saying to you personally through the Psalm?

How can you apply this to your life?

SIXTH DAY   **READ ALL OF THE COMMENTARY**

DEUTERONOMY 26:4-10

Today's reading makes the purpose of tithing very clear: to put God first in our lives. We are called to give God the first and best of what we earn. This means that we give from the heart, and we are to give joyously. What we do with our money shows what we value most. Giving the first part of our paycheck to God, rather than what is left after taxes and bills, focuses our attention on him. A habit of regular tithing can keep God at the top of our priority list and give us a proper perspective on everything else we have.

The Bible and the Christian Church have always supported an organized system of caring for the poor. God told his people then, and he tells us today, to use our tithe for the helpless and poor. These regulations were designed to prevent the country from sinking under crushing poverty and oppression.

We see in today's reading that it was everyone's responsibility to care for the less fortunate and that responsibility still falls upon the body of believers in our church. In the Israelite tradition, each person was required to recite the history of God's dealings with his people. We need to reflect on the history of God's dealings with Christians throughout the ages.

What is the history of your relationship with God? Can you specifically recall what God has done for you? Take some time alone to reflect on the many gifts that God has given you. This will help you to see how all of your gifts and talents really come from God. That is why we can joyously tithe to God, because he has showered us with so much treasure. Remember, where your treasure is, your heart is.

ROMANS 10:8-13

A tremendously powerful statement is made when we say salvation that comes from trusting Christ is already within easy reach of us. In fact, it is as near as our own hearts and mouths. People all through the ages have looked for God through dramatic experiences. Some people have traveled all across the world to meet a spiritual leader.

Today's Scripture reading tells us that God's salvation is right in front of us. He will come to us wherever we are and whenever we call (John 6:37). All we need to do is to respond and accept his incredible gift of salvation. Today many people think that to become a Christian and be the recipient of the gift of salvation is a complicated process, but it is not. If we truly believe in our hearts and this belief is shown in the changes that take place in our lives, and confess that Jesus is the Lord of our lives, then we too will be saved.

Paul is not saying that Christians will be free of all disappointments. There will be many times when people let us down and when circumstances take a turn for the worse. What Paul is really saying is that Jesus Christ will never let us down and that everyone who believes in him will be saved. Today there are some people who say they believe, but there is no fruit of the Holy Spirit visible in their lives. We validate what comes out of our mouths by the way we live our lives. When we really believe with out hearts and confess that Jesus is really the Lord of our life, then others will see in us the fruits of love, peace, joy, patience, kindness, goodness, faithfulness, gentleness and self control (Galatians 5:22-23).

LUKE 4:1-13

Temptations often come after a high point in our spiritual lives or ministries. Sometimes we feel that if the Holy Spirit leads us, it will always be "beside the still waters" (Psalm 23:2). But that is not necessarily true. He led Jesus into the desert and allowed him to experience a long and difficult time of testing.

The Holy Spirit can and does lead us into difficult situations in the desert experiences of our own lives. When facing these trials, first make sure you have not brought them on yourself through sin or foolish choices. If you find no sin to confess or behavior to change, then ask God to strengthen you for your test. Like Jesus did, you are also to follow faithfully where the Holy Spirit leads. We must always remember that Satan is a real being and his temptation of Eve in the Garden and of Jesus in the wilderness is not to be dismissed as just a symbol or an idea. We need to be on our guard in times of victory, just as in times of discouragement. Satan constantly fights against God and those who follow and obey him. We can be assured that knowing and obeying God's Word is a very effective weapon against temptation.

Scripture clearly points out that God's Holy Word is a very powerful offensive weapon that is provided in the Christian's armor (Ephesians 6:17). Knowing Scripture is not enough to defeat Satan because he also knows Scripture. We must have faith in God's promise that he loves us so much that he sent his only begotten Son into the world to die just for us. Jesus tells us that he is the way, the truth, and the life (John 14:6), and Satan can not stand up to that power.

Application

The first reading shows that where your treasure is, your heart is. In the second reading, faith is belief in the giver more than in the gift. In the Gospel, God's love is far more powerful than Satan's fear.

This week, show your family the power that comes from God when you set him in first place in your life. Let your family see that you joyously tithe, and encourage them to give back to God some of the fruits that they enjoy. The simple act of your joyful caring for the helpless with your tithe will be a tremendous witness to your children and your children's children.

SECOND SUNDAY IN LENT - CYCLE C

BEFORE YOU BEGIN:

Pray and ask God to speak to you through His Holy Spirit. "THE PARACLETE, THE HOLY SPIRIT WHOM THE FATHER WILL SEND IN MY NAME, WILL INSTRUCT YOU IN EVERYTHING, AND REMIND YOU OF ALL THAT I TOLD YOU." (JOHN 14:26)

FIRST DAY   **Reread last week's readings.**

1. What was a helpful or new thought from the readings or from the homily you heard on Sunday?

2. From what you learned, what personal application did you choose to apply to your life this week?

SECOND DAY   **READ GENESIS 15:5-12, 17-18**   **FIRST READING**

("I am the Lord who brought you from Ur...")

1. The Lord took Abram outside and said what to him? Genesis 15:5

2. In whom did Abram put his faith, and as what was it credited? Genesis 15:6

3. The righteousness Paul possesses comes from what? Philippians 3:9

4. Read the following scriptures and tell how they apply to you. Romans 4:3, 9, 22, Galatians 3:6, and James 2:23

5. From where did Abram come? Genesis 15:7

6. What question did Abram put to the Lord? Genesis 15:8

7. What did the Lord tell Abram to do, and what swooped down on the carcasses? Genesis 15:9-11

8. What did Abram do when the birds of prey came? Genesis 15:11

9. What happened to Abram as the sun was about to set? Genesis 15:12

10. What are similar ways symbolizing the presence of God in these scriptures? Exodus 19:17-19, Acts 2:3-4

11. What did the Lord do with Abraham on that occasion? Genesis 15:18

12. In whom did the fulfillment of this covenant take place? Joshua 1:1-9

Personal - What is your relationship with God right now? How do you show that you believe the promises God has made in the Bible? What are some of the promises of God, and the covenants he has made with his people? Reflect on this and talk to God about it.

THIRD DAY   **READ PHILIPPIANS 3:17-4:1**   **SECOND READING**

("...continue, my dear ones, to stand firm in the Lord.")

1. Who are we to imitate, and who are we to take as a guide? Philippians 1:1 and 3:17

2. How do many conduct themselves, and what will happen to them? Philippians 3:18-19

3. What is their god and their glory, and with what do they occupy their mind? Philippians 3:19

4. Where do we have our citizenship, and for what do we wait? Philippians 3:20

5. What will the Lord do to our bodies? Philippians 3:21

6. According to what does he remake our bodies, and for what reason? Philippians 3:21

7. Who does Paul love? Philippians 4:1

8. Who does Jesus say his brothers are? Matthew 12:46-50

9. What does Paul tell his brothers? Philippians 4:1

Personal – How much time do you spend taking care of your body? Are you looking forward to the Lord remaking this body? How can you "stand firm," as Paul tells us to do?

FOURTH DAY   **READ LUKE 9:28-36**   **GOSPEL**

("This is my Son, my Chosen One. Listen to him.")

1. What did Jesus say eight days before he took Peter, John and James up onto a mountain to pray? Luke 9:27

2. On what other occasions were Peter, John and James with Jesus? Luke 8:51-52 and Mark 14:32-33

3. What did they go up on the mountain to do? Luke 9:28

4. What happened to Jesus' face and clothes as he prayed? Luke 9:29

5. Who were suddenly conversing with Jesus? Luke 9:30

6. How did they appear, and about what did they speak? Luke 9:31

7. Upon awakening, what happened to Peter and those with him? Luke 9:32

Personal – How do you think you would react if while in prayer you fell asleep and awoke seeing Jesus, Moses and Elijah? Do you think this is possible?

8.   When the men were leaving, what did Peter say to Jesus? Luke 9:33

9.   While Peter was speaking, what overshadowed them? What was the reaction of the disciples? Luke 9:34

10.   What came from the cloud, and what was said? Luke 9:35

11.   Who was standing there when the voice fell silent, and did the disciples tell anyone about this at that time? Luke 9:36

Personal - In what ways have you listened to Jesus this past week? Do you speak to him and then listen to what he has to say through his Word? What is it that God wants to do in you? Are you allowing God to transform you? As you do this you too will be transformed as it says in 2 Corinthians 3:18.

FIFTH DAY   **READ PSALM 27:1, 7-9, 13-14**

("Wait for the Lord, take courage;")

Read and meditate on Psalm 27:1, 7-9, 13-14.

What is the Lord saying to you personally through the Psalm?

How can you apply this to your life?

SIXTH DAY   **READ ALL OF THE COMMENTARY**

GENESIS 15:5-12, 17-18

Abram was not promised wealth or fame, he already had that, but God promised that Abram's descendants would be too numerous to count. Abram was an old man with no heirs to his own fame and fortune and we see God promising to change all that. Abram believes with all his heart, mind and soul. Abram's faith was a strong response to the living presence and power of God in his life and his faith had made him right with God. We too can have a right relationship with God by trusting him with our lives. Our outward actions, church attendance, prayer, good deeds, and even reading Sacred Scripture, by themselves, will not make us right with God. A right relationship is based on faith. We are confident that God is who he says he is, and does what he says he will do. Righteous actions will follow a strong faith naturally as a by-product.

We have read of Abram's mistakes and know that he was not perfect. Though human and sinful, Abram believed and trusted in God. It was faith and not perfection that made Abram righteous in God's eyes. This same principle applies to us. Our first response must be to believe in God and to trust in him completely. God's covenant with Abram was serious business. It represented an incredible promise from God and a huge responsibility from Abram. To confirm his promises to Abram, God gave him a sign, the smoking fire pot and the flaming torch. God confirmed his promise to you and to me when he gave us Jesus Christ, our personal Lord and Savior.

PHILIPPIANS 3:17-4:1

Paul challenges the Philippians to use him as a role model in their attempt to live like Christ. He did not mean that they should just copy him as if he were perfect, but they should focus on their lives being like Christ's life. There was no written Gospel yet, so Paul could not tell them to read the bible to see what Christ was like. Paul therefore urged the people to follow his example as a personal testimony to his character.

We need to ask ourselves about what kind of follower would a new Christian become if he or she imitated us. There is an old saying that is pretty powerful, and it goes like this: "To some people, the only bible that they will ever read will be you." Paul was very strong in his comment about the self-indulgent Christians. These are people who claim to be Christian, but do not live up to the model of being a servant of Christ. There is very little sacrifice in their attitude or actions. They satisfy their own desires before even thinking about the needs of others.

Freedom in Christ does not mean freedom to be selfish, it means the opportunity to serve. We can only become true servants of the Lord when we die to ourselves. This means putting others first, and it means that we all are called to "walk the walk, as well as, talk the talk." Paul was very clear in stating that the bodies we receive when we as Christians are raised from the dead will be like Christ's resurrected body.

Paul is encouraging his listeners to give thanks, and we might all give thanks today, because when Christ returns to take us into his eternal kingdom, we will be glorified and made completely perfect. Paul closes the reading by telling his listeners that he longs to see his brothers and sisters in the Lord. He longs to renew old friendships and he urges them to stay true to the Lord.

Today that plea is extremely important and we are called to hold true to the Lord. The attack on us as Christians is enormous and only by being true to Jesus Christ and staying close in Christian fellowship through his Holy Word, church and sacraments can we be victorious with him.

LUKE 9:28-36

Jesus took Peter, James and John to the top of the mountain to pray together to his heavenly father. He took them there to show them who he really was, not just a great prophet, but God's only Begotten Son. He just recently told them that they would not die before they had seen the kingdom of God (Luke 9:27). He was referring to the transfiguration. Jesus' listeners were not going to have to wait for another future Messiah. He was telling them the kingdom was among them and would soon come in power through the work of the Holy Spirit.

Moses, representing the Law, and Elijah, representing the prophets, appeared with Jesus and God's voice singled out Jesus as the long-awaited Messiah with divine authority. Jesus would fulfill both the law and the prophets because he was the summation of it all. The brightness of Jesus' face was being seen for the first time by the apostles. They were really seeing him for whom he really was. Moses saw the dazzling brightness in the clouds on the mountaintop and in the burning bush on the desert floor, but while he was alive, he never saw the brightness that radiated from the face of Christ on that mountaintop. The transfiguration or change was in the apostles because they were seeing Jesus in a totally new way.

Have you experienced the miracle of the transfiguration in your life? Have you asked Christ to come in and take up residence in your heart? He will gladly abide in you if you will abide in him (John 15:7). Jesus stands knocking on the door to our heart, and he will wait as long as it takes. Open that door of your heart today and look into the radiance and dazzling brightness of his face. He is waiting to share his transfiguration with you, and he wants you to witness to others the miracle of his love and forgiveness.

The apostles did not want to leave that mountain because the change was fantastic, and they did not want to take a chance of losing the excitement of the moment. Jesus is the chosen one and in him is all power and glory. He wants the apostles to come off that mountain and go forth and make disciples of all nations (Matthew 28:19-20). Jesus is giving all of us the same command, and that is to leave the safety of the mountaintop, and go down into the dark, cold valleys and lead our children to safety (Matthew 28:20). And remember, whatever you do to the least of my children, you do unto me (Matthew 25:31-46.)

Application

The first reading shows faith is the response to the living presence and power of God in our life. The second reading challenges faith-filled Christians to be Christ-like role models. The Gospel reveals that conversion to Christ brings upon us a complete transfiguration.

This week, let others see in you a transfiguration. By your actions, show that Christ resides within you. Make a commitment to serve joyfully those around you, and others will notice the radiance and dazzling brightness that comes from you. You will bring more people to Christ by the good fruit you bear. Gal.5:22-23

THIRD SUNDAY IN LENT - CYCLE C

BEFORE YOU BEGIN:

Pray and ask God to speak to you through His Holy Spirit. "THE PARACLETE, THE HOLY SPIRIT WHOM THE FATHER WILL SEND IN MY NAME, WILL INSTRUCT YOU IN EVERYTHING, AND REMIND YOU OF ALL THAT I TOLD YOU." (JOHN 14:26)

FIRST DAY   **Reread last week's readings.**

1. What was a helpful or new thought from the readings or from the homily you heard on Sunday?

2. From what you learned, what personal application did you choose to apply to your life this week?

SECOND DAY   **READ EXODUS 3:1-8, 13-15**   **FIRST READING**

("This is what you are to tell the Israelites:
I Am sent me to you.")

1. What was Moses doing, where did he arrive, and what was it called? Exodus 3:1

2. How did an angel of the Lord appear to Moses, at what was he surprised, and what did he decide to do? Exodus 3:2-3

3. Approximately how old was Moses when the angel appeared to him? Acts 7:23, 30

4. What did God do and say when Moses came near the bush? Exodus 3:4-6

5. What did Jacob say was a gateway to heaven? Genesis 28:17

6. What was Moses afraid to do? Exodus 3:6

7. What did the Lord say he has witnessed, what does he know, and what has he come down to do? Exodus 3:7-8

8. What are we to do to those who are being dragged to death? Proverbs 24:11

Personal - As the Lord has rescued his people from slavery and death, how have you continued to be his hands and feet and rescued those who have been programmed for abortion? What can you do at the abortion mills to make his presence known?

9. What did Moses say and ask God, and what did God say is his name?
   Exodus 3:13-14

10. What did God tell Moses to say to the Israelites? Exodus 3:15

11.   How long does God's name endure, and what is his title? Psalm 135:13

12.   Who will enter the kingdom of heaven? Matthew 7:21

Personal – What do you call the One who has sent you, and what has he sent you to do?

THIRD DAY   **READ 1 CORINTHIANS 10:1-6, 10-12**   **SECOND READING**

*("Therefore, whoever thinks he is standing secure,
should take care not to fall.")*

1.   Of what does Paul not want the brothers to be unaware? 1 Corinthians 10:1-2

2.   Into who and what have you been baptized? Romans 6:3

3.   From what did they all eat and drink, from what kind of a rock did they drink, and who was the rock? 1 Cor. 10:3-4

4.   What spiritual food did he give our ancestors, and what spiritual food does he give us? John 6:31, 6:35

5.   Why were our ancestors struck down? 1 Corinthians 10:5-6 and Hebrews 3:17

6.   What did the Lord do to those who did not believe? Jude 5

7.   What should we not do as some of our ancestors have done? 1 Corinthians 10:10

8.   Why have these things been written down, and of what should you be careful?
1 Corinthians 10:11-12

9.   Why do you not become haughty, and how should you stand? Romans 11:20

Personal – What attitudes that are not pleasing to God have been passed on to you by your ancestors? How can you or how have you overcome them?

FOURTH DAY   **READ LUKE 13:1-9**   **GOSPEL**

("If you do not repent, you will all perish as they did.")

1.   What did some people tell Jesus, and what was his reply? Luke 13:1-2

2.   What did Jesus say will happen if you do not repent? Luke 13:3

3.   What does Jesus say about the eighteen people who were killed when the tower at Saloam fell on them, and what does he repeat? Luke 13:4-5

4.   If you do not believe Jesus is what, what will happen to you? John 8:24

5.   Of what are you to repent, and what will you receive? Acts 2:38

6.   What did Jesus tell the people, and what was planted in the man's orchard? Luke 13:6

7.   What did the man say to the gardener? Luke 13:7

8.   What did Jesus do to the fig tree, and what did he tell his disciples? Matthew 21:19-21

9.   What will happen to every tree that does not bear good fruit? Matthew 3:10

10.   What did the gardener tell the man he would do in hopes it would bear fruit in the future, and what did he say to do if it did not bear fruit? Luke 13:8-9

Personal - Repent means to change. How has your life changed since you have been studied God's Word, and what fruit is evident from this change?

FIFTH DAY   **READ PSALM 103:1-4, 6-8, 11**

*("Merciful and gracious is the Lord,
slow to anger and abounding in kindness.")*

Read and meditate on Psalm 103:1-4, 6-8, 11.

What is the Lord saying to you personally through the Psalm?

How can you apply this to your life?

SIXTH DAY   **READ ALL OF THE COMMENTARY**

EXODUS 3:1-8, 13-15

In today's reading we are shown the startling contrast between Moses' life as an Egyptian prince and his life as an obscure shepherd. As a prince, he had everything done for him, and as the son of an Egyptian princess, he became very famous and very popular. As a shepherd he experienced hard work, little recognition and much loneliness. He was now holding the very job he had been taught to despise. He lived in the hills unknown and as a foreigner. This must have been an incredibly humbling experience for Moses, but God in his infinite wisdom was preparing Moses for leadership. Moses could not see this yet, but God was getting him ready to free Israel.

God spoke to Moses from an unexpected source: a burning bush. When Moses saw it, he went to investigate. God often uses unexpected sources when working in our lives. You can be open to investigate as God speaks through his people. He might speak to your spouse, parents, friend, relative, or anyone. You need to investigate and be open as Moses was open to God's use of people or experiences.

Be ready for God's surprises. He may have guidance for you that can come when you are ready to listen to a "burning bush." God told Moses to take off his shoes because he was standing on holy ground. Moses immediately obeyed and covered his face as well. Taking off his shoes was an act of reverence and conveying to God his own unworthiness. God is our friend, but he is first and foremost our sovereign Lord. When you worship God, do you approach him casually or as though you were an invited guest before a king?

1 CORINTHIANS 10:1-6, 10-12

Today's reading is a powerful example of what happens to a person, a people, or a nation when over confidence and lack of discipline bring about a great spiritual immaturity. This reading encourages us to remember our own Baptism and how we have been blessed to have God within us. Like the people in today's reading, we too have been guided through many raging storms and have been led through to safety by the love and power of God. They followed a cloud by day and fire by night.

We have Christ within us personally. We can have instant access to him if we so desire. The world today, as the Egyptians tried to do to the Israelites, is trying to drive us into the sea of despair and destruction. Because we are temples of the Holy Spirit (1 Cor. 6:19), we can call upon the power of the Holy Spirit within us (1 John 4:4) and calm the storms that rage in different times of our lives.

We need to remember, just as the Israelites needed to remember, that unless we continue to be people of prayer, worship, and doers of God's Holy Word, we will be rebellious, and we will die in our wilderness too. The pressures of today's world makes it easy to forget the lessons of the past, but the daily reading of Scripture will be a powerful reminder of how God wants us to really live. We do not need to make the same mistakes as the people in today's reading. We have been given the tremendous gift of free will. Our God is a God of love, and we have within us the power of the Holy Spirit to help us choose to love.

LUKE 13:1-9

Today's Gospel is a call to repentance. Being killed or staying alive are not measures of righteousness in themselves. Everyone will die at some time; that is part of being human. But not everyone needs to stay dead. Jesus promises all of us that if we believe in him, we will not perish, but instead we will have eternal life (John 3:16).

There are many people in our communities, and even in our families, who are like the fig tree in today's reading. They are being nurtured through life, and they are not producing any fruit. They refuse to listen on how to bear good fruit, and finally, many of them die or are cut down. We need to really hear what is being said in today's Gospel because we are like that tree and we need to repent. We need to be watered and re-cultivated or we will be ripped out and thrown away. Jesus died for us; he has left his Spirit to help us grow. Our church embraces us with the teachings of Christ, the sacraments, Holy Scripture, fellowship; all of this to help us bear the fruits of love. We are bearers of a wonderful kind of life-giving fruit. They will know who we are when they see and taste our fruit of love, joy, peace, patience, kindness, generosity, faithfulness, gentleness, and self-control. This is the kind of fruit we were meant to bear.

Jesus is constantly pleading to save your tree of life within you. Listen to him today. Let him open your roots and root out all the rotten growth through the sacrament of reconciliation. Let Jesus love you through prayer and his Holy Word, and spend time just listening to him. Let him make you his delight once again.

Application

The first reading tells how Moses saw the burning bush and investigates just as we should investigate. In the second reading we see our baptism is constantly being experienced throughout our lives. The Gospel says a Christian is born to never die, but to live forever.

This week, like Moses, look and listen to God speak. He may be speaking through someone in your family. Moses heard him in a "burning bush." Your baptism made you a temple of the Holy Spirit, and your language reflects your attitude of what you think is inside your temple. Let those around you hear only words that are honorable and acceptable in the presence of a king. What kind of fruit do you bear? Ask those closest to you what kind of fruit they see in you? This week, spend time in pruning, nurturing, and watering your tree of life, and your fruit will feed your family.

FOURTH SUNDAY IN LENT - CYCLE C

BEFORE YOU BEGIN:

Pray and ask God to speak to you through His Holy Spirit. "THE PARACLETE, THE HOLY SPIRIT WHOM THE FATHER WILL SEND IN MY NAME, WILL INSTRUCT YOU IN EVERYTHING, AND REMIND YOU OF ALL THAT I TOLD YOU." (JOHN 14:26)

FIRST DAY   **Reread last week's readings.**

1.   What was a helpful or new thought from the readings or from the homily you heard on Sunday?

2.   From what you learned, what personal application did you choose to apply to your life this week?

SECOND DAY   **READ JOSHUA 5:9-12**   **FIRST READING**

("Today I have removed the reproach of Egypt from you.")

1.   What did the Lord tell Joshua he had removed from them that day? Joshua 5:9

2.   What has the Lord removed from those who fear him? Psalm 103:12

3.   Where were the Israelites encamped, and what did they celebrate on the evening of the fourteenth of the month? Joshua 5:10

4.   What was prescribed by the Lord on the fourteenth day of the month? Exodus 12:5-6, 11

5.   What did the Israelites eat the day after the Passover? Joshua 5:11

6.   For what are we to work, and who gives it to us? John 6:27

7.   What did Jesus say is true food and drink, and what happens to whoever eats and drinks it? John 6:55-56

8.   On that same day, after the Passover, what ceased? Joshua 5:12

9.   How long did they eat the manna? Exodus 16:35

10.   How long will you live if you eat the flesh of the Son of Man and drink his blood? John 6:49-51

Personal - What has been removed from you that allows you to participate in communion on Sunday? In your life, what shows that communion is more important than the food on your table?

THIRD DAY   READ 2 CORINTHIANS 5:17-21   SECOND READING

("So we are ambassadors for Christ,
as if God were appealing through us.")

1.   What is "whoever is in Christ," and what has happened to the old things? 2 Corinthians 5:17

2.   To those who accepted Christ, what did he give them the power to become? John 1:12-13

3.   How have we been reconciled to God, and what has he given us the ministry of? 2 Corinthians 5:18

4.   What were we when we were reconciled to God, and how were we saved? Romans 5:10-11

5.   What did God not count, and what did he entrust to us? 2 Corinthians 5:19

6.   What does David declare, and who is blessed? Romans 4:6-8

7.   What are we for Christ, and what is Paul imploring the people to be? 2 Corinthians 5:20

8.   How does Paul want to make known the mystery of the Gospel, and what does that make him in chains? Ephesians 6:19-20

9.   For whose sake did God make Jesus become sin even though he did not know sin, and what did that make us? 2 Cor. 5:21

10. What is Jesus able to do and for what reason? Hebrews 4:15

Personal - If God has entrusted to you the message of reconciliation, how have you shared and acted upon that message to those around you?

FOURTH DAY   READ LUKE 15:1-3,11-32   GOSPEL

("But now we must celebrate and rejoice, because
your brother was dead and has come to life again.")

1.   Who was drawing near to listen to Jesus, and what were the Pharisees and scribes complaining about? How did he address them? Luke 15:1-3

2.   In the parable Jesus told, what happened to the younger son? What did the man long to eat? Luke 15:11-16

3.   Coming to his senses, what did he decide to do, and what was he going to say to his father? Luke 15:17-19

4.   With what was his father filled when he saw his son, and what did he do? Luke 15:20

5.   On who does the Lord have compassion? Psalm 103:13

6.   What did the son say to the father, and what did the father do and say about the son? Luke 15:21-24

7.   What were we following that made us dead in our own transgressions, and how were we brought to life? Ephesians 2:1-5

8.   What was the older son's reaction to all the dancing and festivities for the younger son? Luke 15:25-28

9.   What did the father do at the older son's reaction, and what did he say to his father? Luke 15:29-30

10. What did the father say belonged to the older son, and why did he say it was time to celebrate? Luke 15:31-32

11. What is the will of our heavenly Father, and how should we not feel over one of his little ones? Matthew 18:10-14

Personal – With whom do you relate in this gospel, and why?

FIFTH DAY   **READ PSALM 34:2-7**

("Look to him that you may be radiant with joy.")

Read and meditate on Psalm 34:2-7.

What is the Lord saying to you personally through the Psalm?

How can you apply this to your life?

SIXTH DAY   **READ ALL OF THE COMMENTARY**

JOSHUA 5:9-12

The Israelites were ready to soon enter into the promised land after spending 39 years in the wilderness unnecessarily because they were afraid and underestimated God's ability. The Canaanites heard about Israel's great victories through God (crossing the Red Sea) and were terrified of them. Do not underestimate God. If we are faithful to him, as Joshua and the Israelites were faithful, then God can cause great opposition to melt away. God can change the attitudes of those who oppose us.

The Lord spoke to Joshua and told him that he was to circumcise all the males in his camp because that was the sign of the covenant with him. Then the angel spoke to Joshua and told him to prepare for battle and to listen to God's plan only. They celebrated the feast of Passover before they went on to the battle of Jericho. The celebration reminded them of who they were, and what happened to get them that far.

This was the first celebration of the Passover in the Promised Land. The Israelites remembered how God was with them in their times of danger and hunger. They were now in a land that was overflowing with fruit, vegetables, and water. They knew that God has miraculously provided this land for them. They knelt and in prayer they thanked God for keeping their faith strong enough to get through the wilderness.

They knew, and it is important for us to know too, that prayer is not an alternative to preparing for what needs to be done, and faith is not a substitute for hard, honest work. God can and does provide us with miracles, but he expects us to use our God-given talents and resources to provide for others and ourselves.

2 CORINTHIANS 5:17-21

Christians are brand-new people on the inside when they become baptized. The Holy Spirit dwells within them and gives them a new life, and they are no longer the same. When we become baptized and a new child of the Lord, we are not reformed, rehabilitated or reeducated: we are brand-new creations, living in complete union with Christ (Colossians 2:6,7). It does not mean we are turning over a new leaf when we are baptized. It means we are beginning a new life under a new Master. We are reconciled to God by his wiping out of our sins, or original sin if one is being baptized as a child. We are made righteous. We are no longer strangers or foreigners when we trust in God.

Because we have been reconciled to God, we now have been given the privilege of encouraging others to do the same. We are called to be ambassadors for Christ, and this means we are to be his representatives. As ambassadors of Christ, we are sent with his message of reconciliation to the world. We need not take this responsibility lightly because a hungry, broken, poor, and oppressed world anxiously and hopefully awaits us. How do you see yourself in the role of Christ's ambassador?

While you trust in Christ, you make a trade: your sins for his goodness. He took on unto himself all of our sins at Calvary, and we received his righteousness that he has poured out for us at our conversion. This is what Christians mean when they talk about Christ's atonement for sin. Let us fall on our knees and give God our total gratitude for making this marvelous trade available for us.

LUKE 15:1-3, 11-32

Today's Gospel shows us the conflict between the Pharisees' way of treating a sinner and Jesus' way. To people who did not keep the law, a label called "The people of the land" was given to them. These people were shunned by most Orthodox Jews. A Pharisee was forbidden to have anything to do with a known sinner. They were shocked at the easy way that Jesus got along with them. Their attitude was that to eat with a sinner, to talk to a sinner and to be with sinners must mean that you, too, were a sinner. Their philosophy was to destroy the sinner before God. Jesus, of course, believed in saving the sinner and told them a story about a young man who was very rebellious to his family. Jewish law stated that the oldest son must get twice as much inheritance money as all the other sons combined. In this story the youngest of two sons demanded his share of the money. He was bored and lazy and wanted to leave home to go and enjoy the outside world. He soon ran through the money, and he finished up feeding the pigs at a local farm. This was a job that was forbidden to a Jew because the law stated, "Cursed is he who feeds the swine.

The turning point in the story came when the young man came to his senses and said that he was a sinner. He came back home, not to ask if he could be a son again or even a slave, because there still was some kind of tie to the family being even a slave. But he asked to be a paid servant who had no status or security, only day-to-day existence. He knew that he was a sinner, so he confessed and was repentant.

The father saw the son coming and rushed out to meet his repentant son. His father put a robe of honor on his son, a ring that gave him unlimited buying power, and shoes (a slave or hired servant had no shoes). A feast was ordered so that all might rejoice in that a sinner was lost but now was found, or as the father put it, "My son was dead, but now he is alive." We must never forget that the love of God can defeat even the deliberate rebellion of the heart.

Application

The first reading shows all men that we are not to under-estimate the ability of God. The second reading reveals that a Christian is not reformed or rehabilitated, but is a brand-new creation of almighty God. The Gospel says the Pharisees believed in destroying the sinner, but Jesus believed in saving the sinner.

This week, let people around you see Christ-like actions, not Pharisee-type actions. Show others by your mercy, by your ability to listen, by your not joining in the gossip, and by showing joy when someone apologizes for something they have done wrong. Jesus believed that love will conquer all forms of evil, and your actions will prove to the "people of the land" that he is right. Jesus loved and saved, and you are called to do no less.

FIFTH SUNDAY OF LENT - CYCLE C

BEFORE YOU BEGIN:

Pray and ask God to speak to you through His Holy Spirit. "THE PARACLETE, THE HOLY SPIRIT WHOM THE FATHER WILL SEND IN MY NAME, WILL INSTRUCT YOU IN EVERYTHING, AND REMIND YOU OF ALL THAT I TOLD YOU." (JOHN 14:26)

FIRST DAY	**Reread last week's readings.**

1. What was a helpful or new thought from the readings or from the homily you heard on Sunday?

2. From what you learned, what personal application did you choose to apply to your life this week?

SECOND DAY	**READ ISAIAH 43:16-21**	**FIRST READING**

("See, I am doing something new!")

1. What has the Lord done? Isaiah 43:16

2. Why has he done this? Isaiah 51:10.

3. When was this done? Exodus 14:21.

4. Who lies prostrate never to rise again? Isaiah 43:17

5. What are we not to remember or even consider? Isaiah 43:18

Personal - Memorize Isaiah 43:18. When your mind begins to dwell on the past, from this time forward, repeat this verse and keep your eyes on what Jesus has in store for you.

6. What is the Lord doing in verse 19 of Isaiah 43?

7. Who honors the Lord? Isaiah 43:20

8. Where does the Lord put water and who drinks it? Isaiah 43:20

9. Who are his chosen in the following scriptures: a. Luke 9:35 - b. Acts 1:2 - c. Deut. 7:6-11 - d. Romans 11:5 -

10. For what reason did he form these people? Isaiah 43:21

Personal - In what way do you see yourself as one of God's chosen people. Meditate on this.

THIRD DAY   READ PHILIPPIANS 3:8-14   SECOND READING

("I continue my pursuit toward the goal,
the prize of God's upward calling, in Christ Jesus.")

1.   To what has Paul considered all as loss, what has he accepted, and for what reason has he considered this? Philippians 3:8

2.   What is the righteousness Paul possesses and where does it have its origin? Philippians 3:9

3.   On what is this righteousness based? Philippians 3:9

4.   What three things does Paul wish to know in verse 10 of Philippians 3? 1. 2. 3.

5.   What does Romans 6:3-4 say about baptism?

6.   What must we do in order to be glorified with him? Romans 6:4 and John 3:16.

7.   What does Paul hope to attain? Philippians 3:11

8.   What has Paul not yet reached, what is he pursuing, and who has taken possession of him? Philippians 3:12

9.   What do Philippians 3:13 and Isaiah 43:18 tell us to forget and what are we to do?

10. Toward what is Paul pursuing and what is the prize? Philippians 3:14

Personal – In which of the following ways are you going towards the finish line: sitting, crawling, strolling, fast walking, or running? What is the goal you are pursuing?

FOURTH DAY   READ JOHN 8:1-11 GOSPEL

("Neither do I condemn you.
Go, (and) from now on do not sin anymore.")

1.   Where was Jesus and what did he do when the people started coming to him? John 8:1-2

2.   What two groups of men were there, who did they bring in, and what did they make her do? John 8:3

3.   How did they address Jesus and what did they say to him? John 8:4-5

4.   According to the law if a woman is married and is caught in adultery what will happen to both man and woman? Leviticus 20:10, Deuteronomy 22:22-24

5.   Why did they question Jesus about the adulterer and what did Jesus do when they questioned him about her? John 8:6

6.   When they persisted in their questioning, what did he say to them? John 8:7

7.   How can you avoid judgment, and what must you do to see clearly? Matthew 7:1-5

8.   Who are the sinners among us? Romans 3:23

9. What did Jesus do a second time, what happened to the audience, and in what succession? John 8:8-9

Personal - By whom are you being led? Are you obedient to what your leaders in government tell you? Are you obedient to what your church leaders tell you? Has there been a time when Jesus's Word has been put in conflict to what government or church law has stated? How have you responded to that conflict?

10. What did Jesus say to the woman after they were alone, what was her response, and then what did he say? John 8:10-11

11. In what does God take pleasure? Ezekiel 33:11

Personal - How can you bring pleasure to the Lord today? Take time to examine your conscience and attend the sacrament of reconciliation this week.

FIFTH DAY   **READ PSALM 126:1-6**

(The Lord will lead his people from captivity to freedom)

Read and meditate on Psalm 126:1-6.

What is the Lord saying to you personally through the Psalm?

How can you apply this to your life?

SIXTH DAY READ ALL OF THE COMMENTARY

ISAIAH 43:16-21

The prophet Isaiah continues to proclaim a favorite theme to the exiles in Babylon. It is called, "The New Exodus." God is being shown as the one "creating Israel - opening a way - leading out chariots". The words portray the exodus out of Egypt, ending in the final scene where the Egyptians are lying prostrate and never to be rising. Pharaoh's troops were crushed and drowned as they rushed into the parted sea opened for the Israelites (Exodus 15:19). The Israelites are being warned not to continue glorifying in a past that has no time for application in the present.

The old exodus was temporary; the new exodus is forever. The word Anamnesis is from this great act of exodus. (Exodus 15:19) Anamnesis means to bring back, to continue, to recreate, to live. This is the heart of the Eucharistic prayer that constitutes the new exodus at every celebration of the Catholic Mass. The people are being told to stop looking in the past and look to the future, toward the permanent, new exodus.

PHILIPPIANS 3:8-14

Paul shows us that true freedom can be found only in Jesus Christ, not in observance of a law. He came to God in humble faith, as Jesus told him to do, and he found that fellowship he had sought for so long. Paul discovers that a right relationship with God is based not on law but on faith in Jesus Christ. Righteousness is not achieved by any man but given by God. Paul's understanding of Christ changed his whole value system.

Paul, being a Jew himself, was very much aware of how complete compliance with the law was stressed. He was an educated man, a Roman citizen, and one who hunted down people who did not comply fully with the Jewish belief.

To Paul, salvation meant sharing in the power of Christ's resurrection as well as sharing in the suffering and becoming like him in death. Like Paul, we too hope to share in the power of Christ's resurrection, even as it means sharing in his sufferings and becoming like him in death. Our sharing in his suffering can be through rejection by loved ones, family or friends. Jesus experienced rejection by friends right in his own home town. It is this kind of imitation of Christ that gives us hope that will be completed by our resurrection from the dead, even as Christ also was raised.

Paul tells us that he has not yet reached his goal, that he is not yet been raised and is not yet perfect. Paul tells us in 1 Timothy 6:12 "Fight the good fight of faith, take firm hold on the everlasting life to which you were called, when, in the presence of many witnesses you made your noble profession of faith." We continue to make our profession of faith every time we say the Nicene Creed at a Roman Catholic Mass until we reach the finish line which is life on high in Christ Jesus.

Resurrection and perfection are goals which are pursued, not ones which we already have. The prize of which Paul speaks is "Life on high in Christ Jesus", that is, knowing and experiencing Jesus. Our righteousness and goals come not because of our merit but because of grace which comes from God through Jesus Christ.

JOHN 8:1-11

In the eyes of the Jewish law, adultery was a very serious crime and was punishable by death. The Scribes and the Pharisees were out to get something on Jesus and discredit him.

A scribe was an educated man, an intellectual, maybe a lawyer or even a scholar. They were teachers of the Law. Many were chosen to be Rabbis. A Pharisee was a leader who practiced the observance of the law to its maximum degree. The Pharisees were more concerned with keeping the external tenets of the law than what was in your heart.

The leaders insisted that Jesus give a decision on what to do with this adulteress. They were hoping to trap him. Jesus turned the tables on them by saying, "Let the man that is without sin cast the first stone." The elders were the first to leave and the rest followed. Today, as in the days of Christ, people still follow the lead of influential people in the community, even if they are uninformed. Jesus asked her where did her tormentors go, and who is there to condemn her. Jesus told her that he does not condemn her either and to go and sin no more. In Jesus there is the gospel of the second chance. He didn't say that what she had done did not matter; broken laws and broken hearts always matter; but he was interested in her future more than in her past.

The Pharisees and scribes wished to condemn; Jesus wished to forgive. They knew the thrill of exercising power to condemn; Jesus knew the thrill of exercising the power to forgive. Jesus confronted the woman with a challenge to go out and reach for a life that does not involve sin. He called her to go out and fight, to change her life completely. Jesus showed his belief in her as a person. He did not say "Lady you are a loser." He said, "Go and sin no more." His method is not to blast people with the knowledge which they already knew, that they were miserable sinners, but to inspire them to become living saints.

Jesus also gives a warning, unspoken but implied. She has a choice either to go back to her old life and end up in destruction or to reach out to the new way with him. Jesus tells the man who he had just healed in the pool to stop sinning or something worse may happen to him (John 5:14). He clearly warns all of us that sin leads only to destruction. He offers to all of us the second chance, the gift of forgiveness.

Application

The first reading shows us that to look "back" is not of the Lord. The second reading reveals that only in Christ can true freedom be experienced. The Gospel tells us that Jesus forgives us, he does not condemn us. This week, let your family and your community see and experience you as a person who seeks justice and extends mercy and forgiveness. A person who can forgive and forget is a person who is really free.

PASSION (PALM) SUNDAY - CYCLE C

BEFORE YOU BEGIN:

Pray and ask God to speak to you through His Holy Spirit. "THE PARACLETE, THE HOLY SPIRIT WHOM THE FATHER WILL SEND IN MY NAME, WILL INSTRUCT YOU IN EVERYTHING, AND REMIND YOU OF ALL THAT I TOLD YOU." (JOHN 14:26)

FIRST DAY	**Reread last week's readings.**	

1. What was a helpful or new thought from the readings or from the homily you heard on Sunday?

2. From what you learned, what personal application did you choose to apply to your life this week?

SECOND DAY	**READ ISAIAH 50:4-7**	**FIRST READING**

("The Lord is my help, therefore I am not disgraced.")

1. From where did the well-trained tongue come? To whom has he given it, and for what reason has he been given a well-trained tongue? Isaiah 50:4

2. When and what does he open, that you may hear? Isaiah 50:4

3. What has he not done? Isaiah 50:5

4. What happens to those who rebel? 1 Samuel 12:15

5. What did the servant do to those who beat him and plucked his beard? Isaiah 50:6

6. From what did he not shield his face? Isaiah 50:6, Matthew 26:67 and 27:30

7. Who is the servant's help, and how has he set his face? Isaiah 50:7

8. What does the servant know? Isaiah 50:7

Personal - When do you hear the Lord speaking to you? What is he saying to you? In what way, by using a well-trained tongue, do you rouse the weary in your own household? Pray and ask the Lord to reveal to you how you can train your tongue.

THIRD DAY	**READ PHILIPPIANS 2:6-11**	**SECOND READING**

("Jesus Christ is Lord.")

1. What must be your attitude? Philippians 2:5

2. Of whom was he in the form? Philippians 2:6

3. Who is Christ? John 1:1, 14

4. What was something at which he did not grasp? Philippians 2:6

5. Rather, of what did he become empty and why? Philippians 2:7, 2 Corinthians 8:9

6. Of what did he take the form, and in whose likeness was he born, and of what was he known to be? Philippians 2:7

7. What two things did he do in verse 8 of Philippians 2?

8. For what reason did he do the above two things? Hebrews 2:14,17

9. Because he humbled himself and accepted death on the cross, what two things did God do for him? Philippians 2:9

10. What must every knee do, in the heavens, on the earth, and under the earth, at the name of Jesus, and what must every tongue proclaim? Philippians 2:10-11

11. What does this tell you beyond a doubt? Acts 2:36

12. For whose glory is this proclaimed (Philippians 2:11), and what will happen to you if you confess with your lips that Jesus is Lord and believe in your heart that God raised him from the dead? Romans 10:9

13. Who gives you the power to say "Jesus is Lord?" 1 Corinthians 12:3

Personal – In what way is your attitude that of Christ? In what way have you humbled yourself? What cross have you obediently accepted? Read Mark 8:34 and meditate on this.

FOURTH DAY   **READ LUKE 22:14-23:56**   **GOSPEL**

("Father, forgive them; they do not know what they are doing.")

1. When Jesus took his place at the table what did he tell his disciples he was eager to do, what did he say about the cup, and what did he do and say with the bread and the cup? Luke 22:14-20

2. Who did Jesus say was at table with him, what did he say about him, and about what were the disciples debating? Luke 22:21-23

3. About what were the disciples arguing, what did Jesus say to them, and how did he say he was among them? Luke 22:24-27

Personal – In what ways do you show others that you are a servant?

4. Who did Jesus say stood by him in trials, and what did he say would happen to them? Luke 22:28-30

5. What did Jesus say Satan has demanded, what did Jesus do so their faith would not fail, what did he tell them to do, and what did he say to Peter? Luke 22:31-34

6. What did Jesus tell his disciples to do now in contrast to what they were doing, what did he say about the scripture, and what was his reply to the disciples "Look, look, there are two swords?" Luke 22:35-38

7. When Jesus and the disciples went to the Mt. of Olives, what did he say to them. Withdrawing from them what did Jesus say to his Father, what strengthened him, and what was happening to him? Luke 22:39-44

8. How did Jesus find his disciples and what did he tell them? Luke 22:45-46

Personal - In what way have you failed to stay awake when someone you know was hurting?

9. How did Judas betray Jesus, what did Jesus say to him, what was the disciples response, and what did Jesus do and say? Luke 22:47-53

10. After they led Jesus away to arrest him what happened to Peter, when did Peter remember the word of the Lord, and what was his response? Luke 22:54-62

11. How did the men who held Jesus treat him, what did they say to Jesus when they brought him before the Sanhedrin, what was his response, and what was their conclusion? Luke 22:66-71

12. What did the assembly say about Jesus, what did Pilate ask Jesus, what did he say about his guilt, and how did the people respond to this? Luke 23:1-5

13. Where did Pilate send Jesus, what was Herod's reaction to seeing Jesus, and why did he react that way? Luke 23:6-8

14. How was Jesus treated by Herod, the scribes, chief priest and soldiers, what happened to Herod and Pilate's relationship that day, and what did Pilate say to the chief priest, rulers, and the people? Luke 23:9-17

Personal - Share a time you have been swayed by popular opinion and gone along with the crowd? Did it turn out to be a good or bad decision?

15. What did the people shout, who was Barabbas, what happened to Barabbas, and how many times did Pilate address the people? Luke 23:18-25

16. Who carried the cross behind Jesus, who followed after Jesus, and what did Jesus say to them? Luke 23:26-31

17. Who was led away with Jesus to be executed, what happened at the place called the Skull, and what did Jesus ask the Father? Luke 23:32-34

Personal - In what way does your life show that you have accepted and received God's forgiveness for you?

18. What did the rulers say, what did the soldiers call out to him, and what was inscribed above him? Luke 23:35-38

19. What did each of the criminals hanging there with Jesus say, and what did Jesus tell the one? Luke 23:39-43

20. At noon what happened to the veil in the temple, what did Jesus say before he breathed his last, what did the centurion and the people say and do? Luke 23:44-48

21. Where were his acquaintances including the women, who was Joseph, and what did he do? Luke 23:49-53

22. What day was it, what was about to begin, what did the women do, and what was the commandment they observed? Luke 23:54-56

Personal - Since last year what change has taken place in you life as a result of what Jesus has done for you?

FIFTH DAY **READ PSALM 22:8-9, 17-20, 23-24**

("They have pierced my hands and my feet.")

Read and meditate on Psalm 22:8-9, 17-20, 23-24.

What is the Lord saying to you personally through the Psalm?

How can you apply this to your life?

SIXTH DAY **READ ALL OF THE COMMENTARY**

ISAIAH 50:4-7

The source of strength and courage for all suffering, trial, and tribulations is the suffering and death of our divine Lord Jesus Christ. We need to hold fast to him when the world closes in with its assault, rejection, and abandonment. He not only has traveled this same road before the saints of old, but he travels it today constantly waiting to be with us in our suffering.

Jesus' suffering and death opened the road to heaven for all, even though many refuse the gift. He gave up everything for us, and he bestowed us with love, trust, hope, respect, and eternal life. In return, he was spat upon, ridiculed, beaten, jeered, scourged and mocked. He finally was executed when he was nailed to a cross on Calvary between two criminals.

This is a day of reflection as we are about to enter Holy Week. Let us not forget the actions and the words of this suffering servant of Isaiah. We need to reflect on how quickly the crowd changed from adoring him to jeering him. He had taken up a cross for us, and we must remember that we too are called to carry a cross for someone else. Sometimes we think our cross is too heavy, or that it is unfair to bear such a heavy cross. Dying to self and putting the needs of others first is our daily cross. How heavy is your cross compared to Christ's? How is your Calvary compared to Jesus' Calvary?

PHILIPPIANS 2:6-11

Paul tells us that our attitude should be the same as that of Jesus Christ (Phil. 2:5). He describes putting on the attitude of a servant rather than that of a king. Jesus, though being God, did not demand his rights and privileges of royalty. He deliberately set them all aside and had taken on the role of a servant. There lies the incredible formula of a successful leader. Jesus led by serving all of us. He showed us that by putting others first and by being humble are the only ways a person can become a real leader. The sheep followed the shepherd because they trusted him. People will follow a leader if they know that he has their welfare at heart.

Jesus showed us everything of God's character in human terms. He was obedient even unto death, and the type of death he chose for himself was extremely painful. Jesus is the perfect role model for us in the world today. How many times do you demand your rights when you are being treated less than fairly? The name of Jesus should bring to every Christian person the name of a person who willingly died so that all people could be free, and he died for us absolutely knowing that we are sinners (Romans 5:8).

Jesus voluntarily laid aside his divine rights, privileges, and position out of love for his Father. We, too, are called to lay aside our rights and privileges for our oppressed brothers and sisters in the holy name of Jesus.

LUKE 22:14-23:56

Today's gospel is lengthy and very powerful. It reveals the emotions of the powerful and the lowly. We see Jesus at the Last Supper eagerly waiting for it to begin. He has mixed feelings of joy and sadness, because a betrayer was sitting among a group of very close friends. We see pride and greed being displayed in the question, "Who among them was the greatest?" And the Master knew he was to be betrayed for thirty pieces of silver.

The betrayal of Christ by Judas happens and Jesus is arrested in the dark of night. He is ridiculed, humiliated, tortured, and was denied, rejected and abandoned by his closest followers. He faced the mockery of a trial and his friends and family became unfriendly towards him. Nevertheless, he was not alone in that his Father was with him and in him. He was strengthened and enlightened by the Holy Spirit.

He was humiliated and whipped by the soldiers and dragged through the howling mob to a hill called Golgotha which means Skull. Jesus was flung and nailed onto a cross. The kingdom of God was now about to be inaugurated through his death, and the places on his right and left were to be taken by two dying criminals. Jesus told his two power-hungry disciples, James and John, (Mark 10:35-39) that a person who wishes to be close to him must be prepared to suffer and die as he did. This message is meant for us even today. The way to the kingdom is the way of the cross. Jesus then manifested to the whole world by being on the cross the core to healing is through forgiveness. Jesus asked his Father to forgive all those who were putting him to death. This included the corrupt leaders in the church, politicians, soldiers, and even the bystanders who laughed and ridiculed while he was on the cross. God answered that prayer by opening the way to salvation to all sinners including Jesus' murderers.

Since we are all sinners (Romans 3:23) we have all played a part in putting Jesus to death. The Good News is that God forgives and he gives us a new life through his Son, Jesus. The thief on the right side of Jesus called out to him for forgiveness, and Jesus accepted him and granted the forgiveness to him. This shows that our faith in Jesus is a saving faith, and it is never to late to turn to God. Even in his misery Jesus had mercy on this criminal, and that same mercy is waiting to be granted to us.

Application

The first reading tells us that we are to live in God's light not our own light. The second reading tells us that Jesus was an obedient servant even unto death on the cross. The gospel reveals forgiveness is the core of healing.

This week, let yourself experience what it really means to forgive. Look around and see in your family, job, or school those whom you need to forgive. Jesus tells us that it is necessary to forgive others just as he has forgiven us. You have the power within yourself through the Holy Spirit (1 John 4:4) to hold someone in bondage or you can forgive and give them freedom. The choice is yours, and remember, the truth will set you free (John 8:32).

THE BREAD OF LIFE CATHOLIC BIBLE STUDY

EASTER SUNDAY - CYCLE C

BEFORE YOU BEGIN:

Pray and ask God to speak to you through His Holy Spirit. "THE PARACLETE, THE HOLY SPIRIT WHOM THE FATHER WILL SEND IN MY NAME, WILL INSTRUCT YOU IN EVERYTHING, AND REMIND YOU OF ALL THAT I TOLD YOU." (JOHN 14:26)

FIRST DAY	Reread last week's readings.

1. What was a helpful or new thought from the readings or from the homily you heard on Sunday?

2. From what you learned, what personal application did you choose to apply to your life this week?

SECOND DAY	READ ACTS 10:34, 37-43	FIRST READING

("We have eaten and drunk with him
after his resurrection from the dead.")

1. Who was Peter addressing? Acts 10:24-28

2. What did he say to them? Acts 10:34-35

3. How does Deuteronomy 10:17 describe God, and what does it say he does not do? 2 Chronicles 19:7

4. For what reason does God have no favorites? Job 34:19, Wisdom 6:7.

Personal - In what way do you show partiality with your children, your friends, and your co-workers? Spend time alone with the Lord, repent of this, and ask the Lord to help you look at others through his eyes.

5. What was reported all over Judea about Jesus of Nazareth? Where did it begin, and with what? Acts 10:37-38

6. Who anointed Jesus and who anointed Paul, Silvanus, and Timothy? Acts 10:38, 2 Corinthians 1:21-22

7. What two things did Jesus go about doing and who was with him? Acts 10:38

8. To what are they witnesses, what did they finally do to him, and what did God do? Acts 10:39-40

9. What did God grant, and by whom? Acts 10:40-41

10. Who are the chosen and for what purpose are they chosen? Ephesians 1:13

11. What did he commission us to do? Acts 10:42

12. Whom has he sent to preach to the people? Mark 3:14

13. Who are his disciples today? John 8:31, John 13:35

14. To what are we to bear witness and to what do all the prophets testify?
Acts 10:42-43

Personal – What results and power do you see in your everyday life from your anointing with the Holy Spirit? Does your family see good works and healing taking place from your touch? Reflect on this.

THIRD DAY   **READ COLOSSIANS 3:1-4**   **SECOND READING**

("Be intent on things above rather than things of earth.")

1. With whom have we been raised up, and on what should we set our heart?
Colossians 3:1

2. Where is Christ seated? Colossians 3:1

3. Who raised us up and gave us a place in the heavens? Ephesians 2:4-6.

4. On what are we to be intent and why? Colossians 3:2-3

5. What are things that are rooted in earth? Colossians 3:5, 8, 9

6. How do we become intent on things above? Colossians 3:10

7. Where is our life hidden now? Colossians 3:3

8. Who is Christ to us? Colossians 3:4

9. When Christ appears, what will happen to us and in what way? Colossians 3:4

Personal – As you have died with Christ to your old desires and to things rooted in this earth, do your family, friends, and work acquaintances see you as a reflection of Christ? On a sheet of paper name some of the characteristics of Christ in one column and in another column list your characteristics through a 24-hour day and compare the two columns.

("He saw and believed.")

1. Who came to the tomb, what time was it, and what day was it? John 20:1

2. Where was Mary Magdalene as Jesus hung on the cross? John 19:25

3. What did Jesus drive out of Mary? Mark 16:9.

4. What did Mary see when she arrived at the tomb? John 20:1

5. To whom did she run, and what did she say to them? John 20:2

6. What did Peter and the other disciple do? John 20:3

7. Who reached the tomb first, and how did they get there? John 20:4

Personal – In what way do you see yourself running to see Jesus? Are you persevering in running the race? On whom are you keeping your eyes fixed? Do your family and friends see you as someone with eyes looking up or cast down? Read Hebrews 12:1-2.

8. What did the disciple do when he got to the tomb and what did he see lying on the ground? John 20:5

9. What did Peter do when he got there? What did he observe on the ground, and what did he notice about the cloth which had covered Jesus' head? John 20:6-7

10. What did the disciple who had arrived first do, and what was his reaction to this? John 20:8

11. What does it take to believe? John 1:12

12. What will you receive by believing in the name of Jesus? John 3:36

13. After Jesus rose from the dead, what did the disciples come to understand and believe? John 2:22

14. When did they understand and believe? Luke 24:30-32

15. What does Jesus say about those who believe and have not seen? John 20:29

Personal – How have you seen a change take place in your life through reading the scriptures? Have you come to believe in the spoken word of Jesus through the scriptures? Remember, John tells us Jesus is the Word made flesh. Pray and ask God to fill you with an understanding of the Word through his gift of the Holy Spirit that you received from him.

FIFTH DAY **READ PSALM 118:1-2, 16-17, 22-23**

("The right hand of the Lord has struck with power.")

Read and meditate on Psalm 118:1-2, 16-17, 22-23.

What is the Lord saying to you personally through the Psalm?

How can you apply this to your life?

SIXTH DAY **READ ALL OF THE COMMENTARY**

ACTS 10:34, 37-43

Alleluia is a Hebrew word that means "praise ye the Lord." On this great day of Easter Sunday we give thanks, gratitude and our complete joy in the form of praise to our Lord, Jesus Christ. This passage strongly shows that the resurrection is the basic doctrine and proof of the truth of the Christian faith. We are told in scripture that if Christ has not risen, then our preaching is in vain, and our faith is worthless also (1 Cor. 15:14).

There are many today who disregard the physical resurrection and say that it is no big deal. They say that it is the spiritual resurrection that really matters. St. Paul says just the opposite. Jesus rose from the dead, and then he was seen by witnesses who had not only spoken with him, but had actually eaten with him. The Apostles were devastated on Friday night after the crucifixion. They remained locked in the upper room, fearful of what the Roman soldiers were going to do next. They were even too afraid to do any wishful thinking about their beloved master Jesus. They were hard to convince even when it happened.

We need to reflect on this passage. Have we seen him, have we talked with him, have we eaten with him? he is alive today, and like the Apostle Peter, we too are called to evangelize and teach about Jesus. We are called to fellowship with others who believe that he is risen and that he lives today. We need to discover through Christ something significant about each other, both believers and non-believers. He has risen for the whole world - Alleluia - Alleluia!

COLOSSIANS 3:1-4

In this passage, Paul begins by bringing us into the core meaning of our baptism. In the early days of the church, baptism was by total immersion. When you heard the story of Christ and you were ready to believe in the one true God, the Father, the Son, and the Holy Spirit, you were then immersed in water. You were cleansed from your sins and worldliness. Immersion was a symbol of being drowned or buried with Christ. This signified that the new Christian has died to all earthly attachmentsand desires. He was raised out of the water or the tomb to be with the risen Christ. Paul said, "If you have been raised with Christ, seek the things that are above." This means that we must mean what we say and do.

We have been raised with Christ and we no longer need to dwell on things of the earth. This does not mean we can walk away from responsibility. It does not mean just being obedient to parents and to society. It does not mean just that we have to work to support ourselves or our families. It means that our earthly possessions must not dominate our life.

We are called to love people, not things, money, power, status, etc. Our lives need to show that what we did at baptism has life-long meaning. What we do is far more effective on others than what we say. We were created for unending happiness in heaven and this happiness is now within our grasp, thanks to the death and resurrection of Jesus Christ. We are helped in our daily living by God's holy grace. Remember, God wants us to go to heaven, and he has an Easter resurrection planned for all of us.

JOHN 20:1-9

The divine plan of God for all people was accomplished through the death and resurrection of Jesus Christ. All people would now be eligible to be called sons and daughters of God because of Jesus Christ's perfect act of obedience. Because of him, we will one day like Christ rise from the grave in our glorified bodies. The resurrection was the basis of the new Christian faith. Had it not happened, Christianity would never have started. There would have been no Easter Sunday. Peter would have returned with his companions to their fishing nets and boats, and Jesus Christ would have been forgotten after a few short years.

Mary Magdalene's discovery of an empty tomb brought shock and fear. She ran to Peter and told him that she thought someone had stolen the body of Jesus. Peter had to see for himself and check out the facts. We might take notice of how the clothes were folded after they discovered Jesus' body was gone. They would not have been arranged that way if there had been a robbery. The disciples were completely surprised when they found the empty tomb. It was only then that they remembered that Jesus had said that he would rise again.

Many people today do not believe in Jesus because the "facts" do not check out. We can only accept the fact of the resurrection when we have first personally encountered Jesus Christ. The understanding of the resurrection takes on a special meaning as we commit our life to Jesus and his presence remains with us. Jesus' resurrection is the key to our Christian faith because death, as we know it, is not the end. Jesus' bodily resurrection shows us that he is ruler of God's kingdom. Because of his promise, we who die to ourselves with him will rise from the dead with him. Because of him, you and I can face tomorrow without fear. Because of him, we have his Holy Spirit living within us and protecting us against all evil (1 John 4:4). Because of him, we can witness to all the people in the world that if they believe in Jesus Christ, they will be given eternal happiness. Because of him, all mankind can really be free and live forever. Alleluia - he is Risen - Alleluia - he is Alive.

Application

The first reading shows that "Alleluia" is a Hebrew word that means Praise the Lord. The second reading reveals that Baptism is being drowned or buried with Christ. The Gospel tells us that because of Jesus Christ all mankind can really be free.

Jesus' death brought us freedom from sin and death. We are now called to free others from sin and death here on earth. Some of us can do that by our professions as medical people, legal people, politicians, educators, business people, parents, and children. This week, free someone in your family, home, or workplace from a chore that you know they do not like. Let them see that joy in someone who really knows that he is free. Then each day, have your family gather together to pray that all may become free from sin through Jesus Christ. Because of him, you are free. Let freedom ring throughout this land.

THE BREAD OF LIFE CATHOLIC BIBLE STUDY

SECOND SUNDAY OF EASTER - CYCLE C

BEFORE YOU BEGIN:

Pray and ask God to speak to you through His Holy Spirit. "THE PARACLETE, THE HOLY SPIRIT WHOM THE FATHER WILL SEND IN MY NAME, WILL INSTRUCT YOU IN EVERYTHING, AND REMIND YOU OF ALL THAT I TOLD YOU." (JOHN 14:26)

FIRST DAY   **Reread last week's readings.**

1.   What was a helpful or new thought from the readings or from the homily you heard on Sunday?

2.   From what you learned, what personal application did you choose to apply to your life this week?

SECOND DAY   **READ ACTS 5:12-16**   **FIRST READING**

("Many signs and wonders were done among the people....")

1.   By what means did many signs and wonders occur? Acts 5:12

2.   From where did the power to perform these signs and wonders come? Acts 1:8

3.   This power has been passed on to whom? Acts 2:38-39

4.   In what regard do the people place the apostles? Acts 5:13

5.   What did men and women in great numbers do? Acts 5:14

6.   What did the apostles say that they came to believe? Acts 4:4

7.   As a result of people believing and being added to their number, what did they do, and where did they bring the sick? Acts 5:15

8.   What happened to the sick and those disturbed by unclean spirits? Acts 5:15-16

9.   Read the following Scriptures and tell what constitutes healing: Mark 5:34 - Luke 18:42 - Acts 14:9

10. Read the following Scriptures and tell who was healed: Matthew 8:16 - Matt. 12:15 - Mark 6:56 - Acts 5:16 -

Personal – In what way do you see signs and wonders occurring in your home? In what way do you, your family, friends, and co-workers need healing? What do you think will bring about a healing? Meditate on this and then share it with someone.

("the first and the last and the one who lives")

1. On what island did John find himself? Revelation 1:9

2. See if you can find this island on a Bible map.

3. With whom does John share and what three things does he share with them? Revelation 1:4, 9

4. Why was John sent to the island Patmos? Revelation 1:9

Personal – In what way have you ever felt deserted or isolated for proclaiming God's word and for having borne witness to Jesus?

5. On the Lord's day John heard something. What was it, and what did it say? Revelation 1:10-11

6. For what did John turn around, and what did he see? Revelation 1:12-13

7. What did he hold in his right hand and what came out of his mouth? Revelation 1:16

8. When John caught sight of him, what did he do? Revelation 1:17

9. What did he say to John? Revelation 1:17-19

10. What did he tell him to do when he sees a vision, what he sees now, and what he will see in time to come? Revelation 1:19

Personal – What were some thoughts or visions you had today that you could write down? How can writing your spiritual thoughts in a journal each night help you in your journey through life?

(Blest are they who have not seen and have believed.)

1. On the evening of the first day of the week who appeared to the disciples, what did they do to the door, and for what reason? John 20:19

2. What did he say to them, what did he show them, and what was their reaction? John 2:19-20

3. What did he say again to them? John 20:21

Personal – Reflect on areas in which you do not have peace. Stop what you're doing in that area and ask the Holy Spirit if it is an area that he is sending you or speaking through you, or is it an area of your own doing?

4. In Verse 22 of John 20, what did Jesus do and say to the disciples?

5. What must we do to receive the Holy Spirit? Acts 2:38

6 If you forgive men's sins, what will happen to them; and if you retain them, what will happen? John 20:23

7. What did Jesus say to Peter in Matthew 16:19?

8. Read Matthew 18:18; what does it say about binding and loosing?

9. Who was absent when Jesus came to the disciples, what did they keep telling him, and what was his answer? John 20:24-25

10. What happened a week later, what was the greeting, what did Jesus say to Thomas, and what was his response? John 20:26-28

11. Whom did Jesus say are the blessed? John 20:29

12. What did Jesus do, and why have these been recorded? John 20:30-31

13. Where do you find your life? John 14:6 and John 20:31. Write out John 14:6.

Personal - What areas of life (education, job, athletics, hobbies, etc.) have you been pursuing? In what way can you focus more on the true fulfillment (Jesus) in life rather than on what you have been doing?

FIFTH DAY   **READ PSALM 118:2-4, 13-15, 22-24**

*(The stone which the builders
rejected has become the cornerstone.)*

Read and meditate of Psalm 118:2-4, 13-15, 22-24.

What is the Lord saying to you personally through the Psalm?

How can you apply this to your life?

SIXTH DAY   **READ ALL OF THE COMMENTARY**

ACTS 5:12-16

It was like in the days of Jesus in Galilee all over again, so many were being healed by the apostles. No wonder the Jewish authorities grew jealous of their enormous influence. But threats, imprisonment, even the lash are no weapons with which to resist the power of God. The apostles demonstrated an almost unlimited amount of healing power. The healing was so spectacular that it seemed almost like magic. Peter parallels such items as Paul's handkerchief (Acts.19:12) and the edge of Jesus' cloak (Mt. 9:20). But Peter very carefully tells all that his healing power comes from God in Jesus' name (Acts 3:12-16).

Today, many wonder if God really heals his people. Where are the people like Peter, Paul, and the other apostles? Why are people so reluctant to reach out and call for a healing? We see in today's Scripture a high sense of expectancy by the people. We see them bringing their sick out into the streets and believing that a healing was going to take place. We need to bring that expectancy into our lives, and God's healing power will explode today just as it did in the Scriptures. We need to fall on our knees and repent of our sin of unbelief and let God heal us through his signs and wonders.

We see people like St. Francis of Assisi, Mother Teresa, and many Spirit-filled expectant Christians today who confidently call forth God's healing power through their loving touch to the poor. his healing power was given to all who professed that he was Lord and, as in Scripture, everyone who called on him was healed. His healing power is alive today through his Word, Eucharist, and the loving touch of his children. He is the healer yesterday, today, and forever.

It was common practice for groups to meet for teaching and discussion in the courts of the public buildings. Disciples listened to their teachers in the courts of the Temple. The Christians met in Solomon's Porch; but knowing the authorities' hostilities toward them, many kept their distance. Some Jews were afraid to join the meetings because they were in direct defiance of the Sanhedrin's order as seen in chapter four of Acts.

Because of the fate of Ananias and his wife (Acts 5:1-11), those who want to follow Christ should seriously evaluate the cost of discipleship.

REVELATION 1:9-13, 17-19

Revelation shows us that John was a church leader who was well known to the seven churches in Asia Minor. The churches were located about 50 miles apart and formed a circle in what today is known as Turkey. These churches were like postal centers, and the entire book of Revelation apparently was sent to each one of the seven churches.

The Christians were entering a time of persecution and John, himself, was sent to the Island of Patmos which was a Roman penal colony. Roman authorities at this time were beginning to enforce the cult of emperor worship. Christians who held that Christ, not Caesar, was Lord faced great hostility. John, himself, was exiled for proclaiming the Word of God and the testimony of Jesus (v.9).

John wrote to the believers to resist staunchly the demands of emperor worship. John is also encouraged to write about what is current and what is to happen. We also need to write, read, and reflect on what the Lord is saying to us in our daily living. Like John, we are called to spread the word of God and testimony of Jesus. We need to write in our journal those daily inspirational thoughts that come from the Holy Spirit. We also need to stand up like John did to the idolatry of today's world.

The gods of money, power, sex, and the media are very powerful and demand full tribute. We, like John, may be called upon to pay the price for our belief in Jesus Christ. Jesus tells us to go forth and make disciples of all nations (Mat. 28:16-20). Jesus gave John the great commission; he responded, and we are called to make the same response.

JOHN 20:19-31

There is a story told about a primitive South American jungle tribe that had as its most important member someone who was called "A keeper of the flame." Fire among this primitive people was a precious commodity and to start a fire often took long hours. Keeping the flame going was much easier. It was the very important task of the flame keeper to add wood to the fire at night and to be sure the fire never went out. In today's Gospel we see Jesus' final appearance was to prepare the disciples to continue to carry on his earthly ministry. His final words to his followers are basically words that will equip them to be "keepers of the flame."

Jesus appeared to this small group of frightened men gathered in the upper room. He found them in the darkness of despair. Jesus greeted them, "Peace be unto you" (John 20:19). Oh, how they needed to hear those words from him. A more frightened group of men could not be found anywhere in Jerusalem that night.

Jesus startled his disciples out of their despair by reminding them of a fundamental fact: "As the Father has sent me, I am sending you" (John 20:21). Jesus is saying, " I need you to continue the work that I started." Even though he would be seen leaving to ascend to heaven, the fire started by his life, death, and resurrection must not be extinguished. He must continue to teach, preach, heal, save mankind, and he will do it through his "keepers of the flame." His new body will be composed of believers, and they will become Christ's hands, feet, heart, and life upon the earth.

And what about us? Is the message and mission of Jesus continuing in our world? Are we fulfilling the mission entrusted to the small group of men who followed Jesus of Nazareth? What is our calling? The answer to these questions requires a closer look at this Easter appearance of Jesus. Meeting their Resurrected Savior transformed eleven terrified apostles into courageous "keepers of the flame." The secret of their power is also our secret, and that is the peace of mind and heart.

The real power is the Holy Spirit, who gives us the Peace of Christ, and sends us out to fulfill the Great Commission. He gives us the power to fulfill this mission by giving us what we need most, "His living presence in our life." There are four things we must be ready to do in a moment as "keepers of the flame": pray, preach, give our testimony, and die. The mission of our Lord, Jesus Christ, is ours; and we must be ready to do what he has done also.

Application

The first reading shows that Jesus is the healer yesterday, today, and forever. The second reading shows that like John, we are called to spread the Word of God everywhere. The Gospel tells us that we are called to be "keepers of the flame."

To be a "keeper of the flame" in your family, you must take on the responsibility of making certain that the fire does not go out. You can do this by your prayer, leading your family in Scripture, attending the sacraments with them, encouraging them to give their lives to Christ, and letting them see in your actions that you are a real "keeper of the flame."

THIRD SUNDAY IN EASTER - CYCLE C

BEFORE YOU BEGIN:

Pray and ask God to speak to you through His Holy Spirit. "THE PARACLETE, THE HOLY SPIRIT WHOM THE FATHER WILL SEND IN MY NAME, WILL INSTRUCT YOU IN EVERYTHING, AND REMIND YOU OF ALL THAT I TOLD YOU." (JOHN 14:26)

FIRST DAY   **Reread last week's readings.**

1. What was a helpful or new thought from the readings or from the homily you heard on Sunday?

2. From what you learned, what personal application did you choose to apply to your life this week?

SECOND DAY   **READ ACTS 5:27-32, 40-41**   **FIRST READING**

("We must obey God rather than men.")

1. Who was brought in and made to stand before the Sanhedrin? Who questioned them? Acts 5:17-18, 27

2. What strict orders were the apostles given, and with what did they fill Jerusalem? Acts 5:28

3. Whose name were they told not to speak about, and what did Peter and John say was impossible? Acts 4:18-20

4. What did Peter and the apostles say? Acts 5:29

5. Who raised Jesus, and what did the apostles say they did to him? Acts 5:30

6. Why did God exalt Jesus at his right hand as leader and savior? Acts 5:31

7. What do you receive when you repent? Acts 2:38

8. Who is given the Holy Spirit? Acts 5:32

9. What happened to the apostles, and what were they told? Acts 5:40

10. How did the apostles leave the Sanhedrin, and for what reason did they leave that way? Acts 5:41

Personal – In what way have you gone against the authorities in order to obey God rather than men? In what way have you spoken in the name of Jesus to your family, friends, co-workers or classmates?

("Worthy is the Lamb that was slain
to receive power and riches,...")

1. Who looked again, and what did he hear and see? Revelation 1:1-2, Revelation 5:11

2. As the angels cried out in a loud voice, who did they say was worthy and what did he receive? Revelation 5:12

3. What did John the Baptist call Jesus? John 1:29

4. How can we receive power and riches? Acts 1:8, Matthew 6:33

5. How do we receive wisdom and strength? James 1:5, Philippians 4:13

6. Who is not worthy of Jesus? Matthew 10:37-38

7. Who was heard crying out, and from where? Revelation 5:13

8. Whose knee should bend at the name of Jesus? Philippians 2:10

9. Who should receive blessing, honor, glory, and might forever and ever? Revelation 5:13

10. What did the four living creatures answer, and what did the elders do? Revelation 5:14

Personal – What has made you worthy to bear the name Christian? How do you find your self-worth? Revelation 5:12 and meditate on it.

("Simon, son of John, do you love me?")

1. To whom did Jesus reveal himself, and what were they doing? John 21:1-3

2. What time of day was Jesus standing on the shore, and what did the disciples not realize? John 21:4

3. What did Jesus call the disciples, what did he say to them, and what was their reply? John 21:5

4. What did Jesus tell them, what happened as a result of their doing what he asked, and who recognized the Lord? John 21:6-7

Personal – What has God asked of you, and what has been the result?

5. What did the disciples see on shore, what did Jesus say to them, and what did Simon Peter do? John 21:8-11

6. What did Jesus say to them, what did the disciples not dare to ask, what did Jesus do, and how many times was this that Jesus revealed himself to them since his resurrection? John 21:12-14

7. When they had finished breakfast, what did Jesus ask Simon Peter, what was his response, and what did Jesus tell him to do? John 21:15

8. What was Peter's response the second and third time Jesus asked him if he loved him, and what did he tell him to do? John 21:16-17

9. What did Jesus say would happen to Peter, and what did this signify? John 21:18-19

10. What did Jesus tell Peter to do? John 21:19

11. Why should you follow in Jesus' footsteps? 1 Peter 2:21

Personal – What have you done to show your love for Jesus? Who in your family, friends, work associates, or schoolmates have been fed by you this week?

FIFTH DAY   READ PSALM 30:2, 4-6, 11-13

("I will extol you, O Lord, for you drew me clear.")

Read and meditate on Psalm 30:2, 4-6, 11-13.

What is the Lord saying to you personally through the Psalm?

How can you apply this to your life?

SIXTH DAY   READ ALL OF THE COMMENTARY

ACTS 5:27-32, 40-41

We see in today's reading God's power working through a group of men. We might do well to ask ourselves what would we do if we were threatened by powerful leaders and faced imprisonment for talking about God. These men were beaten, arrested, and jailed and still went back to preaching God's Holy Word when they were released.

When we are convinced of the power of Christ's resurrection and have experienced the presence of his Holy Spirit, then we too will have the confidence to speak out for Christ.

The temple was a very busy place and many people stopped there to pray and worship at sunrise. These were the people the apostles met with the "Good News." Today in our own marketplaces there is a tendency to keep our religion a private affair between us and our God. It is very difficult to see Christian people turn their eyes away from acts of wrongdoing because they "do not want to get involved." Today we are experiencing a great amount of evil that is allowed to continue because the fear of man is greater than the fear of the Lord.

The apostles knew that the penalty for speaking out in the name of Jesus could mean death for them. The apostles knew their priorities. We should always try to keep peace with everyone (Romans 12:18), but conflict with the world and its authorities is sometimes inevitable for a Christian (John 15:18). There will be situations where you cannot obey both God and man, such as accepting the practice of abortion. Then you must obey God and trust in his word and not in man's word or law.

Jesus himself encourages us to follow him in his own words: What happiness it is when others hate you and exclude you and insult you and smear your name because you are mine! When that happens, rejoice! Yes, leap for joy! For you will have a great reward awaiting you in heaven (Luke 6:22-23). We are called to live as Christ has asked, sharing our faith no matter what the cost. We may not be beaten or thrown into jail, but we may be ridiculed, ostracized, or slandered.

To what extent are you willing to suffer for the sake of sharing the Gospel with others?

REVELATION 5:11-14

As Catholic Christians, we have been taught that angels are spiritual beings created by God, who help carry out his work on earth. In some instances they are messengers (Luke 1:26) and in others, they protect God's people (Daniel 6:23). The angels offer encouragement (Genesis 16:7), and give guidance (Exodus 14:9). There are both good and evil angels (Revelation 12:7-9), but because the evil angels follow Satan and not God, they have much less power and authority. The main role of the good angels is to offer continuous praise to God.

Today's reading shows us that only the Lamb of God, Jesus Christ, is worthy to open the scroll. The scroll signifies for us the events of history and it is Jesus Christ who holds it, not Satan. Jesus Christ is Lord, and he alone is worthy to set into motion the events of the last days of history. Jesus Christ is pictured as a lamb which symbolizes his humble submission to God's will. It is the lamb that becomes the focus in John's vision. Christ, the Lamb, was the perfect sacrifice for the sins of all mankind. He alone is the only one who can save us from the terrible events revealed by the scroll.

Jesus is also pictured as a lion symbolizing his authority and power (Revelation 5:5). Christ the Lamb won the greatest battle of all, defeating all the evil forces and death, by submitting humbly to God's will and dying on the cross. Christ the Lion is victorious because of what Christ the Lamb has already done.

We will enjoy the rewards of victory not because of our power and might, but through our humble submission to God. John, through his images of God, has shown us that it is in the act of humbly submitting our lives to God that we receive the power of God's Holy Spirit to do it. We must never forget that anyone who comes in repentance and faith is accepted by God and will be part of his kingdom. Wherever you go, let people see the fruit of humility shine in you and people will see in you, very clearly, the Lamb of God (John 1:29).

JOHN 21:1-19

In today's Gospel Jesus commissions Peter to feed his flock. Jesus appears to the disciples while they are fishing and calls out to them. It is important to remember that these men were tremendously disappointed in the way events had turned out. They had followed a loving Messiah who promised eternal life and now was gone. They decided to go back to doing what they originally did before they heard of Jesus Christ, and that was fishing. It seemed almost comical to recall Jesus' words, "I will make you fishers of men."

When Jesus called out to them and asked if they had caught any fish yet, they said no, and Jesus proceeded to tell these professional fishermen how to fish. These words must have struck them with tremendous force. The thoughts that must have been racing through the minds of these men in the boat must have been awesome and even fearful. They had seen him, they knew him to be dead, and there had been those appearances in the Upper Room; but then he disappeared. They obeyed his command and the result was incredible. John, trying desperately to keep his emotions under control, said to Peter that it must be the Lord on the shore giving the advice.

Peter explodes and jumps into the water to swim, crawl, run, anything to get to Jesus as soon as he can. John knew it was Jesus because he saw him do a similar miracle on Lake Genneserat (Luke 5:1-11). There on the beach, the apostles experience Jesus cooking for them and eating with them.

Jesus leads Peter through the tremendous healing experience that removed the cloud of his denial. Peter denied Jesus three times, and three times Jesus asked Peter if he loved him. When Peter answered yes, Jesus told him to feed his sheep. You need to remember it is one thing to say that you love Jesus, but the real test is your willingness to serve him. Peter had repented and now Jesus asked him to commit his life. Peter's life changed when he finally realized who Jesus was. Peter had faced his true feelings when confronted by Jesus, and we have to confront our true feelings too. How would you respond today if Jesus asked you, "Do you love me, do you really love me?"

Application

The first reading shows that we must obey God rather than man. The second reading reveals worthy is the lamb that was slain for us. The Gospel shows love is a decision, not a sentimental expression.

This week, show those around you that you are in obedience to God's law by your actions, your words, and even in your thoughts. Show your family the humility of the Lamb of God that resides in you by your acts of kindness and gentleness towards them. You can show that you really love Jesus by feeding the sheep in your own household. You can do that by leading them in prayer, scripture readings, church fellowship, and worship through the sacraments.

FOURTH SUNDAY OF EASTER - CYCLE C

BEFORE YOU BEGIN:

Pray and ask God to speak to you through His Holy Spirit. "THE PARACLETE, THE HOLY SPIRIT WHOM THE FATHER WILL SEND IN MY NAME, WILL INSTRUCT YOU IN EVERYTHING, AND REMIND YOU OF ALL THAT I TOLD YOU." (JOHN 14:26)

FIRST DAY   **Reread last week's readings.**

1.   What was a helpful or new thought from the readings or from the homily you heard on Sunday?

2.   From what you learned, what personal application did you choose to apply to your life this week?

SECOND DAY   **READ ACTS 13:14, 43-52**   **FIRST READING**

("The disciples were filled with joy and the Holy Spirit.")

1.   Who arrived in Antioch, and what did they do on the Sabbath? Acts 13:13-14

2.   Who followed Paul and Barnabas, and what did they urge them to do? Acts 13:43

3.   To what is the grace they are to remain faithful? Romans 3:24-25

4.   What did almost the whole city do on the following Sabbath, and when the Jews saw the crowd, what did they do? Acts 13:44-45

5.   How did Paul and Barnabas speak out, what did they say it was necessary to do, and to whom have they now turned? Acts 13:46

6.   What has the Lord commanded them to be, how did the Gentiles react to this, and what did they glorify? Acts 13:47-48

Personal - How has God made you an instrument of salvation to the world?

7.   Who came to believe, and what did the word of the Lord continue to do? Acts 13:48-49

8.   Whom did the Jews incite, and what did they do to Paul and Barnabas? Acts 13:50

9.   Who does not please God, and what do they try to prevent? 1 Thessalonians 2:14-16

10.   Why did Paul and Barnabas shake the dust from their feet, and with what were the disciples filled? Acts 13:51-52

11.   What did Jesus tell his disciples? Matthew 10:14-15

Personal - When you gather to hear the Word of God, what is your reaction to it and to the person proclaiming it? Who are the people who proclaim the Word of God, and how can you affirm them?

THIRD DAY READ REVELATION 7:9, 14-17 **SECOND READING**

("...God will wipe away every tear from their eyes.")

1. Who had a vision of great multitudes, where were they standing, and what were they wearing and holding? Revelation 1:1 and 7:9

2. What was said by one of the elders about those wearing the robes, and how did they make their robes white? Revelation 7:14

3. What does the blood of the Lamb do for you? Hebrews 9:13-14

4. What must you do to be cleansed from sin? 1 John 1:7

5. What do the multitudes do, and what will the one who sits on the throne do? Revelation 7:15

6. From what does the Lord shelter us? Psalm 31:21

7. What will no longer happen to the multitudes? Revelation 7:16, see also Isaiah 49:10

8. What did Jesus tell his disciples? John 6:35

9. Who will shepherd them and lead them to life-giving water, and what will God do? Revelation 7:17

10. Who did Jesus say he was, and what did he say to the woman at the well? John 10:11 and John 4:10

11. Where does God dwell, and what has passed away? Revelation 21:3-4

Personal - How have you been washed by the blood of Jesus? How and where is Jesus leading you today?

FOURTH DAY READ JOHN 10:27-30 **GOSPEL**

("My sheep hear my voice;
I know them, and they follow me.")

1. What does Jesus say his sheep hear, whom does he know, and what do they do? John 10:27

2. Why were they trying to kill Jesus? John 8:37

3. Who hears the words of God? John 8:47

4. What does Jesus give his sheep, what will never happen to them, and what can no one do? John 10:28

5. What is the will of the Father? John 6:39-40

6. To whom does the Lord open his hand? Psalm 145:16

7. Who is the Father greater than, and what can no one do? John 10:29

8. Why did the Father give Jesus authority over all the people, and who belonged to the Father? John 17:2, 6

9. What are the Father and Jesus? John 10:30

10. What did Jesus pray that we all be? John 17:20-23

Personal - How do you recognize Jesus' voice and know when to follow him? When was the last time you felt the protecting hand of God upon you?

FIFTH DAY   **READ PSALM 100:1-3, 5**

("Serve the Lord with gladness.")

Read and meditate on Psalm 100:1-3, 5.

What is the Lord saying to you personally through the Psalm?

How can you apply this to your life?

SIXTH DAY   **READ ALL OF THE COMMENTARY**

ACTS 13:14, 43-52

The Jewish leaders tried to hide behind the shadow of jealousy as they brought legal and religious argu-ments against Paul and Barnabas. The root of their jealousy was that Peter and the apostles were already getting more respect than they had ever received. The difference between Peter, Paul, and Barnabas and the religious leaders was that the Pharisees demanded the respect and reverence for themselves. The goal of the apostles was to bring respect, reverence, and honor to God. The apostles were respected, not because they demanded it, but because they earned it. It is difficult to rejoice with others who are succeeding where we are not; but when we call upon the Holy Spirit, he will give us the strength we need (1 John 4:4).

Jealousy is a human and natural reaction, and it is tragic when we let our own jealous feelings make us try to stop God's work. If a work being done is God's work, then rejoice in it, no matter who is doing it. Paul wanted the Jewish people to join him in proclaiming God's salvation. Unfortunately, many Jews did not recognize Jesus as the Messiah, and they did not understand that in Jesus, God was offering salvation to everyone, Jews and Gentiles. Paul, being a Jew himself, hoped that the people would see that through Israel came Jesus, the light of all nations (Luke 2:32). This light would spread out and enlighten the whole world. The Jewish leaders turned away and like so many people today, when confronted with a disturbing truth, they often turn away and refuse to listen. When God speaks we must listen to him, or else we risk pushing the truth out of our lives.

REVELATION 7:9, 14-17

In today's reading we see a great crowd gathered in front of the throne before the lamb. Some say the crowd was a group of all the martyrs who died preaching God's word. In the face of warfare, famine, persecution, and death, Christians will be called to stand firm for what they believe. These souls were sealed by God and now they are victorious. This crowd in heaven appears to be composed of those who remained faithful to God throughout the generations. The ones who came out of the tribulation washed their souls clean with the blood of Jesus Christ. The blood of Christ is the world's greatest purifier, because it removes the ugly stain of sin. White symbolizes the qualities of sinlessness or holiness which can be imparted by shedding the blood of the sinless Lamb of God.

Some believe the suffering of the martyrs has gone on through the ages, and some believe there will be a specific time of intense tribulation. God will provide for his children's needs in their eternal home. There will be no hunger, thirst, or pain; he will wipe away all tears in his beautiful eternal "Holy City." This is a tremendously comforting verse when you feel that it is hopeless to even go on trying. This truth will sustain you in your time of trial. It is important to remember that all who have been faithful throughout the ages are singing before God's throne. Their tribulations and sorrows are over and all their sins are over. All believers have been resurrected and die no more. Alleluia!

JOHN 10:27-30

The role of a shepherd was very well known in Palestine, and they knew that a flock of sheep knew their master by the sound of his voice. Jesus compared his followers to sheep, and he was their shepherd. When he spoke, the people knew very well what he was talking about. He promised them eternal life if they accepted him as Master and Lord of their lives.

He offers that to us right here and now. All the littleness of our earthly life would be gone and we would know the splendor of being loved by God. He promised a life that would know no end. Death would be the beginning of living forever. He promised a life that was secure. Nothing could snatch that life from his hand. It did not mean that they would be saved from sorrow, suffering, or death. It did mean that they would know the serenity and power of God.

Jesus made a tremendous claim to the crowd of Jews, and he showed them his tremendous trust in God. He had been speaking to them about his sheep and his flock and that no one would ever take them away from him. He revealed that his Father gave him the sheep, and both the sheep and he were secure in his Father's hand. Jesus was so sure of himself because he was sure of his Father. He then told them and us that he and the Father were one (17:11).

Jesus is saying that the unity between himself and the Father is the same unity he wants for us. His prayer is that all Christians be united in love as he is united in love with the Father.

Application

The first reading says faith is a free gift and respect is something you earn. In the second reading we see that only the Blood of Christ can wash away sin. In the Gospel we see prayer as a dialogue between two people in love with one another.

This week let your prayer be that the Lord gives you the courage to confess your sins by receiving the Sacrament of Reconciliation. Then let the power of the Holy Eucharist nurture you and let you approach your family and friends with humility and reverence. Let your faith be shared in unity with members of other denominations in a spirit of joy. Jesus commanded all of us to be filled with his Spirit (Eph. 5:18) and then go out and make disciples of all nations (Matt. 28:19-20). Let your unity begin with God and you; then God, you, and your family; then God, you, your family, and your community. Miracles will then be happening in your neighborhood.

FIFTH SUNDAY OF EASTER - CYCLE C

BEFORE YOU BEGIN:

Pray and ask God to speak to you through His Holy Spirit. "THE PARACLETE, THE HOLY SPIRIT WHOM THE FATHER WILL SEND IN MY NAME, WILL INSTRUCT YOU IN EVERYTHING, AND REMIND YOU OF ALL THAT I TOLD YOU." (JOHN 14:26)

FIRST DAY   **Reread last week's readings.**

1. What was a helpful or new thought from the readings or from the homily you heard on Sunday?

2. From what you learned, what personal application did you choose to apply to your life this week?

SECOND DAY   **READ ACTS 14:21-27 FIRST READING**

*("It is necessary for us to undergo many hardships
to enter the kingdom of God.")*

1. What did Paul and Barnabus proclaim in Derbe, what happened there, and to where did they return? Acts 14:20-21

2. What is the Good News they proclaimed? Acts 13:32-34

3. What did Paul and Barnabas strengthen in the disciples, in what did they encourage them to persevere, and what did they say was necessary? Acts 14:22

4. Where does your strength come from in order to bear your share of the hardship for the Gospel and of what are you not to be ashamed? 2 Timothy 1:8

5. What did Paul and Barnabas appoint for the people, what did they do, and then where did they go? Acts 14:23-24

6. What were the disciples doing when the Holy Spirit spoke to them? Acts 13:2

7. Where did the disciples proclaim the Word of God? Acts 14:25-26

8. Why did Paul and Barnabus call the church together in Antioch? Acts 14:27

Personal - What can you report to your family or friends as to what God has done with you?

9. What happened to the Gentiles who heard the Word of the Gospel and believed, and how did God purify their hearts? Acts 15:7-9

10. For what should you pray, and how should you conduct yourself towards outsiders? Colossians 4:2-5

Personal – How do you approach or talk to those outside your faith? What can you do to bring the Gospel message to those around you who do not believe or know what Jesus has done for them?

THIRD DAY   **READ REVELATION 21:1-5**   **SECOND READING**

("Behold I make all things new.")

1. What was seen and what had passed away? Revelation 21:1

2. What dwells in the new heavens and the new earth? 2 Peter 3:13

3. What was seen coming down out of heaven from God and how was it prepared? Revelation 21:2

4. Of whom is the bride the wife? Revelation 21:9

5. What was heard from the throne, where is God's dwelling, and what will they be to him? Revelation 21:3

6. What are we to the living God and what is he to us? 2 Corinthians 6:16

7. What will God wipe from his peoples eyes, of what will there be no more, and what has passed away? Revelation 21:4

8. What is anyone who is in Christ? 2 Corinthians 5:17

9. What did the one who sat on the throne say and why did he say to write them down? Revelation 21:5

10. What are true and just? Revelation 19:1-2

Personal – In what way does your life show God has made his dwelling place within you? Can you see the old and the new person? Reflect on this.

FOURTH DAY   **JOHN 13:31-35**   **GOSPEL**

("As I have loved you, so you also should love one another.)

1. After Judas left, what did Jesus say? John 13:31

2. How do we glorify the Father? John 15:7-8

3. If God is glorified in Jesus, what will God do to Jesus? John 13:32

4. Whom did Jesus say the Father will honor or glorify? John 12:26

5. How did Jesus glorify God on earth? John 17:4

6. What did Jesus call his disciples, and what did he say about where he was going? John 13:33

7. Where was Jesus going? John 7:33

8. What did Jesus give us, and how should we love one another? John 13:34

9. What did Jesus say about no greater love than this? John 15:12-13

10. How will all know that you are a disciple of Jesus? John 13:35

11. Why do we love, and who is the one who loves God? 1 John 4:19-21

Personal - What do you do to show your love for God and one another?

FIFTH DAY   **READ PSALM 145:8-13**

*("The Lord is faithful in all his words
and holy in all his works.")*

Read and meditate on Psalm 145:8-13.

What is the Lord saying to you personally through the Psalm?

How can you apply this to your life?

SIXTH DAY   **READ ALL OF THE COMMENTARY**

ACTS 14:21-27

Paul tells us in today's reading that honesty and the willingness to accept afflictions was going to be a strong requirement in the new church. He told them that there was no easy way and reminded them that Jesus did not come to make life easy but to make men great. Paul shows them that Christianity must be lived in fellowship.

One of the great fathers of the Church stated, "No man can have God for his Father unless he has the Church for his mother." None of us will go to heaven alone; it will be because someone influenced us to seek Christ, know Christ, and be saved by Christ. To some people, the only bible they will read will be you. We are called into Christian fellowship.

Like a loving mother, the Church teaches, preaches, and rules her children so that they will grow up and die to themselves and live for Christ by living for others. Good parents want their children to grow up, go out and forward. The Church wants the same for her children, to grow up, go out, and bring someone back to Christ. Paul tells about the problem of so many Gentiles coming into the new church. He states the friction over what a Christian is really supposed to be. Gentiles wanted to be Christians. The other side of the problem, Jews were not allowed to have anything to do with Gentiles. The church welcomed all to come into God's family, as they are, not as someone else thought they should be. That is what being a Christian means today. So be all that you can be and be excited in who you are. You are unique, there is no one else quite like you. Remember, all that you do, and all that you say, and all that you are is being brought into perfection in direct proportion to your obedience to God's Holy Word.

REVELATION 21:1-5

Today's passage reveals that the dream of a new heaven and earth was deep in Jewish thought. Today we hear people in many lands still looking forward to a better place than what they have here on earth. Isaiah speaks of the new heaven and earth that God will make, and he calls for the people to make their lives an act of worship (Isaiah 66:22). In the new heaven and earth, there is the eternal hope of no more sorrow, no more tears; sin is defeated, darkness is no more, and joy is forever. This vision has been strongly held throughout the ages because of man's faith in God and his inherent sense of sin.

The ancient people feared the sea because they believed terrible creatures came from the sea. They believed that one day the sea would not be a barrier between God and man. Their beliefs consisted of two concepts regarding the new Jerusalem. The first concept was of Greek origin. It taught that in the invisible world there existed the perfect thing or place of everything visible here on earth. That meant there was a heavenly Jerusalem of which the earthly Jerusalem was an imperfect copy. The ideal is a challenge, in that, even if in this world the imperfect can not be made perfect, it can still be worked out in the next world, because God is the source of all ideals. The second thought or concept is Jewish and it shares the many dreams of the prophets.

The new Jerusalem or the "Holy City" was a constant dream that inspired and sustained the Jew as he was constantly being in the process of being obliterated. The Jews never lost confidence that they were the chosen people and God would someday present them with their "Holy City," the new Jerusalem. They expressed their hope in material things, but these were just symbols for the faithful. We see that God is to make his dwelling place with men. In the wilderness the tabernacle was a tent. Today the tabernacle of God is you. You carry him wherever you go. His power lies within you waiting to be used to make the world "The New Jerusalem."

JOHN 13:31-35

When you look at the word "commitment" you think of someone giving their complete all. The glory of Jesus is the glory of commitment and that is the glory of the cross. Jesus has shown us that the greatest glory in life is the glory which comes from sacrifice. In war time the supreme honor and glory belongs to those who lay down their lives so that others may live. History has taught us that those who have made great sacrifices have entered into great history.

Jesus Christ in his humility and obedience went to the cross for you and me and he brought honor and glory to God. We have found through time tested experience that obedience is the foundation of love. The most notable way a child can honor his parents is by being obedient to them. In Jesus God glories himself in the incarnation and the cross. Jesus's love, for us shows us that there is no glory like that of being loved. Let that sink in for a moment. He died for you because he loved you just as you are, not as you should be.

The enthronement of Christ followed his crucifixion. The crown of thorns has changed into a crown of glory and as scripture tells us "eye cannot see, ear cannot hear, nor can man even comprehend what God has in store for those who love him." Jesus leaves us his stamp of glory and that is we are to love others as he has loved us. We will be asked to love the unlovable, the unwashable, the unkissable, the ugly, the deformed, the sick, the people of the land. We need only to look and see how he loved. He loved deliberately, openly, unhesitantly, completely, gently, unreservedly. He chose to love because simply he is love. His glory will be in you loving others as he has loved you.

Application

In the first reading it brought out to be a Christian in the new church meant equality for all. In the second reading the Holy Spirit resides in you waiting to be used to make the world "a new Jerusalem." The Gospel shows the glory of God lies in the incarnation and the cross.

This week, let yourself be committed to making the world around your home, office, or school "a new Jerusalem" or "Holy City" by seeing in others the signs of Christ. Let yourself, this week, love others as Christ loves you. This especially means those in your family or those around you that you find very difficult to love. Remember, commitment means sacrifice and sacrifice means going to the cross. Your glory will be God's glory in you. You will be his glory as he sees you loving the people around you as Jesus loves you. This will bring the "new Jerusalem" right into your heart.

SIXTH SUNDAY OF EASTER - CYCLE C

BEFORE YOU BEGIN:

Pray and ask God to speak to you through His Holy Spirit. "THE PARACLETE, THE HOLY SPIRIT WHOM THE FATHER WILL SEND IN MY NAME, WILL INSTRUCT YOU IN EVERYTHING, AND REMIND YOU OF ALL THAT I TOLD YOU." (JOHN 14:26)

FIRST DAY	Reread last week's readings.

1. What was a helpful or new thought from the readings or from the homily you heard on Sunday?

2. From what you learned, what personal application did you choose to apply to your life this week?

SECOND DAY	READ ACTS 15:1-2, 22-29	FIRST READING

*("It is the decision of the Holy Spirit and of us
not to place on you any burden beyond these necessities,")*

1. What did some men from Judea begin to teach the brothers in Antioch? Acts 15:1

2. Where did circumcision originate among the Jews? Genesis 17:1-14

3. Among whom did this teaching cause dissension? Acts 15:2

4. What did Paul, Barnabas, and some of the brothers decide to do about this dissension and where did they go? Acts 15:2-3

5. What caused the controversy between them? Acts 15:5, 11

6. What was resolved by the apostles and the presbyters, with whom were they in agreement with, and what were they to deliver? Acts 15:22-23

7. After they sent their greetings, what was it they said they had heard? Acts 15:24

8. What did they unanimously resolve to do? Acts 15:25

9. To whom had they dedicated their cause and, how were they to convey this message? Acts 15:26-27

10. Whose decision was it not to lay on them any burden beyond that which is strictly necessary? Acts 15:28

11. What four things were they advised to avoid? Acts 15:29

Personal – In what way have church members, not under the authority of the church, put a burden on you? How could you resolve this?

| THIRD DAY | READ REVELATIONS 21:10-14,22-23 | SECOND READING |

("I saw no temple in the city,
for its temple is the Lord God Almighty and the Lamb.")

1.   Who was carried away and how was he carried away? Revelation 1:1,
     Revelation 21:10

2.   Where was he taken, what was he shown, and what did the city look like?
     Revelation 21:10-11

3.   Who is the designer and maker of this city? Hebrews 11:10

4.   Describe the following from Revelation 21:12:
     Its walls_____
     How many gates on the walls?_____
     Who were stationed at the gates?_____
     What was written on the gates_____
     Whose names were written there?_____

5.   Who were the twelve tribes of Israel and where were the gates located?
     Ezekiel 48:30-35, Revelation 21:13

6.   The wall of the city had twelve courses of stones as its foundation. Whose names
     were on them? Revelation 21:14

7.   Who were the twelve apostles of the Lamb and who is the Lamb? Matthew 10:2-4,
     John 1:29, Acts 1:20-26

8.   What did John not see, and what did he see as a temple? Revelation 21:22

9.   Of what did the city have no need of and what gave it light? Revelation 21:23

10. Who is our lamp and who is the light for our path? Revelation 21:23,
     Psalm 119:105, and John 1:1,14

Personal – Picture what heaven will look like from what you have just read and studied. How do you think you will respond when you enter its gates? In what way have you been enlightened here and now? How do your family, friends, work acquaintances, or people you come in contact with during the day see the light of Christ in you as his walking, living temple?

| FOURTH DAY | READ JOHN 14:23-29 | GOSPEL |

("Peace I leave with you; my peace I give to you.")

1.   If you love Jesus, to what will you be true, who will love him, and who will come
     to him? John 14:23

2.   Notice in verse 23, it says "we will come to him." To whom is this verse referring,
     when it says we? John 14:11, 17, 26

3. Where will the Spirit make his dwelling place? John 14:17,23

4. Who is it that does not love Jesus, and where does the Word you hear come from? John 14:24

5. While Jesus was with them, what did he tell them? John 14:26

Personal - As you began this study did you read or pray John 14:26. Of what has he reminded you?

6. What is Jesus farewell to you and his gift to you, and what does he tell you not to be? John 14:27

7. What does Jesus say in verse 28 of John 14?

8. If you love Jesus, what would you do when he goes to the Father? John 14:28

9. Who is greater than Jesus? John 14:28, John 10:29

10. Why was he telling them before this took place? John 14:29

Personal - In what specific way have you obeyed the command to "love one another as I have loved you" (John 15:12), in your family, with your friends, at work or school? In what way have you shown your love for the Father?

FIFTH DAY   **READ PSALM 67:2-3, 5-6, 8**

("For you govern the peoples justly,")

Read and meditate on Psalm 67:2-3, 5-6, 8.

What is the Lord saying to you personally through the Psalm?

How can you apply this to your life?

SIXTH DAY   **READ ALL OF THE COMMENTARY**

ACTS 15:1-2, 22-29

Christianity would have become nothing other than a sect of Jews if the condition that new Christians had to be circumcised first, was upheld. There were certain Jews who could never forget their positions as the chosen people. They were willing to accept Gentiles into the church provided they were circumcised first. Paul and Barnabas argued strongly against this attitude and a violent collision seemed inevitable.

An appeal was made to Jerusalem, the headquarters of the church, for a ruling. The principle at stake was quite simple. Was the gift of God for the chosen few or for all of the world? Was the gift of God a privilege or a responsibility? Certain Pharisees who had become Christian insisted that all converts must be circumcised and keep the Mosaic law.

The Mosaic law of Moses stated that on the eighth day the flesh of a male child's foreskin shall be circumcised (Leviticus 12:3). This was submitting of one's flesh to the covenant that originated between God and Abraham (Gen. 17:14). Peter stood up to the apostles and elders and told them that the new covenant is fulfilled by believing the word of the Gospel.

God who knows the heart bore witness to them giving the Gentiles the Holy Spirit, just as he also did to us. This was a circumcision of faith, a cutting off of one's pride and submitting to the will of the Lord. Peter told them that they were saved through the Grace of the Lord Jesus and so also were the Gentiles saved the same way.

The church leaders stated that the men who disturbed the brothers were not given instruction, nor authority, to do what they did. The church leaders, inspired by the Holy Spirit, decided to send authorized representatives with Paul and Barnabas. They did not want to lay upon them a greater burden than the essentials which are: they shall abstain from things sacrificed to idols, from blood, from the meat of strangled animals, and from illicit sexual union.

Today we still can look to the essentials for guidance for our daily living. We are not to sacrifice ourselves to idols such as jobs, power, sex, or money. We are called to stop eating and drinking ourselves into gluttony and sickness. We are called to be chaste in our actions as well as in our thoughts. We must turn away from illicit sexual union such as homosexuality, fornication, pornography, adultery, pre-marital sex, etc.

The controversy about keeping the law is still with us today. There still exists divisions between believers and church authorities. The authoritative teachings of the church are meant to protect the people as well as to preserve the true deposit of faith.

REVELATION 21:10-14, 22-23

John draws much of his imagery from Isaiah Chapter 65:17-24. In this chapter a new heaven is created, things of the past are not remembered, and there is rejoicing and no sadness or pain. John is not concerned about interspace travel or geophysics. Heaven exists because of the moral relationship between God and man.

God has taken the initiative and is the cause of the new order or as we call it the "New Jerusalem" or Heaven. God began by walking with man in the garden of paradise. He sought to dwell near man in the ark and the temple. He made man the holy of holies through his Incarnation. But these former things all passed away when he begins to dwell with them in the immediate personal intimacy of the "New Jerusalem." John has, with much phraseology and repetition, attempted to convey the incomparable beauty of heaven through the use of earthly descriptions.

The radiance of Christ in his eternal home is so dazzling that the lights of the galaxy are not needed. The holy of holies was a cube twenty cubits high, wide, and deep. The cities of Babylon and Nineveh were square. Can you imagine a city as high as it is wide and long. One side would extend from Boston to Chicago (1500 miles). A fence 216' high would hardly seem proportional around this gigantic cube of the heavenly city. We can see that earthly details pale when matched against the concept of spiritual symbolism. The author's main intent is to convey that it is the Divine Presence, radiant and enlivening, that transforms the holy Jerusalem into purest splendor. God began with Paradise. John ends his portrayal of the celestial city with details borrowed from the paradise story. We might all picture ourselves as believers.

JOHN 14:23-29

Before his passion and death, Jesus spoke words of comfort, love and obedience to his disciples. These words brought a sense of serenity and helped them to not be afraid. Jesus promised to provide for them by leaving with them "the Counselor," "The Holy Spirit." Jesus told them that the Father would send them the Holy Spirit in his name. He told them that the Holy Spirit would teach them all things and help them to remember all that he taught them (John 14:26). We have been made by faith, through Gods action in the sacrament of Baptism, temples of the Holy Spirit.

Today, living a life conforming to the prompting of the Holy Spirit is not easy. We have so many distractions in our every day living, that only the Holy Spirit could empower us to remember with clarity the obedience that's needed to walk the Christian walk. We need only to look around us and we can see very easily that unless we control our selfish desires and concerns by submitting them to the word of the Lord, they run wild, quickly overcoming any desire to know and experience God's love.

We can't split our desires evenly between God and the world; we must first seek the kingdom of God (Mt 6:33). We need to ask the Holy Spirit to teach us more about the healing, saving love of Jesus and the Kingdom of God. Pray that you will be open to receive the prompting of the Holy Spirit and to follow and experience the incredible love of Jesus.

Application

The first reading tells us that the gift of God was not for a chosen few, but for all the world. The second reading reveals that Heaven exists because of the moral relationship between God and man. The Gospel shows us that the power to walk the Christian walk can only come from the Holy Spirit.

This week, show those around you at work, at home or in school that God's gift to you has brought you freedom of choice. Choose to love your neighbors, family and friends as yourself. With the power of the Holy Spirit, you can also choose to love your enemies. We can only do this when we seek his kingship first and then everything else is added (Mt 6:33). Remember, the Holy Spirit will teach you in all things (John 14:26).

THE BREAD OF LIFE CATHOLIC BIBLE STUDY

SEVENTH SUNDAY IN EASTER - CYCLE C

BEFORE YOU BEGIN:

Pray and ask God to speak to you through His Holy Spirit. "THE PARACLETE, THE HOLY SPIRIT WHOM THE FATHER WILL SEND IN MY NAME, WILL INSTRUCT YOU IN EVERYTHING, AND REMIND YOU OF ALL THAT I TOLD YOU." (JOHN 14:26)

FIRST DAY   **Reread last week's readings.**

1. What was a helpful or new thought from the readings or from the homily you heard on Sunday?

2. From what you learned, what personal application did you choose to apply to your life this week?

SECOND DAY   **READ ACTS 7:55-60**   **FIRST READING**

("Lord, do not hold this sin against them.")

1. Who was filled with the Holy Spirit, and when he looked up to heaven, what did he see? Acts 6:8, Acts 7:55

2. With what did Ananias tell Paul (Saul) to be filled, and who did he say sent him? Acts 9:17

3. With what were the disciples filled? Acts 13:52

4. What are you not to do, and with what are you to be filled? Ephesians 5:18

Personal - How have you experienced the in-filling of the Holy Spirit?

5. What did Stephen say when he looked up and saw the heavens open? Acts 7:56

6. What happened to Jesus after John baptized him and the heavens opened? Matthew 3:16-17

7. How did the people react to Stephen, and what did they do to him? Acts 7:57-58

8. At whose feet did the witnesses lay their cloaks down, and what did Stephen call out as they were stoning him? Acts 7:58-59

9. What did Jesus say as they were crucifying him, and what were his last words? Luke 23:34, 46

10. What did Stephen say to the Lord just before he died? Acts 7:60

11. How are we to treat our enemies? Matthew 5:44

Personal - Are you holding anything against a family member, friend, or neighbor over a past hurt? Pray about it and do what the Lord is telling you to do?

*("Let the one who thirsts come forward, and the one
who wants it receive the gift of life-giving water.")*

1. When the Lord comes, what will he bring? Revelation 22:12

2. What did Jesus tell his disciples, with whom will he come, and how will he repay us? Matthew 16:24-28

3. Who did the Lord say he was? Revelation 1:8, 22:13

4. Of what is there only one? Isaiah 44:6

5. Who are blessed, what have they done, and to what do they have a right? Revelation 22:14

6. Where is the tree of life, and to whom does the Spirit speak? Revelation 2:7, Genesis 2:9

7. Who does Jesus say he is, and whom did he send to give this testimony to the churches? Revelation 22:16

8. What does the Spirit and the bride say, who is to come forward, and who is to receive the gift of life-giving water? Revelation 22:17

9. Who gives life-giving water? John 4:10

10. What does the one who gives this testimony say? Revelation 22:20

Personal - Do you thirst for the life-giving water that only Jesus can give you, or do you see someone, whom you know, who is thirsty? How can you answer the invitation to "come," or how can you be an instrument in satisfying someone else's thirst?

("...because you loved me before the foundation of the world.")

1. For whom did Jesus say he was praying? John 17:6-9, 20

2. Why does Jesus pray for them, and what does he say about the Father? John 17:21, also see John 10:30 & 14:10

3. What did Jesus give to those who kept his Father's word? John 17:22

4. How are we brought to perfection, and whom does the Father love? John 17:23 and also John 16:27

5. Why did God send his Son into the world? John 3:16-17

6. When did the Father love Jesus, and what are we to Jesus from the Father? John 17:24

7. What has Jesus prepared for us, and how will we get there? John 14:2-3

8. Whom does the Father love and honor? John 12:23, 26

9. Whom does Jesus and his disciples know and who does not know him? What does Jesus call his Father? John 17:25

10. Whom does the world love, and what will they do to you on account of Jesus? John 15:19-21

11. What did Jesus make known, what is he making known, and for what reason? John 17:26

12. What was kept by those to whom Jesus revealed the Father? John 17:6

Personal – What priority have keeping God's Word and speaking God's Word had in your life? Evaluate last week and see what you spent most of your time doing and saying. How do others see the love of Jesus in you?

FIFTH DAY   **READ PSALM 97:1-2, 6-7, 9**

*("The heavens proclaim his justice,
and all people see his glory.")*

Read and meditate on Psalm 97:1-2, 6-7, 9.

What is the Lord saying to you personally through the Psalm?

How can you apply this to your life?

SIXTH DAY   **READ ALL OF THE COMMENTARY**

ACTS 7:55-60

The Jewish leaders were enraged by Stephen's accusation that they were murderers of the prophets and destroyers of God's laws. He accused them of even murdering the Messiah. Stephen's words of seeing Jesus standing at God's right hand supported Jesus' claim and angered the Jewish leaders. In their guilt and rage, they would not tolerate Stephen's words, so they mobbed him and killed him.

Today people may not kill us for witnessing about Christ, but they will let us know they do not want to hear the truth and will often try to silence us. In many lands, those who try to protect the rights of the unborn children against abortion are ridiculed, beaten, and sent to jail. These Christians are responding by not standing by and doing nothing while innocents are being slaughtered (Proverbs 24:11). Keep honoring God in your words, your worship and in your actions. You may experience the rejection of many people to your message, but some will turn to Christ and your effort will be noticed more than you realize.

Paul is introduced into today's reading (verse 58) as a murderer and then later we see him as a changed, repentant apostle of the Lord. This tells us that the power of God's love can change anyone who is open to his call. Paul was tremendously qualified to preach to the Jews because he too had once opposed Jesus Christ and his Christian followers. He understood the opposition and was, therefore, able to be compassionate and forgiving, as well as encouraging them to become free in Christ. Paul never forgot that day when he watched in silence and let the evil actions of those men destroy the life of a very holy man. He knew that he could never be silent again, and he spent the rest of his life preaching the good news of Jesus Christ, Lord and Savior of the whole world. We need to speak out in Jesus' name and let people see in us the holiness of St. Stephen.

REVELATION 22:12-14, 16-17, 20

The Risen Christ is coming, and he makes two powerful claims, that there will be a final judgment and this will not be confined to non-believers. The eternal destiny of a true Christian believer is secure, but Jesus will look at how they handled gifts, opportunities, and responsibilities in their lifetime. He then tells us that he is complete. There is no beginning or end to his existence. Christ is telling us that he is the source and he needs nothing else. He is the alpha and the omega, the beginning and the end. The Jews said that since God was the beginning, he received his power from no one; since he was the middle, he shared his power with no one; and since he was the end, he never handed his power over to anyone.

Those who washed their robes in the blood of Christ were purified and have the right of entry into the "City of God" or the "New Jerusalem." Jesus, through his cross, has provided that grace by which man can be forgiven; but man has to hunger and thirst for that grace, and then he has to make use of that grace. Those who enter into the "Holy City" or heaven are the ones who have accepted Jesus as Lord. In the new and eternal life, people will eat from the tree of life because their sins have been removed by Christ's death and resurrection and they will live forever.

If we have confessed our sins, repented, and accepted Jesus Christ as our personal Lord and Savior, we will have the right to eat from this tree. The church has been the faithful guardian that has protected us, taught us about Jesus Christ, and has presented him to us in sacrament and word. The church, in the name of Jesus, through the power of the Holy Spirit brings glory to God the Father by extending the invitation to the whole world to come to Jesus.

JOHN 17:20-26

Jesus completes his prayer to the Father. He began by asking his Father to glorify him so that he may glorify the Father. He told his Father that he did everything that was asked of him, and now the hour of glory had come. His glory would be the cross; it was not his will but he obeyed his Father's will even unto death on a cross (Phil. 2:2-11). Then he prayed for his disciples and asked God to keep them strong in their faith.

In today's passage Jesus is praying for us. In this prayer, we see his confidence both in his Father and for those who are going to be Christ-followers. He knew that in a very short time he was going to be betrayed, arrested and killed, and he still was confident that his disciples would carry on his name. He was praying for the new church to come. He prayed for a unity of heart, not administration, not a unity of ecclesiastical organization. He prayed for a unity of personal relationships.

We have seen the unity between Jesus and his Father was love and obedience. Jesus prayed for a unity based on the relationships of heart to heart, not denomination to denomination. Jesus prayed that a unity would exist in which people loved each other because they loved him. Christian unity overcomes all differences because it joins people together in love. It is more natural for people to be divided then united. It is more natural for people to fly apart then to come together. But real unity between all Christians would require a "supernatural" solution, and that solution is loving one another as Jesus has loved us.

Application

In the first reading we see that evil can only succeed when good men do nothing. In the second reading we see Jesus is the beginning, middle and the end. The Gospel shows unity does not have to mean uniformity. This week, bring unity into your own heart by praying that God will change your attitude toward others who do not believe and practice their faith in God like you. Then look around you and see who is not of the same faith as you, and then let them experience your respect, your kindness, and your generosity. Then love them just as Jesus loves you. You will be amazed at the power and result of your witness of Christ.

PENTECOST - CYCLE C

BEFORE YOU BEGIN:

Pray and ask God to speak to you through His Holy Spirit. "THE PARACLETE, THE HOLY SPIRIT WHOM THE FATHER WILL SEND IN MY NAME, WILL INSTRUCT YOU IN EVERYTHING, AND REMIND YOU OF ALL THAT I TOLD YOU." (JOHN 14:26)

FIRST DAY   Reread last week's readings.

1. What was a helpful or new thought from the readings or from the homily you heard on Sunday?

2. From what you learned, what personal application did you choose to apply to your life this week?

SECOND DAY   READ ACTS 2:1-11   FIRST READING

("All were filled with the Holy Spirit")

1. What day had come, and where were the disciples gathered? Acts 2:1

2. What day was Pentecost celebrated after the Passover, what are other names for it? Leviticus 23:15-16, Deuteronomy 9:10, Exodus 23:16 and Numbers 28:26.

3. What suddenly happened from up in the sky, and where was it heard? Acts 2:2

4. Read the following scripture, and tell what the Spirit gives to a person? Ezekiel 37:9, 14

5. What appeared, and what did it do? Acts 2:3

6. What was Jesus' promise just before he ascended to heaven? Acts 1:5, 8

7. With what were all filled, and how did they express themselves? Acts 2:4

8. What did the Spirit prompt them to do? Acts 2:4, Acts 4:31

9. Who was staying in Jerusalem at the time, and what did they hear? Acts 2:5-6

10. About what were they confused? Acts 2:6

11. What was their reaction? What did they ask, and about what were they so amazed? Acts 2:7-11

Personal - How can your family or friends identify the Spirit of God's presence in you? What comes forth from your mouth, and what do you need to do so people will be astonished by your words?

THIRD DAY   **READ 1 CORINTHIANS 12:3-7, 12-13**   **SECOND READING**

("No one can say "Jesus is Lord," except in the Holy Spirit.")

1. What is Paul telling the brothers that you cannot do in the Spirit of God, and what can be said only in the Holy Spirit? 1 Corinthians 12:3

2. What is there different, but with the same Spirit? 1 Corinthians 12:4

3. There are different ministries and works but the same God who accomplishes what? 1 Corinthians 12:5-6

4. To each person the manifestation of the Spirit is given for what reason? 1 Corinthians 12:7

5. In what gifts should you try to be rich? 1 Corinthians 14:12.

6. Fill in the following blanks: The body is _____ and has _____ members, but all the members, _____ though they are, are _____ body; and so it is with Christ. 1 Corinthians 12:12

7. In the one Spirit, who were baptized into the one body? 1 Corinthians 12:13

8. What have all of us been given to drink? 1 Corinthians 12:13

9. Into whom have we been baptized? Galatians 3:27

10. When were you chosen and sealed with the Holy Spirit? Ephesians 1:13

Personal - From the above scriptures, how can you identify the manifestation of the Spirit in your life, and in those you come in contact with? Reread 1 Corinthians 12:3, and take note of what comes forth from your mouth this week.

FOURTH DAY   **READ JOHN 20:19-23 GOSPEL**

("Receive the Holy Spirit.")

1. Why did the disciples lock the doors of the place where they were? John 20:19

2. Who came and stood before them, and what did he say to them? John 20:19

3. When he had said this, what did he show them? John 20:20

4. What did the disciples do at the sight of the Lord? John 20:20

Personal - In what way has our Lord appeared to you when you have been gathered with others praying, and what has been your response?

5. What did Jesus say again, and what is his gift to you? John 20:21, John 14:27

6. Whom has the Father sent, and who sends you? John 20:21

7. What did Jesus do to the disciples, and what did they receive? John 20:22

8. How did the Lord God form man, and how did he give him life? Genesis 2:7

9. If you forgive men's sin, what happens to them, and if you hold them bound, what happens? John 20:23

10. What did Jesus say on the cross to the Father, and whom should we imitate? Luke 23:34, 1 John 2:1, 6

Personal - How do others see, spiritually and physically, the breath of his life in you? How do others see you living out your sign of baptism through repentance, which means change? How do others see you as you practice forgiveness of others, and ask others to forgive you? How often do you feel the need for the Sacrament of Reconciliation, and why?

FIFTH DAY　　　　　　　**READ PSALM 104:1, 24, 29-31, 34**

("When you send forth your spirit, they are created.")

Read and meditate on Psalm 104:1, 24, 29-31, 34.

What is the Lord saying to you personally through the Psalm?

How can you apply this to your life?

SIXTH DAY　　　　　　　**READ ALL OF THE COMMENTARY**

ACTS 2:1-11

In today's readings we celebrate the Feast of "Pentecost," which means fifty (50). This was a feast that was celebrated about fifty days after Passover and was a feast of thanksgiving for the harvest. The first fruits of the crop were offered to God that day. All Jewish men were expected to come to the temple for the feast. The city was usually filled to overflowing, and it was fitting that this day was chosen as the day the Holy Spirit descended on the Apostles.

Today is, in reality, the birthday of the church, and the Christian religion was to be a church for the whole world. The old law was given by God to Moses for the Jews only. The new law, given by Christ and confirmed by the power of the Holy Spirit, was for all peoples. That means you, and that means today, right where you are. The very fact that you are reading this Bible Study is proof that the power of the Holy Spirit is drawing you near to him.

Let today be the day that you fall upon your knees and invite Jesus Christ to come into your heart and become the Lord of your life. Take a few moments and confess to the Lord all that is twisted with you, and then ask him to let his Holy Spirit fill you with the power and peace that surpasses all understanding. The celebration of Pentecost is for you as well as it was for the Jews in today's passage. Let the power of the Holy Spirit flow through you, and you will enjoy that same gift that the Apostles had, the gift of speaking in tongues.

The signs and wonders of that incredible day brought huge crowds of Jews in huge crowds to the place where the Apostles were staying. This was the day chosen for the Apostles to go forward and make disciples of all nations. We are called also to go forward and make disciples of all nations (Matthew 28:19). Let us remember, the Jews celebrated the feast of the harvest on Pentecost. Jesus' Holy Spirit breathed life on the universal church on the Feast of Pentecost, or the Feast of Harvest.

We are called today to harvest the crop of souls for the Lord. The Lord needs some good laborers to work in the vineyard. Are you ready to join the workers?

1 CORINTHIANS 12:3-7, 12-13

In this passage, we see that the gifts of the Holy Spirit were given for the good of the whole community to help build up the body of Christ. We should not refuse to use the gifts of the Holy Spirit nor claim them as our own. Paul clearly warns against listening to false teachers and shows us how to check out their credentials. We are to find out what they teach about Christ.

We see people today who mock Jesus Christ, not only with their words, but in the way they live. We see people using their gifts to split communities apart, and then trying to tell us that they are only doing God's will. Anyone can claim to speak for God, and we need only to look at some of the leaders in some countries, and we see a lot of false messiahs running around. God has given us many different gifts, but we must remember they all come from the same Spirit, and they are to be used to help the community or church. They will know we are Christians by the way we love and help one another.

Paul compares the body of Christ to a human body. Every part is an individual, and has a specific job to do. In their differences, all of the parts must work together for the good of the whole body. Jesus Christ is the head, and the rest of us make up the body of Christ. It is very important that we are not too proud of our abilities, and we must not compare ourselves with one another. We are called to use our different gifts together, to spread the "Good News" to a world that is filled with "bad news." The church, which is the people who believe that "Jesus is Lord," must be united in its belief in Christ. It must not let its leaders or members use any gifts to cause divisions or strife.

Faith in Christ is the core of Christian unity. We are one body, with one spirit that is united in Christ with the Father through the power of the Holy Spirit. When we were baptized into the Christian Faith, the Holy Spirit took up residence in us and we became the temple of the Holy Spirit (1 Corinthians 3:16). You, by your baptism, have been born into God's family, and our common goal is faith in our Lord and Savior Jesus Christ.

JOHN 20:19-23

Today's Gospel passage reveals to us the incredible gift of the Holy Spirit being given publicly to the disciples of Jesus by Jesus himself. This is a tremendous feast day in the church. We look back, and we see that Advent was a time to prepare for the Incarnation of God (God becoming man). Christmas was the happening of this great Incarnation act. We then moved into Lent and began to prepare ourselves for the sufferings endured by Christ on our behalf during his holy week. We celebrated victory in Jesus' triumph over death which guaranteed our union with him in heaven.

Today, we celebrate in Pentecost the Holy Spirit coming to abide within his church. This means abiding in you, in me, and all believers of the Lord Jesus Christ. The Holy Spirit gives the power to preserve, teach, explain, and spread the gospel of "Good News," which is a message of hope and love for everyone in the world.

The Holy Spirit that came upon the disciples and all of the people in the upper room is the same Spirit that wants to abide in us. We can let him come into our heart, right now, by getting down on our knees and confessing our sins to the Lord. Invite him to come and take up residence in your heart, his temple, and let him take control of your life. His power will flow through you, and your life will never be the same again. His peace will be your peace, it will be a peace that surpasses all understanding (Philippians 4:7).

The power from the Holy Spirit helps all of us live a life of holiness and wholeness. We need to always remember that God's plan for each one of us is to live a life that is abundant and full (John 10:10). The Holy Spirit gives us the power in the name of Jesus to bind Satan and his cohorts, and in his Name, to loosen the Spirit of Life which is the Lord Jesus himself... to heal, to restore and, to forgive. We can release others from the bondage of sin by our compassion and forgiveness.

We are more than conquerors; we are children of the Living God, we are called to set the captives free and give sight to the blind. We do that by forgiving them, and loving them through the power of the Holy Spirit, and in the mighty name of Jesus Christ, our Lord and Savior. Pentecost - the harvest is now, the Kingdom of God is at hand, come and be fishers of men. I pray that the Holy Spirit today will fill you with his love and power, and fill all of us with gratitude for all that God has done for us.

Application

The first reading tells us that we celebrate the birthday of the church when we celebrate "Pentecost." The second reading reveals that the gifts of the Holy Spirit are to be used to uplift the community. The Gospel reveals to us that the Holy Spirit gives us power in the name of Jesus. This power is a healing power.

Let us take a long look at our gifts, and then share them with others this week. You might visit someone who is sick, or visit someone in jail. You might write a letter to someone who is lonely, or cook someone a special meal. Do something beautiful for God this week, and keep on giving your gift away. God will never let you be without a gift - try it, you'll like it.

TRINITY SUNDAY - CYCLE C

BEFORE YOU BEGIN:

Pray and ask God to speak to you through His Holy Spirit. "THE PARACLETE, THE HOLY SPIRIT WHOM THE FATHER WILL SEND IN MY NAME, WILL INSTRUCT YOU IN EVERYTHING, AND REMIND YOU OF ALL THAT I TOLD YOU." (JOHN 14:26)

FIRST DAY Reread last week's readings.

1. What was a helpful or new thought from the readings or from the homily you heard on Sunday?

2. From what you learned, what personal application did you choose to apply to your life this week?

SECOND DAY   **READ PROVERBS 8:22-31**   **FIRST READING**

("...and I found delight in the sons of men.")

1. What is the firstborn of the Lord's way, and what is the oldest of his words? Proverbs 8:1, 22

2. Where does wisdom cry aloud and raise her voice? Proverbs 1:20

3. When was wisdom poured forth, and what was not settled into place? Proverbs 8:23-26

4. What came with wisdom? Sirach 1:4

5. Where does all wisdom come from? Sirach 1:1

6. When will wisdom not cease? Sirach 24:9

7. How did God establish man? Wisdom 9:1-2

8. When was wisdom beside God? Proverbs 8:27-30

9. How was wisdom beside God, and what was she doing? Proverbs 8:30-31

10. In what did wisdom find delight? Proverbs 8:31

11. Who is the wisdom of God? 1 Corinthians 1:22-24

Personal - In what way can you take delight in those around you and show the wisdom of God? How can you recognize the wisdom of God, and what do you need to do to see it clearly playing on the surface of the earth?

THIRD DAY **READ ROMANS 5:1-5** **SECOND READING**

*("...the love of God has been poured out into our hearts
through the Holy Spirit that has been given us.")*

1.   How have we been justified, and what do we have with God through our Lord Jesus Christ? Romans 5:1

2.   How have we been justified? Romans 4:24-25

3.   How is the manifold wisdom of God made known and where and how do we get boldness and confidence to approach God? Ephesians 3:10-12

4.   To what have we gained access, and in what do we boast? Romans 5:2

5.   Of what else do we boast, and what does it produce? Romans 5:3

6.   What does Christ do in our afflictions, and what does this enable us to do? 2 Corinthians 1:3-4

7.   For what do we need endurance? Hebrews 10:36

8.   What does endurance produce? Romans 5:4

9.   Who will never mature in character? Sirach 23:15

10.   What does hope NOT do, what has been poured out in our hearts, and how has it been done? Romans 5:5

11.   What was Paul's hope? Philippians 1:20

12.   How did God save us, and how did he pour it out on us? Titus 3:4-6

Personal – In what way has affliction produced endurance in your life? What has kept you going on, and how has the peace of God been evident in you during affliction?

FOURTH DAY **READ JOHN 16:12-15** **GOSPEL**

("He will guide you to all truth.")

1.   What was the reason Jesus did not tell his disciples any more? John 16:12

2.   How did Jesus speak the parables to his disciples? Mark 4:33

3.   Whom did Jesus say will guide us to all truth, and what will he speak and declare to us? John 16:13

4.   In what does Jesus ask you to be consecrated, and what is truth? John 17:17

5.   Who will teach you and remind you of everything Jesus did? John 14:26

6.   Who testifies to Jesus, and what are you also to do? John 15:26-27

7.   What did Jesus say you would do if you love him, and for what would he ask the Father? John 14:15-17

8.   What will the Spirit of truth do, and what will he give or tell you? John 16:14

9.   What belongs to Jesus, and what is he giving you? John 16:15

10.   What did the father say to the son who was with him? Luke 15:31

Personal - How has God's Spirit guided you and taught you about Jesus and how to apply what he taught you to your life? Give a specific example.

FIFTH DAY   **READ PSALM 8:4-9**

("You have given him rule over the works of your hands.")

Read and meditate on Psalm 8:4-9.

What is the Lord saying to you personally through the Psalm?

How can you apply this to your life?

SIXTH DAY   **READ ALL OF THE COMMENTARY**

PROVERBS 8:22-31

The Book of Proverbs gives us a person's poetic demonstration of God's wisdom. Christian believers have always read this passage as a prophetic allusion to Jesus Christ, the second person of the Blessed Trinity. This reading was about the word that would be made flesh in Jesus. Nothing is more immediate than the awesome spectacle of life, and nothing is more real than the wonder of creation.

Today's reading shows us how to discern God's hand at work in the world, and how to see the Father's life-giving energy behind every created beauty. The mystic in us "knows God" as we are struck with a sense of the sacred while gazing at a sunset. God is telling us that wisdom is the foundation on which all life is built. Today's reading shows wisdom as being the special attribute of God. Wisdom was present at the creation and works even today with the Creator as in the beauty of the sunset. Wisdom affects every aspect of our entire lives, from beginning to end.

You need to be sure that God's wisdom flows through you and opens all corners of your life to God's direction and guidance. Wisdom will be our main attribute when we put God first in our lives (Matthew 6:33). Look at your values and priorities. What is most important to you? Where is God on that list? Keep him first in everything you do. He will crown your efforts with his wisdom and his understanding. You will see others with spiritual vision instead of plain human vision. Remember, the difference between wisdom and common sense is that common sense is the ability God gives to all people to think and make choices; he only gives wisdom to those who follow him.

ROMANS 5:1-5

In this reading, St. Paul states that the core of our belief in the Trinity, is that we come to the Father through Jesus in the love which is the Holy Spirit. Paul was writing to ordinary Christians, like us, about the experience of God's love flooding the human heart. Nothing is more tangible than an intensely felt love or even our longing for it, and Paul boldly connects that experience with the Holy Spirit.

Paul is speaking about a peace that means being reconciled with God, knowing that he loves you not for what you do but simply because of who you are. Jesus paid the price for this special kind of relationship with his death on the cross. Because of Jesus, we have entry into the presence of the King of Kings and entry into the haven of God's grace.

Our relationship with God has begun in faith which reveals to us that we are delivered from our past by Christ's death. Hope grows as we learn all that God has in store for us, and God's love supplies all our needs and enables us to reach out to others. In the future we will become, but now we must overcome. Scripture tells us that "eye has not seen, ear has not heard, nor can man even comprehend what God has in mind for those who believe in him." (1 Corinthians 2:9).

We can put all of our trust in God because he is in control of our future. We can look at our times of difficulties and know, even if we do not understand how, that we will grow emotionally as well as spiritually. Problems we run into will develop our patience, which in turn will strengthen our character and deepen our trust in God. Thank God for these opportunities to grow, and deal with them in his strength.

JOHN 16:12-15

Jesus teaches the apostles about the availability of the Holy Spirit. He told them that the Holy Spirit would teach them about the nature of their ministry. He also told them that they would face very difficult opposition and that the outcome of their opposition would be revealed by the Holy Spirit. They did not understand any of this until after Jesus' death and resurrection. The Holy Spirit then revealed truths to them, and they in turn formed the writing of the New Testament. It is very important for you to remember that the truth into which the Holy Spirit guides you is the truth about Christ. The name for his followers bringing the revealed truth about Christ to all men through generation after generation is Christian "Tradition."

Understanding of this revelation is bound to be an ongoing process, because Jesus knew that the disciples were not capable of understanding at that point in time. He knew that his Spirit that followed him would enlighten, empower, and sanctify his followers. He knew that they would need time to fully understand their role in bringing Christianity to the waiting world.

He knows of our limitations today, and he has left the same Holy Spirit for us to receive and to empower us. The development of the apostles' faith and the faith of the early church demonstrate to the whole world that the Holy Spirit is revealing the truth of Christ to all peoples. All truth is God's truth, and the revelation of all truth is the work of the Holy Spirit. When you say "Yes, Lord," the power of the Holy Spirit reveals to you that you are at last really set free; Jesus is the truth, and only through him can you really be free (John 8:32).

Application

In the first reading the Word was made flesh and he dwelt in their midst (John 1:14). The second reading shows the core of the Holy Trinity as we come to the Father through Jesus in the power of the Holy Spirit. We see in the Gospel that behind all truth is the presence of God.

This week, let us celebrate the Blessed Trinity by being open to the power that the Holy Spirit has given us. We have seen that the real power is the power of truth. This week, speak to your family only in the Spirit of truth. Truth means being humble, gentle and obedient to God's Holy Word. Your words of truth, matched by your actions of service, will show those around you that the love of God and the fellowship of the Holy Spirit are alive within you and the name of Jesus will set you, as well as others, free.

THE BODY AND BLOOD OF CHRIST - CYCLE C

BEFORE YOU BEGIN:

Pray and ask God to speak to you through His Holy Spirit. "THE PARACLETE, THE HOLY SPIRIT WHOM THE FATHER WILL SEND IN MY NAME, WILL INSTRUCT YOU IN EVERYTHING, AND REMIND YOU OF ALL THAT I TOLD YOU." (JOHN 14:26)

FIRST DAY	**Reread last week's readings.**

1. What was a helpful or new thought from the readings or from the homily you heard on Sunday?

2. From what you learned, what personal application did you choose to apply to your life this week?

SECOND DAY   **READ GENESIS 14:18-20**   **FIRST READING**

("Then Abram gave him a tenth of everything.")

1. What two things was Melchizedek, what did he bring out, and who did he bless? Genesis 14:18

2. What does the name "King of Salem" mean? Hebrews 7:2

3. Where is God's abode, and what is another name for this place? Psalm 76:3

4. Who is Abram, and what did God make him? Genesis 17:5

5. By whom is Abram blessed? Genesis 14:19

6. Why do you praise the name of the Lord? Psalm 148:5

7. Who is blessed by the Lord? Psalm 112:2

8. What did God Most High do? Genesis 14:20

9. What did Abram give, and from what did he give it? Genesis 14:20

10. What is the vow Jacob made to the Lord, and what did he faithfully return to the Lord? Genesis 28:20-22

Personal – In what way have you been blessed by the Lord, and what have you returned to the Lord?

THIRD DAY   **READ 1 CORINTHIANS 11:23-26**   **SECOND READING**

("For I received from the Lord what I also handed on to you.")

1. From whom did Paul receive what he handed on to you, and how did he receive it? 1 Corinthians 11:23, Galatians 1:11-12

2. What was handed on to us? 1 Corinthians 11:23-25

THE BREAD OF LIFE CATHOLIC BIBLE STUDY

3.   What did Jesus do with the bread on the night he was handed over, and who did he say it was for? 1 Corinthians 11:23-24

4.   Of what is Jesus mediator? Hebrews 8:6

5.   What did Jesus say the cup of wine was? 1 Corinthians 11:25

6.   What is the cup of blessing that is blessed and the bread that we break? 1 Corinthians 10:16-17

7.   For whom was his blood shed? Luke 22:20

8.   What do we proclaim each time we eat the bread and drink the cup? 1 Corinthians 11:26

9.   For what are we to wait? 1 Corinthians 1:7

10. In what way are we to speak to one another? 1 Corinthians 14:6

Personal - Each time you receive communion, what do you hand on or pass on to others?

FOURTH DAY   **READ LUKE 9:11-17**   **GOSPEL**

("Give them some food yourselves.")

1.   What did the crowds do when Jesus went to Bethsaida, and what did Jesus do when he saw them? Luke 9:11

2.   As the day was nearing an end, who approached Jesus? For what reason did they ask him to dismiss the crowd? Luke 9:12

3.   What did Jesus tell the apostles to give the people? Luke 9:13

4.   What did Jesus say was true food and true drink? John 6:55

5.   What did Jesus say his food was? John 4:34

6.   What did the apostles tell Jesus was all they had? Luke 9:13

7.   How many men were there, what did Jesus tell his disciples, and what did the people do? Luke 9:14-15

8.   What did Jesus do with the five loaves and two fish? Luke 9:16

9.   What happened to the people when they ate, and how much was left over? Luke 9:17

10. What does the Lord give, and who does he satisfy? Psalm 145:15-16

Personal - How does the food you eat satisfy you? In what way are you satisfied when you receive communion?

FIFTH DAY   **READ PSALM 110:1-4**

("Rule in the midst of your enemies.")

Read and meditate on Psalm 110:1-4.

What is the Lord saying to you personally through the Psalm?

How can you apply this to your life?

SIXTH DAY   **READ ALL OF THE COMMENTARY**

GENESIS 14:18-20

In today's passage we see the powerful bond of family ties which inspired Abram to rescue his nephew Lot from being kidnapped by a powerful and ruthless king of a northern tribe. When Abram learned that his nephew was a prisoner, he immediately tried to help him. Sometime, we must get involved in a very painful situation in order to help others. We should be willing to act right away when others need help (Proverbs 24:11).

Melchizedek was a holy man whose name means "King of Justice" (Heb. 7:2). He was a priest of "the God of Highest Heaven." He recognized that God was the creator of heaven and earth. Abram knew who he was and was paying respect to him. Abram gave Melchizedek one-tenth of the booty. We see that even in the land of pagan gods, tithing was a customary and acceptable action towards the "gods." Abram followed and accepted ancient tradition, but he refused the "booty" won from the war. Abram chose to give his share away because he did not want others to think that he went into battle for greedy reasons.

Abram wanted others to see that his actions were very just and that his life was centered around his God. Abram wanted people to say, "Look what his God has done for him." Abram did not want the attention of his "victory" to be centered on him. He wanted everyone to know that God had won him the victory. When people look at you, they need to see what God has accomplished in you, and what he is doing with you right now.

1 CORINTHIANS 11:23-26

The Lord's supper is a visible representation of the gospel, the death of Christ for our sins. It focuses on the remembrance of Christ's death and the glorious hope of his return. In the Catholic Church we believe in the real presence of Christ in the Holy Eucharist. This worship service is called "The Mass," and it is a celebration of Word and Sacrament. It is also an act of fellowship among all Catholic believers. Our faith is strengthened through fellowship with Christ and with all other believers.

What does the Lord's Supper mean? The early church told that Jesus taught us about the Lord's supper on the night of the Passover (Luke 22:13-20). The Passover celebrated deliverance from slavery in Egypt, and the Lord's supper celebrates deliverance from sin by Christ's death on the cross. All Catholic Christians believe that when the words "This is my body," and "Take this cup and drink" are spoken, the real presence of Christ appears in the bread and wine to become the body and blood of Christ. When we receive Christ in the Eucharist (which means thanksgiving) at a Catholic Mass, we respond by saying "Amen." This means, "I believe it, yes, I am part of the body of Christ."

Through this new covenant that Christ has given us, we can now personally approach God and communicate with him. The old covenant was made on Mount Sinai between God and the Israelites (Exodus 19,20) and was designed to point to the day when Jesus would come. The new covenant completes, rather than replaces, the old covenant. We are recommitting ourselves to this new covenant every time we proclaim his Holy Word and partake of his body and blood at the Catholic Mass.

LUKE 9:11-17

Jesus had tried to slip quietly away from the huge crowds and head for the town of Bethsaida, but they found out where he was going and followed him. He knew the people were hurting and had many needs, so instead of showing impatience at this interruption, he welcomed them and ministered to them. When people interrupt your schedule, do you see this as a nuisance or as a reason for your life and ministry?

Jesus taught mainly about the kingdom of God, and he stressed that the kingdom was here and now, not some place and time in the future. There are many people today who do not believe that the kingdom of God is real and present in the hearts of those who believe in Jesus. It is as present with us today, as it was with the Judeans two thousand years ago.

The disciples displayed a typical, logical, human reaction when told to feed the crowd. They took on the responsibility of having to perform the impossible. They felt that what they had to offer was far too little to get the job done. They were right, and Jesus knew that, but he was not depending on what the people brought. Jesus was giving, simply, because he knew their needs and he wanted to meet them. He does that today with all of us.

Whatever we have, if we bring it to Jesus, he will give thanks, he will bless it, break it, and share it with others. That is the purpose of our life here on earth. Jesus did not have to feed those people. He could have said a prayer and then sent them away. But Jesus does not ignore needs. He is concerned with every part of our lives, physical, emotional and spiritual. Today we are called to continue the miracle of feeding others through him.

Application

The first reading shows Abram's victory was not the battle, but God himself. The second reading explains that "Amen" means "Yes, I believe I am part of the body of Christ." We see in the Gospel Jesus' solution is the same today as it was yesterday - "Feed them."

This week, let the presence of Christ saturate your total being, and take the risk to feed your family and friends the food of eternal life. Witness to them about what Christ is doing in your life.

That is how you feed other people. You pray daily for them, and you encourage them to read and study his Holy Word. Then you show them the Word in action; you minister to their needs. Begin feeding your own family; then feed others. You will be amazed when you discover you cannot run out of spiritual food. Let the "Amen" in you be heard throughout your family and friends.

TWELFTH SUNDAY OF ORDINARY TIME - CYCLE C

BEFORE YOU BEGIN:

Pray and ask God to speak to you through His Holy Spirit. "THE PARACLETE, THE HOLY SPIRIT WHOM THE FATHER WILL SEND IN MY NAME, WILL INSTRUCT YOU IN EVERYTHING, AND REMIND YOU OF ALL THAT I TOLD YOU." (JOHN 14:26)

FIRST DAY	**Reread last week's readings.**	

1. What was a helpful or new thought from the readings or from the homily you heard on Sunday?

2. From what you learned, what personal application did you choose to apply to your life this week?

SECOND DAY	**READ ZECHARIAH 12:10-11**	**FIRST READING**

(The Lord shall pour out a spirit of grace and petition.)

1. Who is speaking in verse 10 of Zechariah 12? Zechariah 12:1

2. Through whom is he speaking? Zechariah 1:1.

3. Who is David? Matthew 1:1, 6.

4. What will the Lord pour out on the house of David and the inhabitants of Jerusalem? Zechariah 12:10

5. What three things will the house of David and the inhabitants of Jerusalem do? Zechariah 12:10.

6. To whom is it that they will do these three things, and what was it they thrust through him? John 19:33-34

7. Who did they mourn in Magiddo? 2 Chronicles 35:22-25.

8. As God will pour out a spirit of grace on us, what are we called to do? Acts 20:24

Personal - In what way have I mourned over the death of Jesus. What does it mean to you to have a spirit of grace and petition poured out on you.

THIRD DAY	**READ GALATIANS 3:26-29**	**SECOND READING**

(All are one in Christ)

1. Who are you and what makes you this? Galatians 3:26

2. All of you who have been baptized in Christ have been clothed with what? Galatians 3:27

3. What does not exist among you? Galatians 3:28

4. What are you in Christ? Galatians 3:28

5. What are you to Abraham and what does that do for you? Galatians 3:29

6. What did God promise? James 2:5

7. How do you inherit the promise and what can hinder this? Galatians 3:26, Hebrews 6:12

8. How does the world look at the heirs of the kingdom? James 2:5

9. Where is the kingdom? Matthew 6:9-10

Personal – In your own words write out what it means to cloth yourself in Christ. How have you been an imitator of Jesus to your family, friends, work acquaintances, those you come in contact with during the day?

FOURTH DAY   **READ LUKE 9:18-24**   **GOSPEL**

(Who do the crowds say I am, who do you say I am?)

1. What was Jesus doing, where was he, and who was with him? Luke 9:18.

2. What did he ask them? Luke 9:18, Matthew 16:13

3. What was their response to him? Luke 9:19

4. What was Jesus question to the disciples, who replied, and what did he say? Luke 9:20

5. What did he strictly forbid them to do? Luke 9:21

6. What title did Jesus give himself and what must he endure? Luke 9:22

7. How would the elders, the high priest and the scribes treat Jesus, and what would they do to him? Luke 9:22

8. What would he do on the third day? Luke 9:22

9. What did Jesus say to all of them and how often must the follower deny himself and take up his cross? Luke 9:23

10. Whose steps must you follow? Luke 9:23

11. What will happen to him who tries to save his own life and what will happen to him who loses his life for Jesus' sake? Luke 9:24

Personal – In what way have you denied yourself to follow Jesus? How can you do this on a daily basis with those you meet each day?

FIFTH DAY   **READ PSALM 63:2-6, 8-9**

("O God, you are my God whom I seek;")

Read and meditate on Psalm 63:2-6, 8-9.

What is the Lord saying to you personally through the Psalm?

How can you apply this to your life?

SIXTH DAY   **READ ALL OF THE COMMENTARY**

ZECHARIAH 12:10-11

In today's reading Zechariah calls the Spirit "the Spirit of grace and prayer." This is the Holy Spirit that was poured out at Pentecost (Acts 2). It is this Spirit who convicts us of sin, reveals to us God's righteousness and judgment. The Spirit helps us to pray even when we don't know how or what to pray for (Rom 8:26).

Eventually, all people will come to realize that Jesus was the one who was pierced with the lance and died for all of our sins. We are experiencing an awakening and a revival today all through out the world. The crucified Christ is being clearly revealed through the power of the Holy Spirit. Many people are beginning to realize that only when God's Holy Spirit is among us can we achieve true peace and prosperity.

We know that obedience to prayer, God's Holy Word, and to the teachings of our beloved church will lead us into the presence of God himself. We will, then, experience the full measure of sorrow that brings us into the revival of repentance. Today's reading reveals that there can be no renewal or revival until there is first a repentance. This is from a Godly sorrow not a worldly sorrow that pierces our hearts. As we yield to the power of the Holy Spirit our hearts become broken, humbled, and contrite (Psalm 51:19).

Some may ask "How do I meet this Holy Spirit?" You will meet him in prayer on your knees, and walking around your room in constant prayer. You don't meet him by just singing a song. Today, let us call out to the Holy Spirit for his anointing, and we do that through prayer and obedience to his Holy Word. Scripture tells us that the yoke shall be destroyed because of the anointing (Isaiah 10:27). This is the Spirit of grace and prayer in today's reading.

Today that same spirit of mercy and spirit of prayer must be manifested in our lives. We need to reflect that when we fail to love others, we are still inflicting pain and humiliation on our Lord Jesus Christ. The people in this reading were being called to remember and repent of their sinful behavior; we are called today to do no less.

GALATIANS 3:26-29

There is a continuing thread running between the reading from Galatians of the past two weeks and this weeks. The thread is the thread of FAITH. Paul tells his brothers of the new - found faith and that it was not based on what he had heard from others but from a personal "revelation from Jesus Christ." What a change this made in Paul! He went on to tell them that "the life I live now is not my own; Christ is living in me. I still live my human life but it is a life of faith in the Son of God." Paul has changed. But Paul does not stop there; he goes on to tell us in this week's reading that "Each of you is son (or daughter) of God because of your FAITH in Christ Jesus."

Our readings for this Sunday's celebration speak to us about FAITH....about our FAITH. We hear Peter telling Christ that he is "the Messiah of God," a statement of FAITH. In Matthew 16:17 we hear Jesus telling Peter that this revelation "did not come from any human being, but it is given you directly by my Father in heaven." Jesus asked his disciples, "Who do you say that I am?" We can ask the same question of others, "Who do you say that I am?" Pray that they can respond with the revelation - CHRISTIAN.

"All of you who have been baptized into Christ" have become children of God. We hear this statement in the baptismal ceremony. But we do not, or should not, consider ourselves to be just mere children who possess a limited awareness about our parent or brother. We are grown-up children of God, children who have, or should have, grown in our FAITH. Paul possessed a faith in God that caused him to resist, out of ignorance, the "new way" being practiced by his fellow Jews. But his faith was increased by an encounter with Jesus on the road to Damascus and the resulting revelation changed him, changed his relationship between God and himself between the people and himself, leading him to profess that we are "all one in Christ Jesus." We were baptized into a relationship with God, into a faith belief in Jesus Christ. We, hopefully, received some "revelation" about Jesus from our parents, clergy, religious teachers and our spiritual friends. We have not remained just "children of faith" but have become adults in the faith. However, the question yet remains to be answered: what degree has this FAITH awareness caused us to change in our relationship with God, with Jesus, and with each other?

LUKE 9:18-24

"Who do you say that I am?" There is that question again, the one that is asked so often in the Gospels. Our reading is situated between Jesus' feeding the five thousand and his transfiguration. In the feeding of the five thousand, Jesus shows us his compassion, care and concern for our well being. The people did not ask to be fed, Jesus knew of their need and he responded accordingly, out of love for his brothers and sisters. If he were to ask the crowd who he was they would probably say that he was a good provider, a worker of miracles; certainly not the "Messiah". This was not seen as a faith experience, but just the receiving of a meal. How often do we receive a gift from Jesus and perceive it to be something other than an experience of faith?

In the transfiguration, Jesus shows his chosen disciples what his relationship with God is really like and who he truly is. He is changed, transfigured, and he shows us that a deepening relationship with God will cause us to be changed. Like the disciples, we might find that difficult to comprehend for we look for change in ourselves and do not necessarily see it. We do not see it because we are not looking through our eyes of FAITH but our human eyes. We look for physical change, and material change. Like the disciples who gazed upon the transfigured image of Christ, our brothers and sisters must be able to gaze upon us and see, in the image they perceive, a person transfigured in their life and be able to respond to the question: "Who do you say that I am" with the response of "A Christian."

Application

The first reading tells us we need to listen, even when it is not pleasant. The second reading tells us that we are to grow up in our faith. The gospel challenges us to ask who Jesus Christ is to us personally.

This week, show those around you that you have been growing in your faith and that you have the strength now to listen to God and to others. Your example of humility and service will help others to see who Jesus really is in their lives. In you they will see Jesus and that is really growing up in your faith.

THIRTEENTH SUNDAY OF ORDINARY TIME - CYCLE C

BEFORE YOU BEGIN:

Pray and ask God to speak to you through His Holy Spirit. "THE PARACLETE, THE HOLY SPIRIT WHOM THE FATHER WILL SEND IN MY NAME, WILL INSTRUCT YOU IN EVERYTHING, AND REMIND YOU OF ALL THAT I TOLD YOU." (JOHN 14:26)

FIRST DAY   **Reread last week's readings.**

1. What was a helpful or new thought from the readings or from the homily you heard on Sunday?

2. From what you learned, what personal application did you choose to apply to your life this week?

SECOND DAY   **READ 1 KINGS 19:16, 19-21**   FIRST READING

(Elisha gave up all that he had to follow the Lord's call.)

1. In 1 Kings 19:16, 19-21 who is speaking and to whom is he speaking? 1 Kings 19:12-15

2. Who was Elijah to name king of Israel? 1 Kings 19:16

3. What was Elijah called and who was to succeed him? 1 Kings 19:16

4. Which of the following show how this was to be done? a. appoint b. assign c. anoint

Personal – What does to anoint mean to you personally?

5. As Elijah set out, who did he come upon and what was he doing? 1 Kings 19:19

6. What did Elijah do to him? 1 Kings 19:19

7. What did Elisha do with the oxen, who did he run after and what did he say to him? 1 Kings 19:20

8. What did Elijah say to him? 1 Kings 19:20

9. When Elisha left him, what did he do to the yoke of oxen and the plowing equipment? 1 Kings 19:21

10. What did he do with the flesh? 1 Kings 19:21

11. After he did all this what did he do and how did he follow Elijah? 1 Kings 19:21

Personal – To what extent have you been called to give up some earthly possessions to follow the Lord's call?

THE BREAD OF LIFE CATHOLIC BIBLE STUDY

THIRD DAY   READ GALATIANS 5:1, 13-18   SECOND READING

(We are called to live in freedom.)

1. Who is writing this epistle? Galatians 1:1

2. Why did Christ free us? Galatians 5:1

3. How must you stand and what must you not do? Galatians 5:1

4. How were you freed the first time? Revelations 1:5

5. How have we been called to live and to what does this not give full reign? Galatians 5:13

6. How are we to place ourselves at one another's service? Galatians 5:13

7. How has the law found its fulfillment? Galatians 5:14

8. What will happen to you if you go on biting and tearing at one another? Galatians 5:15

9. How should you live and what will not happen to you? Galatians 5:16

10. What does the flesh and the spirit do to one another and why do you not do what your will intends? Gal. 5:17

11. If you are guided by the spirit, what are you not under? Galatians 5:18

Personal – In what way are you living in accordance with the Spirit, in your home, work, or at play? In what way are you yielding to the cravings of the flesh? How can you take this situation and live according to the spirit?

FOURTH DAY   READ LUKE 9:51-62   GOSPEL

("Come away and proclaim the kingdom of God.")

1. As the time approached for Jesus to be taken from this world, where did he resolve to go and who did he send ahead of him? Luke 9:51

2. What kind of town did those he sent ahead come to and why were they there? Luke 9:52

Personal – In what way have you prepared the way for the Lord's coming for yourself and for your family?

3. What was the Samaritan's reaction to his coming and what was the reason they acted this way? Luke 9:53

4. What did Jesus' disciples, James and John, say when they saw the Samaritans would not welcome him? Luke 9:54

5. How did Jesus respond to this and where did he turn? Luke 9:55

6. Where did they go? Luke 9:56

Personal – When you find opposition in walking with the Lord, what is your reaction especially in your family? Do you continue walking with him or do you persist on getting through to them?

7. As they were making their way along, what did someone say to Jesus? Luke 9:57

8. What did Jesus say to him? Luke 9:58

9. What did he say to another? Luke 9:59

10. What did Jesus say to him? Luke 9:60

11. Why did Jesus want him to come with him? Luke 9:60

12. What was the stipulation another gave him before he could be his follower? Luke 9:61

13. What did Jesus say about a person who keeps looking back? Luke 9:62

Personal – What blockages or excuses have you had for not following Jesus? He is saying to you "Come after me." In what way have you been going before him instead of after him as a follower?

FIFTH DAY   **READ PSALM 16:1-2, 5, 7-11**

("You will show me the path of life")

Read and meditate on Psalm 16:1-2, 5, 7-11.

What is the Lord saying to you personally through the Psalm?

How can you apply this to your life?

SIXTH DAY   **READ ALL OF THE COMMENTARY**

1 KINGS 19:16, 19-21

One of the most important aspects of this passage, from the Old Testament, deals with the price of discipleship. To follow the call of God means that we surrender our will to God so that we may fulfill the divine will. We "tie" ourselves to the holy will of God. This demands sacrifice, an important characteristic of religion.

Sacrifice means "to make holy." Religion means to bind oneself to almighty God and to promote the kingdom of God in this life.

We share in the mysteries of Christ; we all have the vocation to live out the mysteries of Christ. And in the Old Testament we see the first manifestations of this truth since all mankind is founded on the mystery of the Incarnation (Colossians 1:15-20; Ephesians 1:4-14).

All of the above may be applied to the Jewish prophet, Elisha. Elisha paid the price of discipleship. Indeed, he gave up his worldly possessions to follow God's call, made manifest through Elijah. He was to succeed Elijah to the office of prophecy.

The Old Testament tells us that repeatedly the Jewish nation had fallen into spiritual adultery by following the gods of pagan nations. The Book of Hosea is replete with this sad phenomenon. To recall the Jews to the worship of the true God, God raised up men totally dedicated to this task of restoration.

This was no easy task; paganism offered an "easy" religion, a religion that made few demands on fallen human nature where the gods were made in the image of man and not man to the image of the true God.

The prophets, as we see in the case of Elisha, his predecessor, Elijah, Jeremiah and the other prophets, faced their gigantic task with fortitude - one of the seven gifts of the Holy Spirit. They were men of God, worthy of imitation.

GALATIANS 5:1, 13-18

Above, I mentioned that we should be "tied" and here we have Paul speaking of liberty. Nonetheless, there is no contradiction. To "tie" ourselves, is to bind ourselves, as the word religion suggests (from the Latin religare, to bind) therefore we are bound to the infinite God; there is no constraint whatsoever.

On the other hand, sin can become slavery; temptations are constant demands for self-satisfaction; fallen human nature has the tendency to seek not the kingdom of God but rather the kingdom of instant gratification. To master ourselves calls for the grace of God; to master ourselves is to possess the liberty of Christ as Paul puts it so well: "It was for liberty that Christ freed us. Do not take on yourselves the yoke of slavery a second time!"

In the spirit of true liberty, we are able to give of ourselves to God who is not only within us but within our neighbor as well. In that same liberty, we give ourselves to the service of our neighbor, to the sick neighbor, to the sick in spirit, and to see in all of these the Christ Jesus. (Matthew 25:31-46)

When all this comes about, know that the kingdom of God is near at hand, despite appearances.

LUKE 9:51-62

Today's gospel passage deals with the last stages of Christ's public ministry: "As the time approached when Jesus was to be taken from this world."

Jesus and his disciples were to return to Jerusalem by way of Samaria. At that time bad feelings existed between the Jews and the Samaritans. The Samaritans were a mixed race, descendants of Israelitic-Assyrian colonists, and much hated by the Jews at the time of Christ. For a Jew to go through Samaritan territory was rather a risky thing just as it was risky for a Samaritan to go through Jewish territory.

With this background, we can understand the Samaritan's reluctance to allow Jesus and his followers to pass through their territory. Unlike James and John, Jesus accepted the situation. These two disciples were all for the destruction of the Samaritans: "Lord, would you not have us call down fire from heaven and destroy them?" But this was not the doctrine of Christ. Instead, Jesus had taught: "...love your enemies...If you love those who love you, what merit is there in that?" (Matthew 5:44-46). A true disciple "...must be made perfect as (our) heavenly Father is perfect." (Matthew 5:48)

We come now to the subject of vocations. To follow Christ was never an easy task, and it will always be so. Christ made that clear in today's Gospel. "The foxes have lairs, the birds of the air have nests, but the Son of Man has nowhere to lay his head."

A second example is given: "To another he said, "Come after me." The man replied, "Let me bury my father first." Jesus' answer seems strange. "Let the dead bury their dead." Obviously, Christ did not mean that the dead can perform burials. As commentators (e.g., Stuhlmueller in The Jerusalem Commentary, p.143,#97) point out: "A play on words: Let the spiritually dead bury the physically dead, mine is a message of life." Jesus did not intend to be taken literally, but rather he wanted to stir thought.

Today's gospel gives us a third example concerning the vocation to follow him. Vocation entails a "totality." By this I mean that once we set out to follow Christ we do so wholeheartedly, no half-way measures. We cannot chase after other pursuits; we should not be distracted so as other pursuits gradually become more and more important at the expense of the vocation to follow Christ. In brief, an avocation should never become a vocation; a vocation should never become an avocation.

In following Christ, it is of the greatest importance to pay heed to his words: "Whoever puts his hand to the plow but keeps looking back is unfit for the reign of God." This is a very real admonition. Throughout the course of Church history, "looking back" has sometimes led to disastrous consequences, especially among priests and religious. Witness the spectacle of the worldly priest, the worldly religious and the worldly Christian. Surely, if there were a better way to follow Christ; to help bring about the kingdom of God more effectively, the merciful Christ would have pointed out the way. So we believe that doing the will of God, and not our will, is the only true criterion for putting today's readings into practice.

Application

The first reading shows us that the cost of discipleship is very high. The second reading teaches that mastering ourselves is to possess the liberty of Christ, and the Gospel explains that a true disciple must be made perfect as our heavenly Father is perfect.

This week, let the power of the Holy Spirit come upon you and root out the bigotry that is within you. Examine your speech, thoughts and actions and see if these areas need to be improved. Following Jesus calls for obedience, and obedience is the core of being a disciple. To really be free is to be obedient to the law of Christ, and that is to love one another as he has loved us, without regard for race, creed or color.

FOURTEENTH SUNDAY IN ORDINARY TIME - CYCLE C

BEFORE YOU BEGIN:

Pray and ask God to speak to you through His Holy Spirit. "THE PARACLETE, THE HOLY SPIRIT WHOM THE FATHER WILL SEND IN MY NAME, WILL INSTRUCT YOU IN EVERYTHING, AND REMIND YOU OF ALL THAT I TOLD YOU." (JOHN 14:26)

FIRST DAY   **Reread last week's readings.**

1.   What was a helpful or new thought from the readings or from the homily you heard on Sunday?

2.   From what you learned, what personal application did you choose to apply to your life this week?

SECOND DAY   **READ ISAIAH 66:10-14**   **FIRST READING**

(The Lord's power shall be known to his servants.)

1.   Who will rejoice with Jerusalem and be glad because of her? Isaiah 66:10

2.   What are those to do who were mourning over Jerusalem? Isaiah 66:10

3.   What does the milk of Jerusalem bring? Isaiah 66:11

4.   For what does 1 Peter 2:2 say to be eager, and for what reason?

5.   What will the Lord spread over Jerusalem and how? Isaiah 66:12

6.   As nurslings, how shall you be carried and fondled? Isaiah 66:12

7.   Fill in the following blanks: "As a mother _____ her son, so will I _____ you." Isaiah 66:13

8.   Where will you find comfort? Isaiah 66:13

9.   When this happens, what will your heart and body do? Isaiah 66:14

10.   What shall be known to the Lord's servants and what will be known to his enemies? Isaiah 66:14

Personal – In what way do you find comfort when feeling depressed? To whom do you go to? Write out your thoughts and then meditate on 2 Corinthians 1:3-4.

THIRD DAY   **READ GALATIANS 6:14-18**   **SECOND READING**

(Paul boasts of nothing but the cross of Jesus Christ.)

1.   Who is speaking in Galatians 6:14? Galatians 1:1

2. Paul says he must boast of nothing but what? Galatians 6:14

3. Through the cross of Jesus Christ, what does Paul say about the world and about himself? Galatians 6:14

4. What does not matter? Galatians 6:15

5. What is all that matters? Galatians 6:15

6. In whose image are we created, and of what is this justice and holiness born? Ephesians 4:24

7. What two things are on all who follow this rule of life? Galatians 6:16

8. What does Paul bear in his body? Galatians 6:17

9. How does Paul end this letter? Galatians 6:18

Personal – In what way have you been created anew? How do others see you dying to yourself and boasting in the cross of Jesus Christ? What is the rule of life you follow?

FOURTH DAY **READ LUKE 10:1-12, 17-20** **GOSPEL**

(I have given you power to tread on all the forces of the enemy.)

1. How many did the Lord appoint, and how, when, and where did he send them? Luke 10:1

2. What did Jesus say about the harvest and the workers, and for what did he say to ask? Luke 10:2

3. How did Jesus say he is sending his laborers? Luke 10:3

4. How did he tell them to travel? Luke 10:4

5. When entering a house what did he tell them to say? Luke 10:5

6. If there is a peaceable man, what will your peace do, and if he is not, what will happen to your peace? Luke 10:6

7. Where were they to stay and what did he say about wages? Luke 10:7

8. Where they were welcomed, what were they to do with the food, the sick, and what were they to say to them? Luke 10:8-9

9. What were they to say to people that did not welcome them and where were they to go to say it? Luke 10:10-11

10. What will happen to such a town? Luke 10:12

11. How did the seventy-two return, and what did they say was subject to them and in whose name? Luke 10:17

12. Who did Jesus say fell from the sky like lightning? Luke 10:18

13. What had he given them and what shall not happen to them? Luke 10:19

14.   In what should you not so much rejoice, and in what should you rejoice?
      Luke 10:20

Personal – In what way have you used this power that God has given you in the name of Jesus to get rid of the enemy in your family, or with those you meet each day? Reread verse 19 of Luke 10 and claim the promise given to you.

FIFTH DAY   **READ PSALM 66:1-7, 16, 20**

(Sing praise to the glory of his Name.)

Read and meditate on Psalm 66:1-7, 16, 20.

What is the Lord saying to you personally through the Psalm?

How can you apply this to your life?

SIXTH DAY   **READ ALL OF THE COMMENTARY**

ISAIAH 66:10-14

God will not let his work of restoration go unfinished. In this image of a child nursing at his mother's breast, God shows that he will accomplish what he promised.

This promise of eternal peace and mercy is as unstoppable as the birth of a baby. When all the pain is over, the joy begins. Jerusalem is being presented as the new City of God. The new Jerusalem is a place where safety, peace and plenty will be available to all. All the nations are coming to nurse at the breasts of the "New Jerusalem" and they too, along with the remnant of the old, will find new life in Jesus Christ.

This is a tremendous verse about how God, in his incredible mercy, has left the door open for those who believe and obey him. The faithful remnant asked God for two favors: show them compassion (Isaiah 63:15-19) and punish their enemies (Isaiah 66:6). God today still keeps that promise. He will always preserve a faithful remnant of his people no matter how bad the world. There are always a few who remain loyal to him. This verse shows us how the goodness of God will be seen by the world and yet many will still go on rejecting him. The verse closes with a firm warning that his wrath will come upon his enemies (Isaiah 66:14). The earth, as we know it, will not last forever. God promised Isaiah that he would create a new and eternal earth (Isaiah 65:17, 66:22). We don't really know how it will look or where it will be, but Jesus of Nazareth and his followers will be united to live there forever.

GALATIANS 6:14-18

This passage of Paul to the Galatians boldly declares not only his freedom in Christ but, also, it declares the freedom of all Christians in Jesus Christ. In the days of Paul, there were many who wanted to grow in the Christian life but were being distracted by those who insisted that they had to keep certain Jewish laws.

Some of the "Judaizers," (Jews who insisted that you had to be circumcised before you could become a Christian), emphasized circumcision as proof of their holiness, but ignored other Jewish laws. People often choose a particular principle and make it the measuring rod of faith. Some despise promiscuity but tolerate prejudice. God's word has to be followed in its entirety.

Our world is just like Paul's world, it is full of enticements. We are being barraged daily with both subtle and overt cultural pressures and propaganda by the media. We hear Paul saying that he no longer is bothered by them any more because he is dead to the influence of worldly things.

The only way for us to escape these destructive influences is to ask God to help us die to them just as Paul did. We need to ask ourselves, how much do the interests of this world matter to us? We need also to remember that it is very easy to get caught up in the externals. We need to caution against emphasizing things we should or should not do, with no concern for the inward condition of the heart. We do not do good things to become good, we do good things because of the goodness that is within us, and that is the Holy Spirit (John 14:16). Living a good life without inward change leads to a spiritual walk that is shallow, empty and very frustrating.

Paul is telling us that it really does not matter what the world thinks about him or his accomplishments. What does matter to him is the peace that came to him when he died to himself for Jesus Christ. What matters to God is that we be completely changed from the inside out. Paul was to the world a prisoner, but in reality he was completely free in Christ. We have been set free by Jesus Christ. We do not need to be set back by some form of bondage again. We are all called to use our freedom to live for Christ and serve him as he desires.

LUKE 10:1-12, 17-20

Only Luke tells of this second mission of the disciples. More than just the twelve apostles had been following Jesus. He chose a group of about seventy disciples to prepare a number of towns that he would visit. These disciples were just ordinary men, chosen for a not-so-ordinary assignment. The disciples were not trained in any special categories, nor did they have any unique qualifications. What made them different was their awareness of Jesus' power and their vision to reach all the people through him. We see that having personally experienced his power was much more important than dedicating their skills to God's kingdom. Today, we need to focus on what he wants us to do in the world.

Jesus was sending out teams of two to reach the people. They were not to try to do the job themselves without help; rather they were to pray to God for more workers. In doing the work of evangelizing, we may want to jump out and begin working to save others and bring immediate results. Jesus tells us to first begin by praying for more workers, and before praying for the unsaved people, pray that other concerned people will join you in reaching out to them.

There is no unemployment in Christian service. The Lord Jesus has work enough for everyone. Don't just sit back and watch, look for ways to reap the harvest.

Jesus leaves little room for illusion. He tells the disciples they will be like lambs among wolves. They would have to be careful, for they will meet all kinds of opposition. We, too, are sent into the world as lambs among wolves. So we need to watch out
and remember that we need to face our enemies, not with timidity, but with power, not with aggression, but with love and courage.

The disciples were told to accept hospitality graciously because they were entitled to it. We need to see today that our ministers are supported emotionally and receive plenty of encouragement. The disciples were disciplined to eat what was put in front of them and to go among the sick and heal in the name of Jesus. They were to shake off the dust of any town that refused them and move on with the Good News.

The disciples had seen tremendous results as they ministered in Jesus' name and came back overjoyed. Jesus warned them not to get puffed up with their exploits but to remember their most important victory was that their names were registered among the citizens of heaven. Jesus reminds us, today in our ministry of discipleship, that the victory is being won in Jesus' name. The prize is not human glory through feats of evangelistic power, but of heavenly glory through following Jesus to Calvary.

Application

The first reading shows that God will not let his work of restoration go unfinished. The second reading tells us that our world, like Paul's world, is full of enticements. The Gospel reveals that there is no unemployment in Christian service. Let us boast of nothing but the power of the cross of Christ and his Holy Name. We can be instruments of tremendous deeds in his name. We need to begin everything we do in prayer to our Heavenly Father through the power of the Holy Spirit in Jesus' Name and go forth and make disciples of all the nations. Let us begin with the members of our family.

FIFTEENTH SUNDAY IN ORDINARY TIME - CYCLE C

BEFORE YOU BEGIN:

Pray and ask God to speak to you through His Holy Spirit. "THE PARACLETE, THE HOLY SPIRIT WHOM THE FATHER WILL SEND IN MY NAME, WILL INSTRUCT YOU IN EVERYTHING, AND REMIND YOU OF ALL THAT I TOLD YOU." (JOHN 14:26)

FIRST DAY   **Reread last week's readings.**

1. What was a helpful or new thought from the readings or from the homily you heard on Sunday?

2. From what you learned, what personal application did you choose to apply to your life this week?

SECOND DAY   **READ DEUTERONOMY 30:10-14**   **FIRST READING**

("If only you heed the voice of the Lord, your God,")

1. Who is speaking and to whom is he speaking? Deuteronomy 29:1

2. If you heed the voice of the Lord and keep his statutes and commandments what will God do? Deuteronomy 30:9-10

3. What is this book called? Deuteronomy 30:10

4. In what way must you return to the Lord? Deuteronomy 30:10, 6:5

5. What does Moses say this command is not? Deuteronomy 30:11

6. What two places will you not find it, and what shall you say about it not being there? Deuteronomy 30:12-13

7. What two places will you find this command? Deuteronomy 30:14

8. What are you to do with the Lord's command? Deuteronomy 30:14

Personal - In what way has your mouth spoken about the love that you have in your heart for the Lord? In what way have others in your family, friends, or work acquaintances seen and heard this love in you? Is the way you see yourself confirmed by the way others see and hear you?

THIRD DAY   **READ COLOSSIANS 1:15-20**   **SECOND READING**

("Making peace through the blood of the cross.")

1. Who is the first born of all creatures? Colossians 1:15

2. In the image of whom did he come? Colossians 1:15

3. In whom were heaven and earth created? Colossians 1:16

4.   What are some of the things that were created for Jesus? Colossians 1:16

5.   Apart from him, what came into being? John 1:3

6.   He is before what, and how does everything continue its being? Colossians 1:17

7.   Of what is he the head, and for what reason? Colossians 1:18

8.   What pleased God? Colossians 1:19

9.   How are we reconciled to God, and how has peace been made? Colossians 1:20

10. For what reason has he done this? Ephesians 1:14

Personal – In what way have you personally been at peace with God through Jesus? Write down when and how this happened. In what way have you shared this with someone else?

FOURTH DAY   **READ LUKE 10:25-37**   **GOSPEL**

("Then go and do the same.")

1.   Who stood up to pose a problem, how did he address him, and what did he say to him? Luke 10:25

2.   When Jesus answered him, he answered with two questions. What were they? Luke 10:26

3.   What was the lawyer's reply in verse 27 of Luke 10?

4.   What is the new command that Jesus gave us at his last supper? John 13:34 and 15:12

5.   How did Jesus say the lawyer had answered him and from where did he get his answer? Luke 10:28, Deuteronomy 6:5 and Leviticus 19:18

6.   What did Jesus say would happen to him if he followed that command? See Luke 10:28, and also Leviticus 18:5 to see what happens to a man who obeys his command.

7.   What did he say to Jesus and what was Jesus reply about the man going from Jerusalem to Jericho? Luke 10:29-30

8.   Who was going down the same road and what did he do, and then who came upon him and what did he do? Luke 10:31-32

9.   What did the Samaritan do when he saw the man? Luke 10:34

10. What did the Samaritan do the next day? Luke 10:35

11. What did Jesus ask the lawyer, what was the lawyers answer, and what did Jesus tell him to do? Luke 10:36-37

Personal – In what way has the Lord given you an opportunity to be compassionate to a family member, a friend, a work acquaintance, a stranger this past week? How did you respond?

FIFTH DAY   **READ PSALM 69:14, 17, 30-31, 33-34, 36-37**

("In your great mercy, turn toward me.")

Read and meditate on Psalm 69:14, 17, 30-31, 33-34, 36-37.

What is the Lord saying to you personally through the Psalm?

How can you apply this to your life?

SIXTH DAY   **READ ALL OF THE COMMENTARY**

DEUTERONOMY 30:10-14

This passage states that comfort, forgiveness, and restoration is not only possible for the Israelites but is desired by God. The nation of Israel must turn itself around and come back to the Lord. Only then will God restore his mercy and restore Israel to her rightful place in the land. Only through the covenant proposed by God to his people can the people regain happiness.

We hear in today's reading that the keeping of the command (Deut. 30:11-14) is not as far-fetched as many of the shallow minds of the ages suggested. The author has stressed a powerfully spiritual message. The Law of God is not in some far-off courtroom or in some prestigious university. The Law of God is something very close to the heart of man. If this attitude prevailed toward the Mosaic Law, Jesus would not have had such conflict with the formalism of the lawyer. The Judeo-Christian positive law can be equated simply with God's way of guiding the aspirations of the human heart toward him.

St. Paul shows us how close God's law really is in Romans 10:6-10. Paul tells us that we don't need to search the heavens for Christ to bring him down to help us, and we don't need to go among the dead to bring Christ back to life again! Salvation is trusting in Christ; it is as near as our own hearts and mouths. For it is by believing in his heart that a man becomes right with God and with his mouth he tells others of his faith, confirming his salvation.

People have always looked for God through dramatic experiences, hoping for some life-changing encounter. Some people will travel far and wide to meet some famous spiritual leader, but God's salvation is right in front of us. He will come into us wherever we are. All we need to do is yield and surrender to his gift of salvation. We need to stop searching and start yielding to his love and mercy.

We hear everyday at our Catholic Mass the proclamation of God's Word bringing us salvation, healing and restoration. Let us yield our ears to hear, our hearts to believe, and our tongues to speak and his gift of salvation will spread throughout the land.

COLOSSIANS 1:15-20

This passage has some of the most powerful theological statements about Christ in the New Testament. Christ is praised as the Icon or image of the invisible God. He manifests God's presence in his person. He is called the first born of all creation because everything else was created through his mediation. He existed before all creation and is preeminent among all creation. Paul shows us the scope of creation. He begins with heaven and earth, visible and invisible, power and might, thrones and dominions, principalities or power. This was all created not only for him and through him but, also, in him. Everything is subject to Christ, and through his creative power, creation itself continues on. Paul speaks of Christ as the beginning, the starting point of redemption. He is the first to experience the resurrection of life and, therefore, is the first-born from among the dead. By the frequently used word "all," the cosmic dimension of Christ's power and glory are emphasized. The restoration which he brings about is the peace that was accomplished by the shedding of his blood on the cross.

It is stated that Paul had never visited Colossae, evidently the church had been founded by other converts from Paul's missionary travels. The church, however, had been infiltrated by religious relativism by some believers who attempted to combine elements of paganism and secular philosophy with Christian doctrine. Paul attacks the heresy, confronts these false teachings and affirms the sufficiency of Christ.

We can see in today's passage what happens when the head coach is absent and the team begins to flounder. Paul defends his teachings about Christ in a strong doctrinal discussion of the person and work of Christ. Paul was battling against a group of leaders called "Gnostics." The Gnostics believed it took special knowledge to be accepted by God, even as they claimed to be Christian. They believed that Christ alone was not the way of salvation. Paul's main argument was: it is not what one knows that makes him a Christian, but who he knows. To know Christ is to know God. The same danger exists today, and like Paul, we must accept Jesus as our personal Lord and Savior. Jesus calls for our heart, mind and soul and we need only surrender to him and say yes.

LUKE 10:25-37

The lawyer asked Jesus a question that on the surface seemed simple: "What must I do to receive eternal life?" Jesus, in his role as a Hebrew Teacher or Rabbi, answered him with two questions: "What was written in the Law, and how did he interpret the law?" At that time, to an orthodox Jew, the definition of neighbor would have meant no one else but a Jew. Jesus relates to them a story that draws from them a definition of who is neighbor.

Jesus begins by telling the story of a man who was robbed and beaten and left in the roadway to die. The first person to come by the injured man was a priest, who was probably on his way to the temple to practice his sacred duties. The priest did not even touch the fallen man because, as scripture has it in Numbers 19:11, a priest would be banned from entering into the sacred temple for seven days after touching a dead person. His duty to the temple and community came before helping this particular man. The next person to come by was a Levite who was an assistant to the priests. The priests made the atonement sacrifice and were in charge of the altars and sacred services. The Levite, too, was caught up in his duties to his ministry, and his responsibility which was being an assistant to the priest in the temple and other religious duties.

Finally, along came a Samaritan who not only stopped to see what was wrong, but became involved in trying to help. The man may have not been a Samaritan really, the name itself was used for people who didn't exactly conform to existing standards. Today we might call that kind of a person a "maverick", someone who is willing to take a risk. Jesus was called a Samaritan in John 8:48, obviously they thought he was not orthodox like them. The question Jesus puts to the lawyer, "Who do you think was neighbor to the man?" is the same question that is being asked of you and me. God's love is so great that anyone who is in need is eligible for his help.

God wishes that no man perishes no matter his station in life. We are called to love God with all our heart, soul and strength by loving our neighbor the same way. Jesus even elevates this standard higher in John 15:12 when he calls us to love one another as he has loved us. The Samaritan had the love of God in his heart and he spoke his love into action with his deeds. We will be judged one day, not by our doctrine or creeds, but rather by how we loved our neighbor with all our heart, strength and soul. It is how we love our neighbor that signifies to the world how we really love God.

Application

The first reading tells us that repentance must come before mercy can be expected. The second reading shows that Christ is praised as the image of the invisible God. The Gospel reveals that we will be judged by how we love our neighbor.

We can love, like the Samaritan, when we yield to God's love and allow ourselves to love everyone and anyone just as Jesus loves us. This is a love that is willing to pay any price that is required. Let your family be the first to experience this kind of love from you. You can begin by dying to your own needs, become more aware of the needs of others, and respond to those needs.

SIXTEENTH SUNDAY OF ORDINARY TIME - CYCLE C

BEFORE YOU BEGIN:

Pray and ask God to speak to you through His Holy Spirit. "THE PARACLETE, THE HOLY SPIRIT WHOM THE FATHER WILL SEND IN MY NAME, WILL INSTRUCT YOU IN EVERYTHING, AND REMIND YOU OF ALL THAT I TOLD YOU." (JOHN 14:26)

FIRST DAY   **Reread last week's readings.**

1. What was a helpful or new thought from the readings or from the homily you heard on Sunday?

2. From what you learned, what personal application did you choose to apply to your life this week?

SECOND DAY   **READ GENESIS 18:1-10 FIRST READING**

("...he waited on them under the tree while they ate.")

1. To whom did the Lord appear by the great tree at Mamre, where was he sitting, and what was happening to the day? Genesis 18-1

2. When he looked up, what did he see and what did he do? Genesis 18:2

3. What are two of these men called? Genesis 19:1

4. What did Abraham say to them? Genesis 18:3

5. Why did he want to bring them water? Genesis 18:4

6. What did Abraham call himself, and why did he want them to have food? Genesis 18:5

7. How did Abraham enter the tent, and what did he say to his wife, Sarah? Genesis 18:6

8. How did he go to the herd, and after picking out a tender choice steer, to whom did he give it for preparation? Genesis 18:7

9. What else did he get for them, and what did he do, and continue to do as they sat eating under the tree? Genesis 18:8

10. What did they ask Abraham, what was his reply, what did one of them say about Sarah and what was Sarah doing? Genesis 18:9-10

Personal - In what way do you show hospitality to those passing your way? Who are the messengers of the Lord in your life? How do you treat them?

THIRD DAY   **READ COLOSSIANS 1:24-28**   **SECOND READING**

("Now I rejoice in my sufferings for your sake,")

1.   Who is speaking in verses 24-28 of Colossians, and to what is he a minister? Colossians 1:23

2.   Where does he find his joy? Colossians 1:24

3.   Where does he fill up what is lacking in the sufferings of Christ, and for whose sake does he do this? Colossians 1:24

4.   What does he call his body? Colossians 1:24

5.   What did Paul become to this church, through the commission of whom, and to do what? Colossians 1:25

6.   To whom has he revealed the mystery that was hidden from ages and generations past? Colossians 1:26

7.   What is the mystery that God has willed to make known? Colossians 1:27

8.   What is this for which you hope? Colossians 1:27

9.   What are we to proclaim, and how are we to do it? Colossians 1:28

10. What is useful for teaching and admonishing one another? 2 Timothy 3:16

Personal – In what way has the mystery of Christ in you been revealed to others? When did you first realize that he dwells in you, and what change took place in you when you realized this?

FOURTH DAY   **READ LUKE 10:38-42**   **GOSPEL**

("There is need of only one thing.")

1.   Who welcomed Jesus to her home, and where was this located? Luke 10:38, John 11:1

2.   What was her sister's name, and what two things did she do? Luke 10:39

3.   What did God the Father tell us to do? Mark 9:7

4.   What did Moses say about Jesus? Deut. 18:15 and Acts 3:22

5.   With what was Martha busy, and what did she say to Jesus? Luke 10:40

6.   What did Martha tell Jesus to do? Luke 10:40

7.   What was the Lord's reply? Luke 10:41

8.   What is the one thing only that is required? Psalm 27:4

9.   Who had chosen the better portion? Luke 10:42

10. What did he say would not happen to Mary? Luke 10:42

Personal – This past week in what way have you not been distracted by duty in order to sit at the feet of Jesus and listen to him? In what way have you heard his voice and responded? Share this with someone.

FIFTH DAY   **READ PSALM 15:2-5**

("He who walks blamelessly and does justice,")

Read and meditate on Psalm 15:2-5.

What is the Lord saying to you personally through the Psalm?

How can you apply this to your life?

SIXTH DAY   **READ ALL OF THE COMMENTARY**

GENESIS 18:1-10

The story illustrates near Eastern hospitality in several ways. In Abraham's day, a person's reputation was largely connected to his hospitality, in the sharing of his home and food. Even traveling strangers were accorded treatment that would be given to highly honored guests. Meeting another's need for food or shelter was and still is today one of the most immediate and practical ways to obey God and do his will.

We can see Abraham trying to get a cool breeze and looking out of the opening of his tent on a very hot day in the desert. He probably was startled when he saw the three men coming toward him. He immediately gave them all of his attention. He addressed one of his guests as "my lord" and yet he addressed himself as a servant. He acted like they would be doing him a favor by letting him serve them and attend to their needs. He washed their feet in accordance with the local custom. This was not only a pleasant comfort but also a sign of genuine respect. This was a courtesy to refresh a traveler in a hot, dusty climate like Mamre. He then prepared his food from his best source of crops and the meat came from choice animals. He bowed down to them and stood back and waited upon them like a true servant.

Tradition reflects on the three angels as the Trinity. We may well reflect on the hospitality that Abraham extends to his guests and try to bring it into our manner of conduct. Do people see in my actions the role of a servant, or do we insist on our needs being met first? We are called on to meet the needs of anyone who needs help. Jesus, in Philippians 2:6-11, shows us how to take on the role of a servant. We need to look with humility and joy towards others, and they need to see in our service the sign of God's love and peace in us.

COLOSSIANS 1:24-28

Paul compares his suffering as completing the sufferings of Jesus Christ. Jesus died to save the church; but the church must continue on in a broken lonely world. Paul experienced incredible rejection and physical danger in bringing his message of Good News to a many times more hostile world. Paul's legacy to us is that we too are called today to bring the marvelous mystery of Christ to all people, and if such service involves suffering, sacrifice and even death, then that is the filling up and sharing the suffering of Christ. Paul's task was to bring to men a new discovery, a mystery that was now revealed.

Paul's great gift to our Christian faith and to the world itself was that Christ was the God of not just the Jews, but the Gentiles as well. Paul totally destroyed the idea that God's love and mercy were for only a special nation or a privileged people. Our God is a God of all people, poor people, rich people, young people, old people and all nationalities.

Had it not been for Paul we might have been nothing more than a new sect of Judaism. The Jews would have refused to believe that he was the God of Gentiles, and that would have been blasphemous. The gnostic would have never believed that every man could be taught enough knowledge necessary for salvation. The gnostics believe that salvation was only for the spiritual elite and the chosen few.

Most educators today have agreed that it is impossible to teach knowledge to every person, because not everyone is capable of learning it. We can look around today and see that not everyone has the same gifts. There are gifts which some will never attain. There are those who are color-blind and to whom the wonders of art mean nothing. There are those who are tone deaf and the glory of music does not exist. Not everyone can be a singer, a writer, a student, or a preacher. These are gifts which some will never possess. There are privileges a person will never enjoy. There are some heights of fame and glory that some will never scale but the mystery that Paul brought to the world through his preaching was that to everyone there is available the Good News of the Gospel, and that is the love of God in Christ Jesus who dwells within each one of us.

This Good News is the transforming power which brings holiness into life itself. That is why Paul can say he rejoices in his suffering for us. He was bringing the Good News, and making the Word of God fully known. Today you and I are called to continue and we too are to rejoice in our sufferings as we bring the Good News, and, like Paul, make the Word of God fully known to all men.

LUKE 10:38-42

In the first reading Abraham's anxiety to entertain his guests leaves us almost winded. Abraham hastened into the tent. He ran to the herd. He had a servant quickly prepare a meal. Then in our Gospel reading we see Martha rushing about and even complaining about Mary's lack of concern. To judge from the story of the Samaritan, Martha should have been praised for her practical service to Jesus. Jesus, in fact, challenges her priorities.

The whole gospel is not contained in loving your neighbor, no matter how important that is. Christian discipleship is first and foremost surrendering to a personal relationship with Jesus Christ. There must be a quiet time to listen to his Word. Devotion to Jesus is the "one thing" that is required. Matthew 6:33 "Seek ye first his kingship and all else will be added unto you." This kind of a relationship shows itself in loving service, but without prayer, care for other's needs may not be love.

Today's Gospel shows us a tension between temperaments. Some people are naturally dynamos of activity; others are normally quiet. Some people find it very hard to just sit and meditate alone with the Lord. There are those who would find it very uncomfortable to go into an active ministry. God needs his Mary and Marthas too. Ecclesiastes tells us, "There is an appointed time for everything and a time for every affair under the heavens." (3:1).

In today's Gospel Luke shows us how the incident between Mary and Martha illustrates the primary love of God with all one's heart, soul, strength and mind. Jesus points out to Martha that there is a proper time for prayer and contemplation, for studying scripture and listening to God, just as there is a proper time for action.

We need only to think where Jesus was going when this happened. He was on his way to Jerusalem - to die. His whole being was taken up with the intensity to bend his will to the will of God. Jesus wanted comfort, peace, solace and Martha wanted to lay on him a fantastic meal and a spotlessly clean house. That was not what Jesus needed or wanted but it was what Martha wanted. Mary listened to his needs and Martha in her kindness assumed his needs. Jesus said "one thing is necessary," and in probability, a small simple meal would have of been enough. This is one of our great difficulties in life. We want to be kind to people, but we want to be kind to them in our way. We get hurt when our way is not the necessary way. We need to forget our plans and listen to what he or she needs. Mary understood Jesus' needs but Martha did not. Let us, as Mary, listen, listen...

Application

The first reading tells us that a person's reputation was largely connected to his hospitality. The second reading tells us that the Good News of the Gospel is available to everyone. The Gospel reveals that it is God's agenda not ours that is to be followed.

Let us be available as Abraham and a servant to others, and let the mystery of Christ's presence within us be available to all we meet. Mary listened to Christ and she heard his heart as well as his words; let us do no less.

We can be present to our families only when we are listening and understanding what they are saying and not saying. The essence of the Christian life is not doing, but rather it is dying. It is in dying to one's own needs and being available to listen and respond to other's needs.

SEVENTEENTH SUNDAY IN ORDINARY TIME - CYCLE C

BEFORE YOU BEGIN:

Pray and ask God to speak to you through His Holy Spirit. "THE PARACLETE, THE HOLY SPIRIT WHOM THE FATHER WILL SEND IN MY NAME, WILL INSTRUCT YOU IN EVERYTHING, AND REMIND YOU OF ALL THAT I TOLD YOU." (JOHN 14:26)

FIRST DAY   **Reread last week's readings.**

1. What was a helpful or new thought from the readings or from the homily you heard on Sunday?

2. From what you learned, what personal application did you choose to apply to your life this week?

SECOND DAY   **READ GENESIS 18:20-32**   **FIRST READING**

("The outcry against Sodom and Gomorrah is so great,
and their sin so grave,")

1. What did the Lord say about Sodom and Gomorrah? Genesis 18:20-21

2. What was one of the sins of Sodom and Gomorrah? Genesis 19:4-9

3. Why did the Lord go down to Sodom and Gomorrah? Genesis 18:21

4. Who were the two men that walked on further while Abraham remained standing before the Lord? Genesis 19:1

5. What did Abraham say to the Lord in Genesis 18:23?

6. What did he say about fifty innocent people? Genesis 18:24

7. What was Abraham's statement to the Lord, and what was the Lord's reply? Genesis 18:25-26

8. How did Abraham see himself, with what did Abraham persist in questioning the Lord, and what was the Lord's answer? Genesis 18:27-32.

9. How many times did he persist with his questions? Genesis 18:24-32.

10. As soon as the Lord had finished speaking to Abraham, where did he go, and where did Abraham go? Genesis 18:33.

Personal – In what specific area have you been persistent in praying to the Lord? How often do you get into conversations with the Lord as Abraham did?

("God gave you new life in company with Christ.")

1. What two things happened to you in Baptism? Colossians 2:12

2. In whom did these two things happen and why? Colossians 2:8-9 Colossians 2:12.

3. Who raised Jesus from the dead? Colossians 2:12

4. What condition were you in when God gave you new life? Colossians 2:13

5. When you were dead in sin, to whom did you give allegiance? Ephesians 2:1-2.

6. With whom was this new life that God gave you? Colossians 2:13

7. How can we partake of this new life? Romans 6:3-4

8. What did he do with all of our sins? Colossians 2:13

9. What did he cancel, and taking it; what did he do with it? Colossians 2:14

10. What did Jesus do in his own flesh, what did this create in him, and what was the result? Ephesians 2:14-15

Personal – In what way do people see in you a person who has been pardoned of all your sins? Take time to thank God for freeing you from the bondage of sin which he did by sending Jesus to die on the cross for you. Spend time in conversation with our Father this week.

("Lord, teach us to pray.")

1. What did the disciples of Jesus observe him doing in a certain place, and what did they ask him? Luke 11:1

2. To whom did Jesus say you first address your prayer, and what two things do you say to him? Luke 11:2

3. Next, what do you ask him to do? Luke 11:3

4. What do we ask him to do for us as we do the same to others? Luke 11:4

5. From what do we ask him to forgive us? Luke 11:4.

Personal – How have you used the five levels of prayer in the Our Father this past week? (Praise; Acceptance; Petition; Forgiveness; Protection). Let this include your family life and work.

6. Jesus tells a parable on prayer in Luke 11:5-8. What is a reason he gives for prayer to be answered? Luke 11:8.

7. What does Jesus say will happen when you ask, when you seek, and when you knock? Luke 11:9.

8. What does he repeat in verse 10 of Luke 11?

9. What analogy does he use about our earthly fathers? Luke 11:11-12

Personal – When did you personally ask God to give you the Holy Spirit? What change took place in your life?

FIFTH DAY   **READ PSALM 138:1-3, 6-8**

("I will give thanks to you.")

Read and meditate on Psalm 138:1-3, 6-8.

What is the Lord saying to you personally through the Psalm?

How can you apply this to your life?

SIXTH DAY   **READ ALL OF THE COMMENTARY**

GENESIS 18:20-32

Abraham introduces to us the idea that prayer is the means through which we can better comprehend the mind of God. Abraham is well aware of the evil that is going on in Sodom, and he begins his prayer for the Lord's people, including Lot, his nephew and Lot's family. It appears that Abraham was attempting to change God's mind but in the process Abraham's mind was changed.

Abraham never doubted that God hated sin and that sinners would be punished. But he may have been confused on just how merciful God really is. He is seen probing the mind of God and ending his prayer convinced that God is both kind and fair. Abraham's prayer is in many ways like ours, always subject to change. We might question why God let Abraham intercede for a city of people who were so wicked. God wanted Abraham to personally experience God's mercy towards sinners. God knew that there were not ten righteous people in the city of Sodom, but he was delighted with Abraham's intent to intercede for them.

God wants us to constantly intercede for others, so that they can repent and come back to the kingdom of righteousness. It is very important that we see God, not as one who enjoys destroying the wicked, but as one who must punish sin. God was fair in testing the men of Sodom. He told Abraham that he was going to see for himself how wicked the people of Sodom were and then he would decide what to do (Genesis 18:20). God was not ignorant of the perversion that was going on in the city (Gen. 19:4-9), but in his mercy he gave the people one last chance to turn to him.

God is still waiting for his people to turn to him (2 Peter 3:9). We are that people. We too can suffer the same fate as the people of Sodom. We need only to look around and see the moral perversion that has become so common and acceptable in our society. Abraham prayed that God would not destroy the city if only ten people were righteous. We need to reflect and pray that there are enough good people in our community. God wills that none of us should perish. God was not unfair to the people of Sodom. He showed great mercy to Lot, who had only a mild relationship with him. We are told in scripture, "Repent, the Kingdom of God is at hand" (Mark 1:15). Let us not be like the Sodomites who risked God's patience wearing out. Rather, let us imitate Abraham and be people of prayer and righteousness.

COLOSSIANS 2:12-14

In Paul's day, the Church's common form of Baptism was total immersion. This was because the majority of new Christians were adult converts. The Christian family had not yet come into existence which led naturally to infant baptism.

The new Christians were completely submerged in water. This submersion symbolized the death and burial of their old way of life. The coming up out of the water symbolized the resurrection of Christ from the dead. We who have been baptized need only think of our old sinful life as dead and buried. Then we will have a powerful motive to resist sin. We do not want to empower that ugly part of our past.

Through faith in the Lord Jesus Christ and the power of his Holy Spirit, we can consciously choose to treat the old nature as dead and enjoy our wonderful new life with Jesus Christ. Through our baptism, we now have a new nature. God crucified the old one (Romans 6:6) and replaced it with a new loving nature (Colossians 3:9-10). It is important for us to realize that God does not take us out of the world and make us into religious robots. We still have that tendency to sin occasionally and sometimes we do sin.

Incredibly, before we were saved we were slaves to a sinful nature, but now, through faith in Jesus Christ, we can choose to live for Christ. We can enjoy our new life in Christ because we have joined him in his death and resurrection. Our evil desires, our love of sin, and our bondage to sin have died with him. Now, joining him in his resurrection, we can have unbroken fellowship with God and freedom from sin.

Our debt for sin has been paid in full, our sins are swept away and forgotten. We can be clean and new. We need not be torn apart by the distractions in our society, families and even within ourselves. We have been saved from the grasp of Satan by Christ through Baptism. We have become heirs of the King and children of God. We need only remember that because of our baptism "the Spirit that is within us is greater than anyone in the world." (1 John 4:4).

Our baptism brings into our temple the awesome power of the Holy Spirit. The Holy Spirit makes us far more than just conquerors. Spend time with our heavenly Father this week. Giving prayer and praise will strengthen our response in faith. Those around us will see that we are people of prayer and power.

LUKE 11:1-13

After finishing a regular, much needed, and fulfilling time of prayer, Jesus was asked by his disciples to teach them how to pray. Jesus was a devout Jew who practiced his faith very diligently by reading his scripture and spending time in prayer. He knew that his power and success in his mission came from his heavenly Father. We too can take on this attitude of humility especially when we look around and see the accomplishments that we have made in our families, jobs, etc. We need to remember that we can't do anything of lasting value by ourselves.

Our only power and success comes from God (2 Cor. 3:5). This is why praying is so powerful and so needed in our lives today. Jesus taught them what we call today the "perfect prayer." First, he identifies God as "Father," which immediately ties him into a special relationship. The Hebrew word for father is "Abba" or daddy. Jesus, by calling him that name, states that he knows him personally. Not only he but all who make this prayer can be included in this intimate relationship. He lets us know right from the beginning that Our Father can be trusted completely.

Jesus praises his Father and then he makes his requests. Praising God first puts us in the right frame of mind to tell him about our needs. The most powerful way to break out of a depression is through praise. We step out of ourselves when we are truly praising someone else.

Many times our prayer is a shopping list, and not a conversation, between two people who love each other. We see his precious name being hallowed or blessed. This makes sense when we realize that in Hebrew times a person's name was his entire character, his strength, and his reputation. God's name was blessed because all who called on it would also be blessed. His kingdom was not only coming to earth but was in fact already here, transforming and saving the earth through the death and resurrection of our Lord Jesus Christ.

God's provision of bread is daily, not once but for all. We can't just store it up and then cut off communication with God. We dare not become fully self-satisfied. If we are running low on strength, we need only to ask ourselves how long have we been away from the source. The cornerstone of this prayer is forgiveness. Forgiveness, like love, is a decision that must be made in our relationship with God. We can choose not to forgive and hold someone else in bondage, or we can choose to forgive and loosen someone from the bondage of being imprisoned.

Jesus very clearly shows us that his love is a love of forgiveness. We are to love as his Father loves and to love as Jesus loves. We must forgive those who have wronged us just as he has forgiven us who have wronged him. To remain unforgiving shows that we have not understood that we ourselves, along with all others, deeply need to forgive.

After the Lord's prayer, Jesus continues to explain the need for persistence in prayer by an example of a friend waking his neighbor in the middle of the night asking for food. We need to be as persistent in our prayer as the man knocking on his neighbor's door.

God who loves us receives our prayers as a perfect Father would and we should be persistent in praying to him. His response to us is always for our own good, even if we don't understand fully the response at the time. He is our Father, he is blessed, and he forgives us. We as his children honor him by our prayers, our praise, and our forgiveness of others.

Application

The first reading shows that Abraham prayed constantly and with great persistence. The second reading tells us that we are dead to the old sinful nature through Christ, and the Gospel introduces us to the perfect prayer.

Let us pray that all will accept the Holy Spirit from our heavenly Father. If you have not asked to receive him, I pray that you will take this time now and invite the Holy Spirit to take up residence in your heart. This is the essence of our "perfect prayer." The result of this will be a hunger to know his will for your life by getting to know what he says in his Word.

EIGHTEENTH SUNDAY IN ORDINARY TIME - CYCLE C

BEFORE YOU BEGIN:

Pray and ask God to speak to you through His Holy Spirit. "THE PARACLETE, THE HOLY SPIRIT WHOM THE FATHER WILL SEND IN MY NAME, WILL INSTRUCT YOU IN EVERYTHING, AND REMIND YOU OF ALL THAT I TOLD YOU." (JOHN 14:26)

FIRST DAY   **Reread last week's readings.**

1. What was a helpful or new thought from the readings or from the homily you heard on Sunday?

2. From what you learned, what personal application did you choose to apply to your life this week?

SECOND DAY   **READ ECCLESIASTES 1:2; 2:21-23**   **FIRST READING**

*("For what profit comes to a man for all the toil and
anxiety of heart with which he had labored under the sun.")*

1. Who is Qoheleth, and what are his words? Ecclesiastes 1:1-2

2. How has a man labored, over what has he labored, who must he leave it to, and besides vanity what is it? Ecclesiastes 2:21

3. Why do we do honest (labor) work? Ephesians 6:7-8

4. What question is asked over that which a man labors? Ecclesiastes 2:22

5. For the sake of profit, what do many do, and what does the struggle for wealth do? Sirach 27:1

6. What chokes the word and bears no fruit? Mark 4:19

7. What did Jesus tell Martha? Luke 10:41-42

8. What is a man's occupation, what happens to him at night, and what is this? Ecclesiastes 2:23

9. What has God made the wisdom of the world, and what will he do with it? 1 Corinthians 1:19-20

10. What is there in much worldly wisdom and sorrow? Ecclesiastes 1:18

Personal – In what way have you worked so hard that worry has kept you awake at night over your work? What is your purpose in doing this?

| THIRD DAY | READ COLOSSIANS 3:1-5, 9-11 | SECOND READING |

("Stop lying to one another, since you have taken off
the old self with its practices.")

1. What did you do with Christ, what do you seek, and where is Christ seated? Colossians 3:1

2. Through what have we grown in union with him, and through what shall we also be united with him? Romans 6:5

3. About what are we to think, about what are we not to think, and for what reason are we to think this way? Colossians 3:2-3

4. About what things are we to think, with what are we not to occupy our mind, and where is our citizenship? Philippians 4:8, Philippians 3:19-20

5. What will happen when Christ your life appears, and what are we to put to death? Colossians 3:4-5

6. What should not even be mentioned among us? Ephesians 5:3

7. What are we to stop doing, and what have we taken off? Colossians 3:9

8. What is being renewed, and for what is it being renewed? Colossians 3:10

9. What are we to put away, and in what are we to be renewed? Ephesians 4:22-24

10. Between what is there no distinction, and who is everything and in everything? Colossians 3:11

Personal – What are the things you seek in life, and about what do you spend most of your time thinking? What do you need to do to think about the things above and not of these earthly things?

| FOURTH DAY | READ LUKE 12:13-21 | GOSPEL |

("Take care to guard against greed, for though one
may be rich, one's life does not consist of possessions.")

1. What did someone in the crowd say to Jesus, how did Jesus address him, and what did he say? Luke 12:13-14

2. Against what did Jesus tell the crowd to guard, of and what did he say one's life does not consist? Luke 12:15

3. What comes from a man's greed, and it is better to be a poor man than what? Proverbs 19:22

4. What does not satisfy a man's greed? Ecclesiastes 4:8

Personal – How can you guard against greed in your home or work?

5. What did Jesus go on to tell the crowd? Luke 12:16

6. What did the rich man ask himself, and what did he say he would do to store his bountiful harvest? Luke 12:17-18

7.   Now that he had so many good things stored, what did he say he could do?
     Luke 12:19

8.   About what should you not boast, and for what reason? Proverbs 27:1

9.   What are you to tell the rich? 1 Timothy 6:17-18

10. What did God say to the man? Luke 12:20-21

Personal - What are the things you are storing that matter to God, and what do you need to give away?

FIFTH DAY   **READ PSALM 95:1-2, 6-9**

("Come, let us bow down in worship.")

Read and meditate on Psalm 95:1-2, 6-9.

What is the Lord saying to you personally through the Psalm?

How can you apply this to your life?

SIXTH DAY   **READ ALL OF THE COMMENTARY**

ECCLESIASTES 1:2, 2:21-23

Today's reading is taken from the Book of Qoheleth, which in Greek means Ecclesiastes. The book is presented as coming from David's son, King in Jerusalem. We see the author as a man of numerous experiences. His interest of human life and experiences is very broad.

This reading challenges us and raises more questions than it answers. We see man constantly searching for more out of life, and while he achieves a great deal, he seems frustrated and unfulfilled. He talks about vanity in the sense that everything is only temporary and to put all of our energy into things is foolish as well as in vain. He states that the wise man and the fool both die, and whatever they have on earth goes to someone else to enjoy. He sees in the vanity of life that a man is blessed if he reverently honors his promise to God. The unjust man, on the other hand, will some day face great punishment.

A strong vanity of life appears to be great wealth, because it also causes a man much worry and loss of sleep due to his fear of losing his wealth. Wisdom seems to help a man from being depressed and fills his life's emptiness, but death seems to put an end to wisdom. Qoheleth showed through experience that even the just suffer and the unjust seem to go unpunished for a long time. He calls for patience and wisdom. He links obedience with authority to obedience to God. He sees life as something to be enjoyed rather than something to be endured. This reading brings to us the example of life's experiences.

Today we see people who are very wise with very little formal education. We see in the wise person the knowledge that God is the only one who is permanent. Today's passage tells us that to put our complete trust and faith in anything or anyone, other than God, is indeed this vanity of vanities.

COLOSSIANS 3:1-5, 9-11

In today's passage, true Christian behavior is demonstrated by putting on a new nature and accepting Christ, and then letting the old nature die. In Baptism, the Christian dies and rises again. Baptism means to submerge, drown, and sink. This is the death of the old nature. To rise is when we come up out of the water and, like Christ did in the resurrection, take on a new life. We rise from the waters of Baptism, a different person.

We change our behavior when we let Christ live within us, so that he can shape us into what we should be, rather than what we may want to be. While the Christian's real home is in heaven, it does not mean that he is to withdraw himself from the work and activities of the world. God never did tell us to leave this world; he did tell us to win over the world. The Christian sets his eye, his standard, and his ideal, not on the world but on that which is of God. He will go on using the things of the world, but he will use them in a new way.

As Christians, we are invited to place giving before getting, serving before ruling, and forgiving above avenging. The Christian's standard of values will be God's standards, not men's. The early Christians regarded Baptism as a dying and rising again. The Greeks spoke of a man who was dead and buried as hidden in the earth, but the Christian who has died a spiritual death in Baptism is not hidden in the earth, but hidden in Christ.

Today, the world tells us that the treasury of wisdom is hidden, acquired knowledge. Christians have the treasury of all wisdom in Jesus Christ. The Christian is in a continuing educational program. The more we know about Christ, the more we are being changed to be like him. Christ breaks down all barriers and accepts all people who come to him. As Christians, we are called to build bridges, not barriers.

LUKE 12:13-21

Today's Gospel brings us right into the conflict that is threatening to tear the heart out of our communities. The conflict is between the people who have much of the so-called good life and those who are struggling just to make ends meet. Jesus is pointing to a higher issue, a correct attitude toward the accumulation of wealth. He tells us that life is far more than material goods, and most important is our relationship with God.

When we bring our problems to God in prayer, he often shows us how we need to change and grow in our attitude toward these problems. Jesus tells us that we do not always have to wish for what we do not have, and he tells us the existing good life has nothing to do with being wealthy. This is the exact opposite of what the world is telling us. Advertisers spend fortunes telling people that if they buy a certain product, their lives will be happier, and more comfortable. In your community, how do you respond to the constant pressure to buy?

We must learn to concentrate on the good life; that is to live in a relationship with God and do his work. The man in today's reading died before he was able to use what he had saved. Jesus asks what good is it to put all of our energy into what we need here on earth and not to prepare for our inevitable death. When a rich man or a poor man dies, they both will stand in judgment. It makes no difference how well they did in their earthly life. How powerful, rich, or educated you are will not be the question asked by the Lord. He will say, "What you did to the least of my people, you did to me." (Mat. 25:31-46). You are to plan and save and be prudent with your life, but it is most important to make your life worthwhile by living it for others through Christ. When Christ one day asks you, "What did you do when you were on earth?" and if you say, "I loved others as you have loved me," you will be one of the richest saints in heaven.

Application

The first reading tells us "that you can not take it with you." The second reading tells us to give before getting, serve before ruling, forgive before avenging. The Gospel shows that we should seek first the kingdom of God and all else will be given to us.

This week, use what you have to help others and let your example be passed on to others. Let your comments be positive and offer to help whether it is a big project or a small one. Share your wealth generously. Your wealth is far more than your money. To those who love you and know you, your presence is priceless to them. Let people see the Christ in you as you speak. Listen to them with the ears of Christ and see others through the eyes of Christ. You will be the richest person in your community because Christ wants you to give him away, so he can stay with you.

NINETEENTH SUNDAY OF ORDINARY TIME - CYCLE C

BEFORE YOU BEGIN:

Pray and ask God to speak to you through His Holy Spirit. "THE PARACLETE, THE HOLY SPIRIT WHOM THE FATHER WILL SEND IN MY NAME, WILL INSTRUCT YOU IN EVERYTHING, AND REMIND YOU OF ALL THAT I TOLD YOU." (JOHN 14:26)

FIRST DAY   **Reread last week's readings.**

1. What was a helpful or new thought from the readings or from the homily you heard on Sunday?

2. From what you learned, what personal application did you choose to apply to your life this week?

SECOND DAY   **READ WISDOM 18:6-9**   **FIRST READING**

("Your people awaited the salvation of the just.")

1. What night was known beforehand to our fathers? Wisdom 18:5-6

2. Fill in the following blanks: "With sure knowledge of the oaths in which they put their _____ they might have _____. Wisdom 18:6

3. What is faith? Hebrews 11:1

4. How does faith come to us? Romans 10:17

5. They put faith in the knowledge of what in order to have courage? Wisdom 18:6

6. What did the people await? Wisdom 18:7

7. Who was punished and in this, what happened to those who had been summoned? Wisdom 18:8

8. What were the holy children offering and what were they putting into effect with one accord? Wisdom 18:9

9. What two things would the holy ones share alike and what had they previously been doing? Wisdom 18:9

Personal - In what way have you been "singing the praises" of what your forefathers, those who believed, have passed on to you? In what way have you passed this faith on to your family?

| THIRD DAY | READ HEBREWS 11:1-2, 8-19 | SECOND READING |

("Faith is confident assurance concerning what we hope for,..")

1. Fill in the following blanks: "Faith is the confident assurance concerning what we _____ for, and conviction about things we do _____ _____." Hebrews 11:1

2. Why were the men of old approved by God? Hebrews 11:2

3. What did Abraham do when he was called, where did he go, and did he know where he was going? Hebrews 11:8

4. What did Abraham do in the promised land as in a foreign country and with whom did he dwell in tents who were heirs to the same promise? Hebrews 11:9

5. To what was he looking forward, and who is the designer and maker of this? Hebrews 11:10

6. What did Abraham do by faith, and of what did he think the one who made the promise was worthy? Hebrews 11:11

7. In whom are we to trust? Hebrews 2:13, Isaiah 8:17

8. As a result of this faith, what came forth from the one man? Hebrews 11:12

9. What happened to those who died in faith and for what were they searching? Hebrews 11:13-16

10. What is God not ashamed to be called, what has he prepared for them, what did Abraham do by faith and what would happen through Isaac? Hebrews 11:16-18

11. What did Abraham reason that God was able to do; in so doing, as what did he receive Isaac back? Hebrews 11:19

Personal – List the things you have given up by faith and trust in the Lord. This list can include monetary things or people.

| FOURTH DAY | READ LUKE 12:32-48 | GOSPEL |

("Do not live in fear, little flock")

1. In what must you not live, and what has pleased our heavenly Father? Luke 12:32

2. What must you do, what must you give and what must you get? Luke 12:33

3. Fill in the following blank: "Wherever your treasure lies, there your _____ will be." Luke 12:34

4. What must you do, with whom will it go well when the master returns, and what will the master do with them? Luke 12:35-37

5. If the head of the house knew when the thief was coming, what would he not do? Luke 12:39

6. What are we to be and when will the Son of Man come? Luke 12:40

7. What was the question Peter asked Jesus when the Lord replied with a question and then gave an example? Luke 12:41-42

8. What is the servant doing who is fortunate, and who will the master rank undeserving of trust? Luke 12:43-46

9. What will happen to the one who knew his master's wishes and what will happen to the one who did not know them? Luke 12:47-48

10. When much has been given a man what will be required of him and what will be asked of a man to whom more has been entrusted? Luke 12:48

Personal - How have you been preparing for the day when you will be face to face with the Lord. Pray and ask the Lord to show you where to spend your money, where to spend most of your time and what you should be doing with your talents (natural gifts God has given you). Repent and receive the Sacrament of Reconciliation this week in order to receive the added grace to change.

FIFTH DAY   **READ PSALM 33:1, 12, 18-22**

("Happy the nation whose God is the Lord.")

Read and meditate on Psalm 33:1, 12, 18-22.

What is the Lord saying to you personally through the Psalm?

How can you apply this to your life?

SIXTH DAY   **READ ALL OF THE COMMENTARY**

WISDOM 18:6-9

The Exodus was Moses leading his people out of bondage in Egypt and into freedom in the new land. The angel of death went from house to house and killed the first-born baby. The only ones spared were in the homes that had the blood of the slain lamb spread around its doorsill. The Israelites, rather than succumb to the darkness of false religions and immoral culture, remain loyal to genuine wisdom of their faith.

This passage was written for the Jews who found it essential to keep that night (Exodus) vividly implanted in their minds for maintaining spiritual balance. On that night, all of Egypt's first-born died.

We see incredible contrasts in this passage, the Hebrews sharing the same things, blessings and dangers, and all the time singing praises to their heavenly Father. We can also hear the despairing cry of their enemies lamenting for their dead children. All suffered, slave, master, common man, even Pharaoh's first-born died that night. Finally he saw that the faith of the Hebrews was far too strong for him to defeat. He told them to take their God with them and flee from Egypt.

The Jews were delivered from Pharaoh by the power of God's Holy Word. In faith they read, believed, and lived his word. The Lord delivered them and he will deliver us if we keep his Holy Word in our minds, on our lips and in our hearts. He has given us the gift of faith and in that faith we will find the courage to profess that Jesus Christ is our Lord and Savior.

Jesus is the new and permanent passover. Through Moses the people passed over from bondage to freedom and then finally they died. Through Jesus we have passed over from death to life and with him we will have eternal life.

HEBREWS 11:1-2, 8-19

This passage challenges us to question the very meaning of faith. What is faith?

Faith is the response to the living presence of the power of God in our lives. It is a response, an acceptance, a belief of a very special gift from God. A birthday always brings the excitement and anticipation of receiving gifts. You knew you would receive some things but there would always be something that was a surprise. Birthdays combine assurance and anticipation and so does faith. Faith is the conviction based on past experience that God's new and fresh surprises will surely be ours.

We describe faith with words like confidence and certainty. These two qualities need a secure beginning and ending point. The beginning point of faith is believing - "He is what he says." The end point is believing in God's promises - "He will do what he says."

Abraham believed in who God was and he believed in what God promised. His faith was anchored by obedience. It is not enough to believe, we must also, through obedience, RESPOND. Abraham left his home and went to another land, obeying without question. Abraham was even willing to sacrifice his son, Isaac. We should not be surprised if God asks us to give up the security of the familiar to obey him and what he promised. Many people of faith listed in scripture died without receiving all that God promised, but they never lost their vision of heaven.

Today many Christians become frustrated and defeated because their needs, wants, expectations, and demands are not immediately met when they believe in Christ. Many become impatient and want to quit. We need to take courage from those heros of faith who lived and died without seeing the fruit of their faith on earth, and yet they continued to believe. We can in faith trust God with our most prized possessions (our families, etc.). We may not receive what we want immediately, but by responding in faith he will do what he says, when the time is appropriate.

LUKE 12:32-48

This passage tells us that to worry is not of the Lord. Jesus tells us that it gives his Father great pleasure to give us the kingdom. To understand this verse we must know that when a person was adopted into a Hebrew family, he became legally eligible for all the benefits that were due to him; therefore, he was now a full fledged heir to the estate. Through the blood of Jesus Christ we all become eligible heirs to the King. We need only to accept Jesus as Lord to become an heir to the kingdom.

That is why we do not have to worry, we are heirs of the King. We do not need to worry about how much money we have to make, God will provide for us. This does not mean that we do not need to be responsible or to plan to provide for our families. Money used as an end in itself quickly traps us and cuts us off from both God and the needy. We need to see how much of our money can be used for God's purposes. Does God's love touch your wallet? Does your money free you to help others? If so, you are storing up lasting treasures in heaven. We cannot separate what we do from what we believe. What we treasure reveals our true priorities. If your priorities were judged by where you put your time, your money, and your energy, what would be the verdict?

NINETEENTH SUNDAY OF ORDINARY TIME

Not only does Jesus tell us to not worry but also to be prepared for his return. Our faith is a response to the living presence of God in our lives. It is through the gift of faith that we can draw on the resources of Jesus Christ. It is Jesus who will supply all of our needs from his riches in glory (Phil. 4:19). We must stop worrying about what the world thinks of us and in faith live in preparation for his return.

Jesus tells us that a kingdom is being prepared for his followers. Furthermore, we are told in this passage that much is required from those to whom much is given, for their responsibility is greater. You and I have much; we have been blessed in many ways. We have a loving, compassionate, forgiving God, who calls on us to be the same as he. Our faith, which is a gift from him, gives us the courage to say "Yes Lord."

To prepare for the Lord's return, we must not be hypercritical, but sincere, fearless, and ready to witness. We need not be anxious, but trusting. We should not be greedy but generous, not lazy but diligent. In faith, we can be ready for his return.

Application

"That night," in the first reading, was a flight of faith out of Egypt. In the second reading, we saw a journey through darkness by our spiritual heroes that was illuminated by their faith. The gospel tells us to be prepared and through the gift of faith, be ready for the Lord's return.

Today, through our own gift of faith, by daily prayer, reading scripture and receiving the sacraments, we can keep ourselves ready for when the Lord appears personally to each one of us.

TWENTIETH SUNDAY OF ORDINARY TIME - CYCLE C

BEFORE YOU BEGIN:

Pray and ask God to speak to you through His Holy Spirit. "THE PARACLETE, THE HOLY SPIRIT WHOM THE FATHER WILL SEND IN MY NAME, WILL INSTRUCT YOU IN EVERYTHING, AND REMIND YOU OF ALL THAT I TOLD YOU." (JOHN 14:26)

FIRST DAY   **Reread last week's readings.**

1.   What was a helpful or new thought from the readings or from the homily you heard on Sunday?

2.   From what you learned, what personal application did you choose to apply to your life this week?

SECOND DAY   **READ JEREMIAH 38:4-6, 8-10**   **FIRST READING**

("King Zedekiah answered: 'He is in your power.'")

1.   What did the princes say to the king? Jeremiah 38:4

2.   What was it Jeremiah said that caused the princes to say this? Jeremiah 38:1-3

3.   What did the princes say Jeremiah did to the soldiers and all the people and in what did they say was his interest? Jeremiah 38:4

4.   Who was the king at that time, how did he answer them and for what reason? Jeremiah 38:5

5.   What did they do with Jeremiah? Jeremiah 38:6

6.   Who was Ebed-melech and what did he do? Jeremiah 38:7-8

7.   What did he tell the king about the men who had Jeremiah put in the cistern? Jeremiah 38:9

8.   What did he say would happen to Jeremiah and for what reason? Jeremiah 38:9

9.   What did the king order to be done? Jeremiah 38:10

Personal – In what way are you influenced by the opinions of others? This past week how have you obeyed God's Word, which was against what others thought you should do.

THIRD DAY	READ HEBREWS 12:1-4	SECOND READING

("For whom the Lord loves, he disciplines;")

1. By what are we surrounded? Hebrews 12:1

2. What are we to lay aside? Hebrews 12:1

3. In what are we to persevere? Hebrews 12:1

4. On whom are we to keep our eyes fixed, and what does he do for us? Hebrews 12:2

5. What lay before him and what did he endure, heedless of its shame? Hebrews 12:2

6. Where has he taken his seat? Hebrews 12:2

7. What are we to remember and what are we not to become? Hebrews 12:3

8. Who was it that opposed him? Hebrews 12:3

9. Who are the sinners? Romans 3:23

10. Where do we get our strength in the struggle against sin? Isaiah 40:28-31

11. What have we not yet done? Hebrews 12:4

Personal - How have you resisted sin in your life? What does
it mean to you personally: "In your fight against sin you have not yet resisted to the point of shedding blood?"

FOURTH DAY	READ LUKE 12:49-53	GOSPEL

("I have come to set the world on fire,")

1. What has Jesus come to do on the earth? Luke 12:49

2. What does he wish? Luke 12:49

3. What does he have to receive and what does he feel, until it is over? Luke 12:50

4. What is the baptism to which he is referring? Mark 10:38 and John 19:28-30

5. What question does Jesus ask and how does he answer it? Luke 12:51

6. Why did he come? Luke 12:51

7. What is the division to which he refers? Matthew 25:32-46, Ezekiel 34:17

8. What will happen to a household of five? Luke 12:52

9. What will happen to fathers and sons, mothers and daughters, mother-in-law and daughter-in-law? Luke 12:53

10. What will happen to you because of Jesus and when will this happen? Matthew 10:21-23

11. Who will be our enemies? Matthew 10:36

Personal - In what way has following Jesus separated you from family members? How have you dealt with the rejection? Meditate on Matthew 11:28-30.

FIFTH DAY **READ PSALM 40:2-4, 18** **PSALM**

("He put a new song into my mouth.")

Read and meditate on Psalm 40:2-4, 18.

What is the Lord saying to you personally through the Psalm?

How can you apply this to your life?

SIXTH DAY **READ ALL OF THE COMMENTARY**

JEREMIAH 38:4-6, 8-10

King Zedekiah and his officials did not want to listen to Jeremiah's words, but they were in need of blessing from his prayers. The King went back and forth from surrender to resistance. The King was in turmoil with everyone. He was told by Jeremiah that if he accepted Egypt's help and stayed in Jerusalem, he would be destroyed by the Babylonian army. He asked Jeremiah to come secretly to the palace, hoping for some better news from God. The King was in a panic, he wanted to hear God's word but he had no desire to enter into a political conflict with some of his public officials.

King Zedekiah was a leader who was incapable of making firm decisions. He agreed with everybody, which resulted in his nation's being in turmoil. He listened to Jeremiah (37:2); and then by another's advice, he agreed that Jeremiah should be killed (38:5). Finally, he had Jeremiah rescued by advice from yet a different person (38:10). Jeremiah was not popular, his words were misinterpreted as being those of a traitor. He was, in fact, stating God's prophecy that Jerusalem was going to be destroyed because of its sins. He warned the people to flee to Babylon but they refused to listen. Jeremiah was proclaiming God's word for 40 years and was rejected, persecuted, and had no followers encouraging him. He finally was forced to leave his homeland, and even the pagan Babylonians treated him with more respect than did his own people.

Today, we need to recognize that God does not guarantee that his servants, even one with the stature of Jeremiah, will escape persecution, even when they are faithful. But God does promise us, as he promised them, that he will be with us and will give us the strength to endure. As you minister to people, remember that your service is for God and not for man's approval. Jerusalem had several gates, including the gate of Benjamin, where legal matters were handled. Ebed-melech, a public official, went immediately to the gate of Benjamin to protest to the King about the injustice being done to Jeremiah. This public official stood alone in his protest of the murder plot. His obedience could have cost him his life, but God spared him when Jerusalem fell (39:16-18).

You can either go along with the crowd or speak up for God when someone is treated unjustly. You may be the only one, and when you are being treated unjustly yourself be sure to thank the Lord when he sends an "Ebed-melech" your way.

HEBREWS 12:1-4

Living a Catholic Christian Life, or as they say in the street, not only talking the talk but also walking the walk, involves hard work. We are called to let go of anything or anyone who endangers our personal relationship with the Lord. We are to run patiently and to struggle against sin in our lives with the power of the Holy Spirit (2 Timothy 1:7). To live this type of life, we must constantly keep our vision on the Lord Jesus Christ. We stumble and eventually fall when we take our eyes off Jesus Christ and look at ourselves or the circumstances surrounding us. We need to remember that we are running Christ's race and we must always keep him in sight. When hardship and discouragement come, it is easy, sometimes, to lose sight of the big picture.

Jesus is always with us, encouraging us in our struggle. We must not back away from suffering either, because suffering is the training for our Christian spiritual maturity. Jack LaLayne, the body builder, canned the phrase "no pain, no gain." It is true that suffering develops our patience and makes our final victory sweeter. Jesus endured the ultimate suffering and it was for us all. He suffered to the point of shedding his blood, so that all mankind might be free.

Many of us face tremendous physical, emotional or spiritual difficulties but it is in knowing that he is within each of us that makes the race endurable. Jesus sweat great drops of blood over the sin and temptation to which all are subject. Jesus did not give up his vision for our freedom, and neither should we give up our vision of running his race in the same manner as he did his.

Today we hear of many ways to run in the race of life. An athlete has to train diligently if he expects to be successful. You and I are called to look together to Jesus, and he will be in concert with us. His love will become obvious in the way we respond to the needs of others.

LUKE 12:49-53

Jesus warns that his coming to the earth was about to bring division between many close groups, including families. He tells us that he came to bring a fire to the earth and that, of course, was his Holy Spirit. We think of the coming of the Holy Spirit as little tongues of fire over the heads of the Apostles (Acts 2:3). Fire is used for cleansing and purifying precious metals. Fire strips and burns away all imperfections. Fire is powerful and painful.

Jesus' terrible baptism was his coming crucifixion. He talked of the incredible physical, emotional, and spiritual pain of complete separation from God which was necessary to pay for the sins of the whole world. That's right, he had to take on the pain of all the sins of the world. He died for you and me, while we yet were sinners (Romans 5:8). His death released all of us from our slavery to sin. It is easy for us to say we will suffer anything for Christ, and yet most of us complain every day when even little irritations come. If we say that we are willing to face suffering on a large scale for Christ, we must be willing to suffer in little ways for Christ.

Jesus had revealed that his coming would result in conflict even between family members. He demands a response, and many groups are torn apart when some choose to follow him and incur suffering in his name, while others refuse to do so. There is no middle ground with Jesus; you are either with him or against him. We need only look at places in our world where families are pitted against each other. We are called to declare our loyalty to Christ and make our commitment to him. This might involve cutting off some relationships, possibly in our own family. Are you willing to risk the approval of your friends or even that of your families to gain eternal life?

Application

In the first reading we see Jeremiah being persecuted and rejected for forty years in his ministry. The second reading tells us that we must keep our eyes on Christ as we run the race of life, especially when suffering comes our way. The gospel tells us not to give up, that Christ is always with us even in our darkest moments of life.

This week, let us be especially aware of others, particularly our family members. If we experience rejection and persecution because of our commitment to Christ, let us, through our prayers, and knowledge that Jesus is always with us, respond in a manner that will show others that nothing can separate us from God's love.

TWENTY-FIRST SUNDAY IN ORDINARY TIME - CYCLE C

BEFORE YOU BEGIN:

Pray and ask God to speak to you through His Holy Spirit. "THE PARACLETE, THE HOLY SPIRIT WHOM THE FATHER WILL SEND IN MY NAME, WILL INSTRUCT YOU IN EVERYTHING, AND REMIND YOU OF ALL THAT I TOLD YOU." (JOHN 14:26)

FIRST DAY Reread last week's readings.

1. What was a helpful or new thought from the readings or from the homily you heard on Sunday?

2. From what you learned, what personal application did you choose to apply to your life this week?

SECOND DAY	**READ ISAIAH 66:18-21**	**FIRST READING**

("As a mother comforts her son, so will I comfort you.")

1. Who does the Lord come to gather and what will they see? Isaiah 66:18

2. Who will we set among the nations? Isaiah 66:19

3. What does Matthew 24:30 say about a sign and the glory of the Lord?

4. Who will he send to the Nations? Isaiah 66:19

5. What had the coastlands never heard, what had they never seen, and what shall the fugitives do? Isaiah 66:19

6. Who shall they bring from all the nations as an offering to the Lord and how will they bring them? Isaiah 66:20

7. Where will they bring them and what is this place called? Isaiah 66:20

8. How did the Israelites bring their offerings to the house of the Lord? Isaiah 66:20

9. What will the Lord do with some of them? Isaiah 66:21

Personal - As you approached the altar of the Lord this past week, in what way has your vessel (your body) been made clean and in what way can you make it clean now?

THIRD DAY	**READ HEBREWS 12:5-7, 11-13**	**SECOND READING**

("For whom the Lord loves he disciplines;")

1. What kind of words were addressed to you as sons and what were they?
Hebrews 12:5-6

2. With what should you not disdain nor lose heart? Hebrews 12:5

3. Who does the Lord discipline and who does he scourge? Hebrews 12:6

4. What are you to endure as the discipline of God and how does he deal with you? Hebrews 12:7

5. At the time discipline is administered, what does it seem like? Hebrews 12:11

6. What does it bring forth later to those who are trained in its school? Hebrews 12:11

7. Where do you find peace and how is peace made? John 16:31,33, Colossians 1:19-20

8. What are the fruits that come from the Holy Spirit? Galatians 5:22

9. How did God manifest his own justice? Romans 3:24-25

10. What must you strengthen? Hebrews 12:12

11. What are you to do with the paths on which you walk, and what will happen when you do this? Hebrews 12:13

Personal - In what way has God, who loves you, disciplined you this week? In what way can you make straight the paths you walk on and what are you looking toward, according to this lesson?

FOURTH DAY   **READ LUKE 13:22-30**   **GOSPEL**

("Try to come in through the narrow door.")

1. What was Jesus doing as he went through cities and towns and where was he going? Luke 13:22

2. What did someone ask him about being saved? Luke 13:23

3. What did Jesus say about the narrow door and what will happen to many? Luke 13:24

4. What did he say about the master of the house? Luke 13:25

5. Knocking on the door, what would you say to the master and what will be his reply? Luke 13:25

6. What will they then begin to say and what will they say he did in the streets? Luke 13:26

7. What will he say about where they come from and then what does he say to them? Luke 13:27

8.   What does he call these people? Luke 13:27

9.   Who will enter the kingdom and how do you know if you will enter? Matthew 7:16-21

10.   What are the fruits of the Holy Spirit? Galatians 5:22

Personal - On a daily basis, what fruits of the Holy Spirit are most evident in your life? Which ones are not evident? What can you do so that all of the fruits are evident in your life especially to your family?

FIFTH DAY   **READ PSALM 117:1-2**   **PSALM**

("Steadfast is his kindness towards us.")

Read and meditate on Psalm 117:1-2.

What is the Lord saying to you personally through the Psalm?

How can you apply this to your life?

SIXTH DAY   **READ ALL OF THE COMMENTARY**

ISAIAH 66:18-21

The incredible gift of being able to participate and to see God's glory is now granted to all nations and tongues. Many nations and people will go against Jerusalem and God will bring his wrath against them and send those who escape as missionaries to all those foreign lands. They will bring back to Jerusalem the good news and will behold the sign that the new heavens and the new earth have come. The list of foreign people was symbolic of all the world: Tarshish in Southern Spain, Put and Lud in Africa, Tubal around the Black Sea, and Javan representing Greece.

These nations will bring back God's people to the holy mount of Jerusalem. We might reflect on this passage that as Israel brought the good news of salvation to tie nations, so will these nations in turn be responsible for Israel's final conversion to the Lord Jesus Christ. Today we are one of those Gentile foreign nations. The question we might ask ourselves is: "Is our country an example of God's holy nation?" If not, what must we do to become, once again, God's holy people?

Today we see in our Gentile religion of Catholicism, priests and deacons performing priestly functions; we need to pray for them, bless them, and above all love them. The Israelites made their special offerings to the Lord in clean vessels. We are called to make our offerings, which will be ourselves to the Lord and we have to be clean vessels. We do this by loving God with all our mind, heart and soul (Deut. 6:4-5) and then by loving others as he has loved us (John 15:12).

HEBREWS 12:5-7, 11-13

This passage from Hebrews exhorts us to pattern our lives after Jesus Christ and to allow God to discipline us as we are establishing this pattern. It is never pleasant to be corrected and disciplined by God, but like a loving Father, he does not want his child to do anything that will bring harm to himself. Who loves his child more, the father who allows the child to do what will harm him or the one who corrects, trains and even disciplines the child to help him learn what is right.

A loving Father's discipline is a sign of God's deep love for us. When we are being corrected by God, we need to see it as proof of his love and ask him what he is trying to teach us. We can respond to discipline in several ways: (1) we can accept it with resignation; (2) we can go into self pity, thinking we do not deserve it; (3) we can be angry, resentful, and bitter at God for it; or (4) we can accept it gratefully as a proper response from a loving Father.

God pushes us to our limits and requires of us a disciplined life. We will be able to continue as we follow Christ and draw upon his strength. It is then that we can use our strength to grow and to help those who are weak and struggling. We must live our lives so that others will follow our example. We have a responsibility to them if we claim to live by Christ. We have to ask ourselves, "Does my example of life make it easier for others to believe, follow and mature in Christ?" We also must be sure that our actions will not confuse and mislead others into following a life of sin.

Our daily response to prayer, scripture and church fellowship will help us to establish the pattern of being a disciplined disciple of our Lord and Savior, Jesus Christ.

LUKE 13:22-30

This is the second time Luke has reminded us that Jesus was intentionally going to Jerusalem (Luke 9:51). Jesus knew that he would be faced with persecution and death in Jerusalem, yet he pressed on toward the city. His determination to follow the will of the Father should characterize our lives too. When our Lord gives us a course of action, we must steadily move toward our goal, regardless of the obstacles along the way or the potential hazards that await us. Even the prospect of death did not turn Jesus away from his mission.

The question, "Will only a few be saved?" (v.23) was asked by one of his followers. This gave Jesus the opportunity to mention once again the many difficulties encountered in following him. He does not directly answer the question, but he does say that many will not be saved. Finding salvation requires more concentration and commitment than most people are willing to bear. Salvation is not a doctrine or a set of rules, it is a person and his name is Jesus Christ.

It is obvious that we cannot save ourselves and it is not possible to work our way into God's favor. But, there are many who are under this illusion today, like the ones in this passage who were following Jesus but had no intimate fellowship with him. They heard his teaching but did not accept it as the word of God to be put into practice. The work Jesus referred to is the establishment of a deep personal relationship with him, whatever the cost is here on earth. We need to have a hunger and thirst for his Holy Word, we need to establish a quiet time every day of our lives and learn to abide in him (John 15:7). We dare not put off this work, the door will not stay open forever.

Jesus words, "away with you evildoers," (v.27) are meant as a challenge to you and me to redirect our steps toward Jerusalem with Jesus while there is still time. The people in this passage were eager to know who would be saved, and Jesus explained that while many people knew a lot about him, only a few had really accepted his forgiveness. Just listening to his Word, attending church services or admiring a few miracles is not enough. We need to turn away from sin and turn to and trust in Jesus Christ to save us.

There will be many surprises in God's kingdom. Many great people here on earth (in God's eyes) are virtually ignored by the rest of the world. What matters to God is not one's earthly popularity, status, wealth, or power, but one's personal commitment to Jesus Christ. We need to make sure that we put God in first place, so that we will join the people from all over the world who will find their places in the kingdom of heaven.

Application

The first reading tells us that God's glory is available to all nations. The second reading challenges us to pattern our lives after Jesus Christ. The Gospel clearly reveals that we cannot save ourselves.

Let us take the incredible gift of faith and become disciplined in our response to that gift and develop a deeper personal relationship with Jesus by accepting his forgiveness of ourselves. Then let others see the fruit of our faith by forgiving others, especially those who are close to us.

TWENTY-SECOND SUNDAY IN ORDINARY TIME - CYCLE C

BEFORE YOU BEGIN:

Pray and ask God to speak to you through His Holy Spirit. "THE PARACLETE, THE HOLY SPIRIT WHOM THE FATHER WILL SEND IN MY NAME, WILL INSTRUCT YOU IN EVERYTHING, AND REMIND YOU OF ALL THAT I TOLD YOU." (JOHN 14:26)

FIRST DAY	**Reread last week's readings.**	

1. What was a helpful or new thought from the readings or from the homily you heard on Sunday?

2. From what you learned, what personal application did you choose to apply to your life this week?

SECOND DAY	**READ SIRACH 3:17-18, 20, 28-29**	**FIRST READING**

("Conduct your affairs with humility.")

1. How are we to conduct our affairs? Sirach 3:17

2. What will happen to us if we conduct ourselves this way? Sirach 3:17

3. What are we to do all the more, the greater we are? Sirach 3:18

4. With whom will we find favor? Sirach 3:18

5. For what are we not to seek or search? Sirach 3:20

6. What does the mind of a sage appreciate? Sirach 3:28

7. What is the wise man's joy? Sirach 3:28

8. What quenches a flaming fire and what atones for sin? Sirach 3:29

9. What makes a person great and what happens to the person who exalts himself? Matthew 23:11-12

10. What must we do to our soul and where do we put our hope? Psalm 131:1-3

Personal – In what way have you taken on a servant's attitude at home, with family or friends or at work? What is your attitude about being a servant to all with whom you come in contact?

THIRD DAY	**READ HEBREWS 12:18-19, 22-24**	**SECOND READING**

("Jesus, the mediator of a new covenant")

1. To what have we not been drawn near, that those who heard begged that it not be addressed to them? Hebrews 12:18-19

2. Where have we drawn near and whose city is it? Hebrews 12:22

3. Who is there and how are they gathered there? Hebrews 12:22

4. Of whom is it the assembly, where are they enrolled, and who is the judge of all? Hebrews 12:23

5. Who has been made perfect? Hebrews 12:23

6. How can we be made perfect? Matthew 5:43-48

7. Of what is Jesus mediator? Hebrews 12:24

8. What speaks more eloquently than that of Abel? Hebrews 12:24

9. What is the new covenant of which Jesus is mediator? Hebrews 8:6-12

10. How was this new covenant made? Hebrews 9:11-14

Personal – In what way have you accepted the new covenant of God? How has the shedding of Jesus' blood washed you clean?

FOURTH DAY   READ LUKE 14:1, 7-14   GOSPEL

("Everyone who exalts himself shall be humbled
and he who humbles himself shall be exalted.")

1. What day did Jesus come to eat a meal, to whose house did he come, and who were they observing closely? Luke 14:1

2. What did Jesus go on to do to the guest, and what had he noticed happening? Luke 14:7

3. What did he say we are not to do if we are invited to a wedding, for what reason, and what might the host do? Luke 14:8,9

4. How would we proceed to the lowest place, and what should we do when invited so the host will say, "My friend, come up higher?" Luke 14:9-10

5. What will this do for us in the eyes of our fellow guest? Luke 14:10

6. What happens to everyone who exalts himself, and what happens to everyone who humbles himself? Luke 14:11

7. Who was humble and how did he humble himself? Philippians 2:5-8

8. What did Jesus say to the one who had invited him? Luke 14:12

9.   What are we to do when we have a reception? Luke 14:13

10.   About what should we be pleased, and how will we be repaid? Luke 14:14

Personal – How have you demonstrated humility in your home, at work or at social functions? When is the last time you entertained someone who could not repay you the honor? Be specific.

FIFTH DAY   **READ PSALM 68:4-7, 10-11**

("God gives a home for the forsaken.")

Read and meditate on Psalm 68:4-7, 10-11.

What is the Lord saying to you personally through the Psalm?

How can you apply this to your life?

SIXTH DAY   **READ ALL OF THE COMMENTARY**

SIRACH 3:17-18, 20, 28-29

To have a clear picture of who you really are is to be humble. Paul tells us in Romans 12:3 that we should not get too enthused about our own self-importance. While a healthy self-esteem is important, we should not go too far in self-love. Humility is the key to an honest and accurate evaluation of our self-worth, our own identity in Christ. Being humble does not mean that we should put our self down, because we know that we are sinners, and are saved only by God's grace. We also know that we are saved and therefore have great value in his eyes and in his kingdom. We must yield to him completely and put ourselves in his hands to be used as he wants, in order to spread his Word and share his love with others.

Our conduct speaks volumes about our humility. Humility is the call to servanthood, it is totally opposite of one who is selfish. A humble person is one who is selfless and thinks of others more than of himself. This is what Christ preached, believed, and lived. Being humble is a guard against selfishness, prejudice and jealousy. Showing genuine interest in others is one way to strive actively to put on the "mind of Christ" (Philippians 2:5-11). The attitude of humility was the kind that Jesus has shown to all mankind. He didn't demand or cling to his rights, or cry out for vengeance. He called us out to love our enemies and forgive over and over. Jesus was humble, he was God yet he took on the role of a servant. He was willing to give up his rights in order to obey God and serve his people.

We must be just like Christ, in fact he calls us to do even greater things than he (John 14:12). We can strive to be more like him by being more humble than we have ever been before. Like Christ we must serve out of love for God and for others, not out of guilt or fear. Jesus humbled himself on a cross and to his death. We are called to follow him by humbly going up on our own cross and dying to ourselves in his Holy Name.

HEBREWS 12:18-19, 22-24

Paul describes what it must have been like on that flaming Mount Sinai. The people were probably terrified with all of the commotion going on the mountain. A great ball of fire was present, then out of nowhere a great storm sprung up. Paul told them that they did not have to face anything as terrifying as the people of Moses time did on that mountain. He goes on to tell them about the incredible contrast to their being able to be on the special mountain and into the city of God. This contrast between the old and new covenant was like pointing out the differences between a photograph of a person and the actual person. The photograph is in reality a shadow of the real person, and the old covenant of God handing Moses the ten commandments was a shadow of the new covenant.

The old agreement was a covenant of Law between God and Israel. The new and better way is the covenant of Grace. The new covenant is Christ forgiving our sins and bringing us to God through his sacrificial death. This covenant goes beyond Israel and Judah to all the gentile nations of the world. Jesus is the source of this new agreement, and his blood was shed in forgiveness not in vengeance as was Abel's. This new covenant is written in our hearts and minds. Our bodies have become the sacred temple of this Lamb of God. This new covenant offers a new way to forgiveness, not through animal sacrifice, but through faith. We need to reflect and ask ourselves, "Have I entered into this new agreement and begun to walk in the better way."

The invitation to partake in this new covenant is open to all of us. Before Jesus came God seemed distant and threatening, as we can imagine on that night on Mount Sinai. Now God welcomes us through Christ into his presence.

LUKE 14:1, 7-14

Jesus accepted this invitation to a Pharisee's home even though he knew they were trying to trap him into saying or doing something wrong. He was criticized for defending the integrity of a woman who came uninvited to the home of the Pharisee who had invited Jesus. Their trap to get Jesus to do something wrong, so that they may get him arrested, did not scare him.

Jesus began to teach them about honor. He told the guest not to always be seeking places of honor, rather they should seek ways to be of service. Today, just as it was then, service is more important in God's kingdom than status. He told them not to be so particular about who is invited, because he knew that this select group of people would invite them to one of their special functions.

Jesus really hit a nerve with them when he told them that if they try to impress others with their own status and demand to sit up front, they might be terribly embarrassed if someone who has more status shows up and forces them to sit in the back. We might ask ourselves, "Does this apply to me?". When you go out to some function, such as a dinner, do you demand quick service and complain if the service or food is not quite the best? Do you expect people to cater to you because you are a religious person or maybe a professional person like a lawyer, doctor, teacher, etc.? Jesus' message to the Pharisees who lived two thousand years ago applies today to all of us. We are all called to be humble, to defer to others. We are called to die to ourselves, to think about meeting the needs of others and not just our own. Jesus tells us to think about inviting someone to our house who will not be able to repay the invitation. He tells us to serve someone who is not of any high status personally. He is not asking us to join some organization, or help out at a soup kitchen. He is saying that we need to reach out in humility to someone who is poor in spirit. To be poor in spirit is to have material things and yet be emotionally and spiritually hungry and looking for a personal relationship with Christ.

Spiritual leadership, which means taking on the humility of Christ and becoming a servant, is desperately needed in our own homes. It is certainly needed in our jobs, schools and churches. God will reward us for inviting the uninvited, for loving the unlovable. He will say to us one day, "My loving friend, I have a better place for you; come, be here with me in heaven forever."

Application

The first reading tells us that our conduct speaks volumes about our humility. The second reading shows that the old agreement was a covenant of law between God and Israel. The new and better way is the covenant of grace. The Gospel reveals that we are all called to be humble.

This week, put on a heart of humility (Col.3:12) and be clothed in humility toward one another (1 Peter 5:5). We can only love one another when we serve each other in Jesus' holy name.

Let us begin at home by helping one another in simple chores around the house. Look around to see where you can serve instead of being served. We really love one another when we serve one another.

TWENTY-THIRD SUNDAY IN ORDINARY TIME - CYCLE C

BEFORE YOU BEGIN:

Pray and ask God to speak to you through His Holy Spirit. "THE PARACLETE, THE HOLY SPIRIT WHOM THE FATHER WILL SEND IN MY NAME, WILL INSTRUCT YOU IN EVERYTHING, AND REMIND YOU OF ALL THAT I TOLD YOU." (JOHN 14:26)

FIRST DAY	**Reread last week's readings.**	

1. What was a helpful or new thought from the readings or from the homily you heard on Sunday?

2. From what you learned, what personal application did you choose to apply to your life this week?

SECOND DAY	**READ WISDOM 9:13-18**	**FIRST READING**

("Or whoever knew your counsel, except you had given wisdom...")

1. Fill in the following blanks: For what man _____ _____ _____, or who can _____ what our _____ _____? Wisdom 9:13

2. What are the deliberations of mortals, and of what are we unsure? Wisdom 9:14

3. What does the corruptible body do to the soul? Wisdom 9:15

4. What does the earthen shelter weigh down? Wisdom 9:15

5. What do we find with difficulty? Wisdom 9:16

6. What does Wisdom 9:16 say about things that are in heaven?

7. You had to be given _____ in order to know his counsel. Wisdom 9:17

8. What was sent from on high? Wisdom 9:17

9. By sending your Holy Spirit from on high, what would happen to the paths of those on earth? Wisdom 9:18

10. What did men learn and by what were they saved? Wisdom 9:18

11. What happens to the man who walks in wisdom? Proverbs 28:26

Personal – In what way have you been following God's wisdom and counsel in your everyday affairs, or have you not thought to seek it?

THIRD DAY	**READ PHILEMON 9-10, 12-17**	**SECOND READING**

("I prefer to appeal in the name of love.")

1. In the name of what does Paul prefer to appeal? Philemon 9

2. As what does Paul refer to himself? Philemon 9

3.   For whom is Paul appealing to Philemon? Philemon 10-11.

4.   Where was Paul when he had begotten him? Philemon 10

5.   In sending Onesimus to Philemon what did that mean that Paul was really sending? Philemon 12

6.   What reason did Paul want to keep Onesimus with him? Philemon 13

7.   For what reason was Paul in prison? Philemon 13

8.   How might kindness be bestowed? Philemon 14

9.   Onesimus was separated from Philemon for what reason? Philemon 15-16

10. By regarding Paul as his partner how would Philemon welcome Onesimus? Philemon 17

Personal – In what way have you defended a brother or sister in the Lord this week? In what way can you make an appeal for the unborn who is about to die at the hands of an abortionist?

FOURTH DAY　　　　**READ LUKE 14:25-33**　　　　**GOSPEL**

*("Anyone who does not take up his cross and
follow me cannot be my disciple.")*

1.   To whom was Jesus speaking on one occasion? Luke 14:25

2.   What must a person do to become Jesus' follower? Luke 14:26

3.   What two things must we do to become Jesus' follower? Luke 9:23 and 14:27

4.   How often must we take up our cross? Luke 9:23

5.   How do we discover who we really are? Matthew 10:37-39

6.   What would a person do if he decides to build a tower, and for what reason? Luke 14:28-29

7.   What would people say if he could not finish the tower? Luke 14:30

8.   What will a king who is about to do battle sit down and do first? Luke 14:31

9.   If he cannot withstand the enemy while he is at a distance, what will he do? Luke 14:32

10. In the same way, if we want to be Jesus' disciple, what must we do? Luke 14:33

Personal – What are you still possessing that is holding you back from completely dying to self in order to peacefully and joyfully follow Jesus? How can you give up all of your possessions?

FIFTH DAY   **READ PSALM 90:3-6, 12-17**

*("Teach us to number our days aright, that
we may gain wisdom of heart.")*

Read and meditate on Psalm 90:3-6, 12-17.

What is the Lord saying to you personally through the Psalm?

How can you apply this to your life?

SIXTH DAY   **READ ALL OF THE COMMENTARY**

WISDOM 9:13-18

The book of Wisdom is addressed to Jews around 50 B.C. These people were so impressed by Hellenistic learning and civilization that their faith was in danger. The author combats their materialism, Hedonism and idolatry by taking full aim at the renegade Jews. Wisdom is a gift of God; genuine wisdom means belief in the one God of Israel and fidelity to his Law.

Wisdom delivers the believer from all evil. This is illustrated by a review of the saving deeds of God for the patriarchs and for the Israelites in Egypt, the very country where Jews were beginning to abandon their faith. We are told that man's counsel can never conceive the Lord's counsel. We see in these passages thanksgiving for the excellence of wisdom. We experience folly when we trust in ourselves and our peers (Ps. 49:13).

Our plans can only be stable and successful when our source is the scriptures. We become eligible for salvation only through faith in Jesus Christ (2 Timothy 3:15). Our corruptible body is called an earthen tent and that is what weighs down our minds. This idea of a body as a tent is found in Pythagoreanism and Platonism. In other words, it is a conception of stoicism. The Greeks look at wisdom as knowledge of natural science; the Hebrews looked at wisdom as the chief servant of the Creator. We have in the final verses the realization that only the wisdom of God can really grasp all that happens and is about to happen to the earth and all of its creatures (Ps. 104:24).

The Lord, through his grace, has given us the gift of faith which is born of a "Fear of the Lord." Wisdom is this fear of the Lord, and to these who have this wisdom, the Lord also gives knowledge and happiness (Ecc. 2:26). Let us look not to ourselves or to our peers for wisdom, rather let us yield to the healing power of Jesus Christ. Let us say, "Lord, come into my heart, renew my mind, and let me have a tongue that professes your glory." Lord, I pray that you will give all of us wisdom, and I stand on your Word for this request." (James 1:5).

PHILEMON 9-10, 12-17

Paul wrote this letter from Rome in about 60 A.D., when he was under house arrest (Acts 28:30, 31). Onesimus was a runaway slave of Philemon's; he robbed his master and fled to Rome (verse 15). He then came under the influence of Paul and was converted into Christianity (verse 10). This letter to Philemon was a very exceptional one for Paul, for in it we see him asking a favor. He is asking a favor for Onesimus who had taken the wrong turn and whom Paul was helping to find the way back.

Paul could have demanded whatever he wished from Philemon, simply on his authority as an Apostle. His was a humble request and he realized that a gift must be given freely and with good will; if it is forced, it is not a gift at all. Paul based his request, not on his own authority, but on Philemon's Christian commitment. We might ask ourselves the same question, "If when you know something is right and you have the power to demand it, do you appeal to your authority or the other person's commitment?" Paul gives us a great example here of how to deal with a possible conflict between Christian friends.

Paul wrote this letter on behalf of Onesimus who feared for his life. A master had the legal right to kill a runaway slave, and Paul wanted to help him understand his new relationship with Onesimus. Paul calls Onesimus his child whom he has "begotten" in prison. To bring someone to Christ is like giving him a new birth, and that is exactly what Paul did to Onesimus.

Paul would like to have kept Onesimus with him but he would do nothing without the consent of Philemon. Paul was sending him back, not as a slave, but as a brother and partner in Christ. Paul tells Philemon that if he agreed that Paul is his partner in the work of Christ, he must receive Onesimus as he would receive himself.

The tone of this letter reflects against what was a common occurrence, and that was human slavery. Paul does not come right out against the unjust law; but through the power of Christian love, he presents to Philemon the obviousness of its injustice. The fact that Onesimus, the runaway slave, was returned as a brother to Philemon was a powerful statement against slavery. We need to reflect that all are equal in God's family, and how we treat our brothers and sisters in Christ's family reflects our own true Christian commitment to Christ.

LUKE 14:25-33

This passage is one of the strongest in the New Testament about the cost of discipleship. Jesus told them that nothing or no one can come between the love of a disciple and his master. To make this point even more pronounced, he then tells them that they have to carry their own cross every day and follow him. The people were very much aware of what that meant. They knew from the criminals who went to be crucified in their hometown that to carry one's cross in public was an act of submission to Rome. This warned others that they had better submit and turn away from their rebellious actions.

Jesus gave this message to the crowd so that they might reflect on what it really costs to follow him. You and I need to reflect on this message also. There is no room for a disciple who looks for "cheap grace" in the Kingdom of God. "Cheap grace" is what we sometimes think our devotions and sacraments bring. They are not magical toys that prevent us from suffering and yet deliver us into glory. Following Christ calls for a total submission to him. This means letting everything go and putting him first. It could mean great financial, social, and even physical loss, even death itself. We are called to carry our cross every day, not just once in a while. We must count the cost of becoming a disciple, so that we know what we are getting into and are not tempted to turn back.

As Christians we are called to be "the salt of the earth." We will be of no value if our flavor is lost or dried out. We must not just blend into the world and avoid the cost of standing for Christ. We are faced today, in our society, with the direct challenge of driving out the scourge of abortion. If we fail to do this, then our flavor of being the salt of the earth becomes worthless. Just as salt flavors and preserves foods, we are to preserve the good in the world. This calls from us a willingness to sacrifice everything for Christ. If we take up our cross and follow him daily, all that will change in our lives is everything.

Applocation

The first reading tells us that wisdom is the "fear of the Lord." The second reading shows that a gift must be given freely and joyfully. The Gospel reveals that there is no "cheap grace" in the kingdom of God.

This week, let us be the salt of the earth to our families by taking up our cross and dying to ourselves by serving them and not judging them, even if we are rejected by them. To serve them as a Christian means to bring out the best in them, like salt brings out the flavor. Let them see that you care enough to give them your personal attention as well as your affirmation. We cannot expect to be the salt of the earth until we have become the salt for our families.

TWENTY-FOURTH SUNDAY IN ORDINARY TIME -CYCLE C

BEFORE YOU BEGIN:

Pray and ask God to speak to you through His Holy Spirit. "THE PARACLETE, THE HOLY SPIRIT WHOM THE FATHER WILL SEND IN MY NAME, WILL INSTRUCT YOU IN EVERYTHING, AND REMIND YOU OF ALL THAT I TOLD YOU." (JOHN 14:26)

FIRST DAY   **Reread last week's readings.**

1. What was a helpful or new thought from the readings or from the homily you heard on Sunday?

2. From what you learned, what personal application did you choose to apply to your life this week?

SECOND DAY   **READ EXODUS 32:7-11, 13-14**   **FIRST READING**

*("They have soon turned aside from the way
I pointed out to them.")*

1. Why did God tell Moses to go down to his people? Exodus 32:7

2. From what had they turned away? Exodus 32:8

3. What was the way God pointed out to them? Exodus 20:1-17.

4. What did they do with what they had made and what did they cry out? Exodus 32:8

5. How did the Lord see the people? Exodus 32:9

6. What did the Lord say to Moses about his wrath? Exodus 32:10

7. What did the Lord say he would do for Moses? Exodus 32:10

8. What was the question Moses asked the Lord? Exodus 32:11

9. Who did Moses ask the Lord to remember and what did the Lord say he had promised for their descendants? Exodus 32:13

10. What did the Lord relent in doing? Exodus 32:14

Personal - How do you, like Moses, stand in the gap and plead for God's mercy, rather than his wrath, for your country, community, parish, family, and finally for yourself? What promises that God has made to us from his Word, can you use for your defense?

THE BREAD OF LIFE CATHOLIC BIBLE STUDY

THIRD DAY   **READ 1 TIMOTHY 1:12-17**   **SECOND READING**

*("The grace of the Lord has been granted me
in overflowing measure.")*

1. In 1 Timothy 1:12 who has been strengthened by Christ and been made his servant? 1 Timothy 1:1

2. How has he been judged? 1 Timothy 1:12

3. Who keeps faith with us and strengthens us and guards us from the evil one? 2 Thessalonians 3:3

4. What three things was Paul at one time? 1 Timothy 1:13

5. For what reason was he treated mercifully? 1 Timothy 1:13

6. What has the Lord granted Paul in overflowing measure plus two other things which are in Christ Jesus? 1 Timothy 1:14

7. What can you depend on as worthy of full measure? 1 Timothy 1:15

8. What kind of a sinner does Paul see himself? 1 Timothy 1:15

9. Are we any different than Paul? Romans 3:23

10. How was Paul dealt with, what did Jesus display and for what reason? 1 Timothy 1:16

11. What is Paul's response to what God has done for him? 1 Timothy 1:17

Personal – In what way have you seen yourself as a sinner saved by the grace of God? What has your response been to this?

FOURTH DAY   **READ LUKE 15:1-32**   **GOSPEL**

("Father, I have sinned against God and against you.")

1. As the tax collectors and sinners were gathering around to hear Jesus, about what were the Pharisees and Scribes murmuring? Luke 15:1-2

2. In the parable Jesus addressed to them, to what was he referring as being lost? Luke 15:3-4

3. What does the owner of the sheep do when he sees one is lost, and what is his response when he finds it? Luke 15:5-6

4. In verse 7 of Luke 15 Jesus goes from speaking of sheep (an animal) to speaking about people. What does he say about people?

5.   Jesus goes on to speak another parable and this time it is not an animal but an object. What is it and what does the woman do when she loses one? Luke 15:8

6.   When she finds it, what is her reaction? Luke 15:9

7.   What is the reason for the joy of the angels of God? Luke 15:10

8.   Jesus now tells the story of the man and his two sons. What did the younger son say to his father, and what did the father do? Luke 15:12

9.   When the son collected his inheritance, where did he go and what did he do? Luke 15:13

10. When the famine broke out and the son found himself in dire need, what did he do? Luke 15:14-16

11. When he finally came to his senses, what did he say and do? Luke 15:17-19

12. In verse 18 of Luke 15, who does the lost son say he had sinned against?

Personal – When you come into repentance over something you know you did wrong, are you sorry because you got yourself into a mess or are you sorry because you offended God and others? What do you see as the difference between worldly repentance and Godly repentance?

13. When the son set off for the father's house, what happened when he was still a distance away? Luke 15:20

14. What did the son say to the father and what did the father tell the servants to do? Luke 15:21-24

15. Meanwhile what happened with the elder son, and what was his reaction? Luke 15:25-30

16. What was the father's reply to the older son? Luke 15:31-32

Personal – In what way, this past week, have you been angry or jealous over what has happened to someone in your family, a friend, a church member or a work acquaintance? Come into Godly repentance.

FIFTH DAY   **READ PSALM 51:3-4, 12-13, 17, 19**

("My sacrifice, O God, is a contrite spirit.")

Read and meditate on Psalm 51:3-4, 12-13, 17, 19.

What is the Lord saying to you personally through the Psalm?

How can you apply this to your life?

EXODUS 32:7-11, 13-14

This passage clearly defines the consequences of what happens when idols become the god of our lives. The people were beginning to panic and become very unruly. Moses had been up on the mountain for a long time (over 40 days) and the fire, smoke and thunder continued to terrify them. They wanted to see a familiar God and wanted to shape him into an image that they could understand and worship. They wanted a god made into their image and a god that was convenient to either obey or ignore.

Today our temptation is still to shape God to our liking or to make him in our image. We need only to look around and see some of the golden calves that we have made into gods. The cow or calf was one of the most popular idols in the pagan world at that time. They were a symbol of power and fertility and were, therefore, connected with immoral sexual practices.

The Lord saw how stubborn and rebellious these people were and he responded in great anger as he does even today when his mercy is trampled on. The people in today's passage were blind to the love that God wanted to shower upon them. Their blindness came from their idols and useless worship. We need to reflect on our rebelliousness and stubbornness. Some of the golden calves in our lives are power, sex, money, pleasure, education, youth, health, big homes, fancy cars, athletic ability, marriage, family, etc.

We need to ask ourselves if any of these things come before our total commitment to our Lord and Savior, Jesus Christ. Moses begged God not to destroy those foolish people, and then he called on God to remember his promise to the servants of Abraham, Isaac and Israel. God had promised that these descendants would inherit the kingdom forever, so the Lord heard this plea and changed his mind and spared them. You and I have to get down on our knees and pray the same prayer that Moses prayed. There are so many people today worshipping false idols and many times they are right in our own families. We have a loving, merciful and just God, and he will hear our prayer of intercession. We need to put down our false gods and become repentant and change the way we live. Our God is the One True God, and his name is Jesus Christ.

1 TIMOTHY 1:12-17

Praise God, praise God, for being so merciful. Paul probably said this kind of prayer day and night. He is telling Timothy that God's mercy is so powerful that no one has to feel unworthy or abandoned. Paul tells about how he was a blasphemer of the Lord and how he hunted down people who believed in Jesus. Paul was an educated man with a zealous vengeance that produced terror in the hearts of Christians. He not only hunted Christians, but he had them arrested and murdered before he, himself, came to Christ in faith (Acts 9:1-9).

Paul tells us about a God that not only loves and forgives, but he forgets our wrongful past. Some people feel so guilt-ridden by their past that they think God could never forgive and accept them. That is what we call today "stinkin' thinkin'." We are called to renew our minds (Romans 12:2), to put on the mind of Christ (Philippians 2:5), and fill our minds with thoughts that are pure and honorable (Philippians 4:8).

The call to renewal has to begin with the call to repentance, and repentance begins with the confession of our sins. Even Paul admitted he talked violently against Jesus through unbelief and arrogance and was a persecutor of innocent people. God forgave Paul, and he can forgive you and wants to forgive you. Take this time now to reflect on what is going on in your life. Ask, "Do I blaspheme God with my tongue?" "Do I attack others with my criticalness?"

We as Catholic Christians have a tremendous opportunity to be reconciled with the Lord through the sacrament of Reconciliation (being brought back to a loving relationship with God). Forgiveness is a decision and God wants to forgive us more than we want to be forgiven. God wants to love us more than we want to be loved. His love for us is unconditional - no strings attached. Paul wants Timothy to spread the news that God took a sinner like Saul and made him into a loving servant called Paul. We need to let the healing power of God's love and forgiveness soak into us and repent, because the Kingdom of God is at hand (Mark 1:15).

LUKE 15:1-32

In this passage, Jesus defends why he associated with the unwashed, the unclean, and the unsaved people by sharing with them a story about sheep, coins and a human being. Jesus knew that the pharisees were always very careful to stay clean and safe according to the Old Testament law. They avoided unsafe people and unsafe conditions to make sure they did not violate any legal restrictions.

Jesus was a complete contrast to them, in that he risked defilement by touching lepers, eating with tax collectors, being seen in the company of public sinners (like Mary Magdalene). Jesus came to love the sinner and hate the sin. He came to show that God loves them no matter what they have done or where they have been. He continued going to those who needed him, regardless of what that might do to his reputation. Jesus' love for the individual is so great that he seeks out each one and rejoices when he or she is "found."

Jesus connects sinners being lost to sheep that are lost, as both depend very heavily on the shepherd. The shepherd will go through the most dangerous situations to save one lost sheep. They would fight off robbers, wolves, and thunderstorms. Dangerous rocky cliffs were places where a valiant shepherd would find a lost sheep and be returned safely to the flock. Sinners who were beyond hope were found and saved through the good news of God's Kingdom. Our God is like the shepherd. He searches for lost people and then he save them.

Jesus then shows us the incredible power of God's love for the lost in the story of the prodigal son. You first need to understand that the oldest son receives more than one-half of the father's estate. The rest was divided up equally by the remaining sons. This young man received one-third of the estate when he demanded his share. The remaining two-thirds of the estate went to his older brother. In most cases this would have been done after the father's death, but this showed the contempt he had for his father's authority as head of the family. His son took the money and left for a distant land and he squandered it on parties and prostitutes. After a while his money was gone and to survive he got a job feeding the pigs at a local farm. For a Jew to stoop to feeding pigs was a great humiliation. According to the law of Moses, the pigs were unclean animals (Deut. 14:8). The son had hit bottom and finally he came to his senses. The key to this passage is his saying "Father, I have sinned against both heaven and you; and I am no longer worthy to be called your son." He confessed his sin and in a spirit of true Godly sorrow and repentance, he went home to be accountable to his father. His father ran out to meet him and instantly restored him to his former position of honor.

We need to reflect on this message. It may take a great tragedy to cause us to look up to the only one who can help. Are you trying to live your life this way? Don't take foolish chances, stop and look before you hit bottom, and save yourself and your family much grief. God, like the father in this story, waits patiently and lovingly until we come to our senses.

Application

The first reading tells us of the consequences that happen when idols become the God of our lives. The second reading shows that the call to renewal has to begin with the call to repentance. The Gospel reveals that God waits, patiently and lovingly, until we come to our senses.

In the spirit of mercy, select someone in your family, or among your friends, and make a decision to forgive all the wrongs of this particular person; and for one whole week, affirm what he/she does right. You will be astonished at the result.

TWENTY-FIFTH SUNDAY IN ORDINARY TIME - CYCLE C

BEFORE YOU BEGIN:

Pray and ask God to speak to you through His Holy Spirit. "THE PARACLETE, THE HOLY SPIRIT WHOM THE FATHER WILL SEND IN MY NAME, WILL INSTRUCT YOU IN EVERYTHING, AND REMIND YOU OF ALL THAT I TOLD YOU." (JOHN 14:26)

FIRST DAY   **Reread last week's readings.**

1.   What was a helpful or new thought from the readings or from the homily you heard on Sunday?

2.   From what you learned, what personal application did you choose to apply to your life this week?

SECOND DAY   **READ AMOS 8:4-7**   **FIRST READING**

("Hear this, you who trample upon the needy.")

1.   Who is speaking and to whom is he speaking in Amos 8:4-7? Amos 8:1-2

2.   On whom do you trample, and whom do you destroy? Amos 8:4

3.   What do you ask about the new moon and what is the new moon? Amos 8:5 and Numbers 28:9-15

4.   For what reason did they want to know if the new moon was over? Amos 8:5

5.   What does the Lord tell his people in Leviticus 19:35-36?

6.   How can you have a long life on this earth? Deuteronomy 25:13-16

7.   What will they buy for silver and for a pair of sandals? Amos 8:6

8.   What will they sell? Amos 8:6

9.   By what has the Lord sworn, and what will he never forget? Amos 8:7

10.   What does the Lord say about the pride of Jacob? Amos 6:8

11.   When does the Lord forget what we have done in the past? Ezekiel 18:21-22

Personal - In what way have you cheated a poor person by remaining silent or by giving from your surplus rather than from your needs, at home, or at the offering at church on Sunday?

THIRD DAY **READ 1 TIMOTHY 2:1-8** **SECOND READING**

("God is one. One also is the mediator
between God and men, the man Jesus Christ.")

1. Who is writing this letter and to whom is he writing? 1 Timothy 1:1-2

2. What four things is he urging be offered for all men? 1 Timothy 2:1

3. For whom is he especially urging this and for what reason? 1 Timothy 2:2

4. What does he say about prayer of this kind and how does God feel about it? 1 Timothy 2:3

5. What does God want and for whom does he want this? 1 Timothy 2:4

6. What does he want all men to come to know? 1 Timothy 2:4

7. What is the truth and who is the truth? 1 Tim. 2:5, John 14:6

8. As what did Jesus give himself and for whom? 1 Timothy 2:6

9. When was this truth attested to? 1 Timothy 2:6

10. What has Paul been made and what is his wish? 1 Timothy 2:7-8

11. What is his wish that every man be free from? 1 Timothy 2:8

Personal – In what way have you been set free from anger and dissension? In what way are you following the example of Paul and teaching those around you what verse 5-6 of 1 Timothy 2 says?

FOURTH DAY **READ LUKE 16:1-13** **GOSPEL**

("You cannot give yourself to God and money.")

1. As Jesus was speaking to his disciples what did he say the steward of a rich man was reported doing? Luke 16:1

2. What did the rich man say to his steward? Luke 16:2

3. What did the steward say to himself? Luke 16:3

4. As he thought of an idea, what would be the result of the people toward him? Luke 16:4

5. When the steward called in each of his master's debtors what did he ask them, what was their answer, and what were the steward's instructions? Luke 16:5-7

6. For what did the master give his devious employee credit, and for what reason? Luke 16:8

7.   What are you to gain from this world's goods? Luke 16:9

8.   How are you to use this world's goods? Matthew 25:35-36

9.   When the goods of this world fail you, what will be yours? Luke 16:9,
       Matthew 25:34

10.   Fill in the following blanks: The person who is _____ in very small matters
       is also _____ in great ones; and the person who is _____ in very
       small matters is also _____ in great ones. Luke 16:10

11.   In verses 10-12 of Luke 16, what is the key quality being brought out in regards to
       money?

12.   What must you do first before providing for yourself and family? Matthew 6:33

13.   What can a servant not do? Luke 16:13

Personal – In what way have you shown responsibility in your use of your worldly goods? Examine the last twenty-four hours. How much of your time was spent earning and spending money for this world's goods and how much time was spent loving and giving to your brother or sister in need? "You cannot give yourself to God and money."

FIFTH DAY   **READ PSALM 113:1-2, 4-8**

("High above all nations is the Lord.")

Read and meditate on Psalm 113:1-2, 4-8.

What is the Lord saying to you personally through the Psalm?

How can you apply this to your life?

SIXTH DAY   **READ ALL OF THE COMMENTARY**

AMOS 8:4-7

This passage is spoken to us by a person who was a shepherd. He was not a prophet or the son of a prophet. He did not go to some prestigious school, but he was called by God to bring a message of obedience to the people without any special preparation, education or upbringing. Amos obeyed God's call to go and prophesy to the people of Israel.

Obedience, then, as it is today, was the test of a faithful servant. He spoke out to the people in a time of peace and affluence, and his message was not well received. He told them, you do all the external things that are required of you very well, but in your hearts you are corrupt. The merchants kept the religious holidays, but not in spirit. Their primary goal was in making money, even if that meant not being really honest. We see that today in our society on special days like Christmas and Easter. The message on the surface is peace and good will but the bottom line to many is to make money.

The humanist call Christmas "Winter Vacation" and Easter "Spring Vacation," and many Christians go right along with it, and their conduct is no different than the pagans in this passage or the ones that are right here in our present-day society.

They used phony weights and measures and cheated the poor. We do that today by electing corrupt politicians who make it legal to cheat the poor and make millions of dollars doing it. We need to reflect on this passage on our time that we call our "day off" (Sunday). Do we give that day to the Lord? Is that a day that our family knows will consist of praising the Lord and visiting family? Or is it a day when what we should get done during the week is being done because we are too busy making money on the other days? We need to reflect in prayer that God will give us the strength to open our hearts and give to him the first fruits of our efforts. We are these people in this passage, and we must respond in obedience to God's call to feed his hungry, clothe his poor, visit his sick because what we do to the least of our brother and sisters we do unto him (Matthew 25:31-46).

1 TIMOTHY 2:1-8

The church has a great calling. We are not only called upon to plead with men to turn to God, but to plead with God the cause of men. Our God is so fantastic, he has let us have the incredible privilege of helping him change the world through our prayers. Our understanding of this can never be fully grasped because it is a true mystery of faith. But it is a reality because Paul urges us to pray for one another and he even tells us to pray for our rulers.

We might well remember that Nero was the emperor at this time (A.D. 54-68). It was under this wicked emperor that Paul was imprisoned, and he knew that soon he was to be beheaded. This proves to us that we must pray for bad rulers as well as good rulers.

Paul wrote this during a great persecution of the believers. Paul tells us that God longs to save us just as Peter did in Scripture (2 Peter 3:9). This means that while God wanted all to be saved, all did not accept his invitation. Paul tells us that the power of prayer affects all men and that power is available to us through intercessory prayer.

When we pray for someone else we stand in God's presence, pleading for that person. Our Lord Jesus binds and casts out the demon spirit and leaves the person the freedom to choose to return to God's loving way. Some people refuse this incredible gift and fail to become healed. Paul makes it clear that when we pray for someone we can go straight to our Lord and stand in his Presence, pleading for that person.

There is an old story about a Roman warrior who returned home in victory to find his brother about to be put to death in the Roman court. He stood in the back of the courtroom and without a word he held up the bleeding stub of the arm which had been cut off in battle. As the judge looked upon the wound, he said "For the sake of this brave warrior, his brother is counted innocent and free." We should be condemned for our sins, but we look and see Jesus holding up his nail-printed hands, presenting his pierced feet and wounded side, pleading for you and me.

That is what the power of prayer can do. It brings the healing power of Jesus to anyone who is truly sorry. We need to be people of prayer and people of pure conduct. We are the temples of the Holy Spirit (1 Cor. 3:16) and the prayers of the righteous man are very powerful (James 5:16).

LUKE 16:1-13

Jesus tells the parable of the shrewd accountant in this passage. The story is about an accountant being confronted by his boss on charges of cheating the company. We will have to give an account of our actions to God someday just like the accountant had to do in this story (Romans 14:12). This man wasted the resources that he had through the use of his conniving and cheating with others in the business world. His love for money determined his course of conduct and he exercised corrupt authority and power with it. We need to reflect on these few verses about our involvement with money, trust and integrity.

We are called by God to use our material goods in a way that will help us as we stand face to face with God on judgment day (Luke 12:33, 34). We notice the admiration coming from the boss toward the accountant for his shrewdness. We can easily be influenced by what the world calls admirable behavior, because worldly people are very clever, more so than Godly people. We are children of the light (John 12:36), and we are not called to be clever, we are called to be honest. We are not called to buy friendship through cheating or granting special favors.

Our entry into heaven is not based on how clever we are, or how many good deals we make in business, or how close we come to the line of integrity and still be legal. We are called to be righteous in all matters, small or large, profitable or otherwise. We can only be trustworthy in large matters by being trustworthy in small ones. We can only be trustworthy to others when we are always trustworthy to ourselves. Heavens riches are far more valuable than earthly wealth and power.

Many people have let money take the place of God in their life, and it has become their master. Make a few observations and see if you have become a slave to money. Do you worry about money frequently? Do you give up doing what you should in order to make more money? Do you spend a great deal of time in caring for your possessions? Do you find it difficult to give away your money?

We can see that money is a hard and deceptive master. Money always promises power and control, but it often can not deliver on its promises. Money cannot buy health, joy, or eternal life. We are so much wiser, happier, and at peace when we let God be our master. Money is meant to be a servant of man and man is called to be a servant of God. God's servants have peace of mind and security both now and forever.

Application

In the first reading we saw the dangers of greed, and in the second reading we saw the power of prayer. We are told in the gospel that we cannot serve two masters.

This week, look around in your family or parish and pick out someone with whom you can share your worldly goods. Do something for that person without their knowing that it was you—like paying a bill, having the lawn mowed, or doing an errand, etc. In short, do something beautiful for God this week; and remember, before you do anything for that person, pray that the Lord fill his or her life as he has filled yours.

TWENTY-SIXTH SUNDAY IN ORDINARY TIME - CYCLE C

BEFORE YOU BEGIN:

Pray and ask God to speak to you through His Holy Spirit. "THE PARACLETE, THE HOLY SPIRIT WHOM THE FATHER WILL SEND IN MY NAME, WILL INSTRUCT YOU IN EVERYTHING, AND REMIND YOU OF ALL THAT I TOLD YOU." (JOHN 14:26)

FIRST DAY   **Reread last week's readings.**

1. What was a helpful or new thought from the readings or from the homily you heard on Sunday?

2. From what you learned, what personal application did you choose to apply to your life this week?

SECOND DAY   **READ AMOS 6:1, 4-7**

FIRST READING

("They are not made ill by the collapse of Joseph.")

1. Woe to whom in Zion, and to whom on the mount in Samaria? Amos 6:1.

2. With whom do the people of Israel have recourse? Amos 6:1

3. What do you eat and on what do you lie? Amos 6:4

4. What does the Lord say about those who take care of themselves and feed off of choice lambs and fatted calves? Ezekiel 34:3, 10

5. On the day the Lord punishes Israel for her sins, what will he tear down? Amos 3:14-15

6. Like David, what do they do? Amos 6:5

7. What do they drink and what do they do with the best oils? Amos 6:6

8. By what are they not made ill? Amos 6:6

9. What did those in Sodom do? Ezekiel 16:49

10. What will they be the first to go into, and what will be done away with? Amos 6:7

Personal – In what way have you become complacent with what you eat and where you sleep? In what way do you have more than you need? In what way can you benefit others by your excess?

("He is the blessed and only ruler,
the King of kings and Lord of lords.")

1.   Man of God that you are, from what are you to flee? 1 Timothy 6:10

2.   What six things are you to seek? 1 Timothy 6:11

3.   Of what are you to fight the good fight and take hold of? 1 Timothy 6:12

4.   You were called to this when you did what, and in whose presence? 1 Timothy 6:12

5.   What did Paul say awaited him for fighting the good fight of faith? 2 Timothy 4:7-8

6.   What does God do for all and what did Jesus do? 1 Timothy 6:13

7.   With what are we charged, how are we to do this, and until when? 1 Timothy 6:14

8.   When will God bring this appearance to pass? 1 Timothy 6:15

9.   Who is Jesus Christ? 1 Timothy 6:15

10.   What does he alone have, and where does he dwell? 1 Timothy 6:16

11.   What can no human being do and what two things must we show Jesus?
      1 Timothy 6:16

Personal - This past week, what have you been seeking, and what has occupied your mind the most? Who or what has been your ruler? If you can see the opposites of the six things you are to seek according to 1 Timothy 6:11, and if any of these have crept into your life, confess them; then come back to seeking what God's Word tells you.

("They have Moses and the prophets, let them hear them.")

1.   As Jesus spoke to his disciples, what did he say there once was? How was he dressed, and how did he eat? Luke 16:19

2.   Who was at his gate, what was he, and with what was he covered? Luke 16:20

3.   What did Lazarus long to eat and what did the dogs do? Luke 16:21

4.   What eventually happened to the beggar, and what happened to him after that?
      Luke 16:22

5.   What happened to the rich man and what happened to him after that? Luke 16:22

6.   Where was the rich man, what was happening to him, and what did he see?
      Luke 16:23

7.   What did he call out and what was Abraham's response? Luke 16:24-25

8.   What was fixed between them and what happens to those who try to cross from either side? Luke 16:26

9. What did the rich man ask Father Abraham to do, for what reason, and what was his reply? Luke 16:27-29

10. What did the rich man say and what did he say they would do? Luke 16:30

11. Abraham said if they did not listen to whom, they would not be convinced even if one should what? Luke 16:31

Personal - In what way have you noticed a poor person and responded to his need this week? A poor person is one lacking in knowing God's love through Jesus, a lonely person, a widow, an orphan, or someone lacking their daily bread and shelter.

FIFTH DAY   **READ PSALM 146:7-10**

("The Lord sets captives free.")

Read and meditate on Psalm 146:7-10.

What is the Lord saying to you personally through the Psalm?

How can you apply this to your life?

SIXTH DAY   **READ ALL OF THE COMMENTARY**

AMOS 6:1, 4-7

In Amos we find God calling a man when he was occupied in his daily work (1:1). God called him with his shepherd's crook in his hand, and sent him forth to gather straying people instead of straying sheep. Amos was not the only prophet of his day. No doubt, as a boy, he had known Jonah, and possibly Elisha. Hosea was a co-worker of his. When Amos' work was ending, the great Isaiah and Micah appeared.

These men, when they were boys, might have heard Amos proclaim the word of God on one of his tours. The two kingdoms of Israel (Northern Kingdom) and Judah (Southern Kingdom) were entering tremendous prosperity. The idea of surrounding nations giving them any trouble was not even imagined. The nation was at peace and all that the people thought of was pleasure and having a good time. God tried to arouse his people to a sense of their danger by sending them Amos.

Amos told them about the great cities to the north, east, and west (including Gath, the hometown of Goliath) that once were greater than Israel and Judah but that they had been destroyed because of the pride of their people. He warned that this was going to happen to Israel also because of the arrogance and pride of her people. Amos leveled his attack at the people living in a lifestyle that consisted of wealth and being very comfortable. He said this was a false security and that God was displeased with people who did not use their wealth to help the unfortunate.

Ivory symbolizes great wealth and extravagance. This gross waste of resources should have been used to help the poor. Amos told them that God wanted them to be concerned for others, especially those who could not help themselves. The kingdom of God has no place for selfishness or indifference.

We, in the United States, need to really reflect on this passage, because we too indulge in incredible extravagances with our desires and wishes. We spend billions of dollars on cosmetics, while millions of people are starving. We spend more on dog food in this country than many nations spend on their entire budget. We kill more unborn babies in one year than all of the military personnel who have died in battle since the country began. In less than fifty years, Israel was destroyed because she did not listen to God through his prophets. We need to pray that the United States will heed God's powerful warning and repent and return to his Holy Word.

1 TIMOTHY 6:11-16

Paul is telling Timothy that when you are involved in a spiritual battle, it is as important knowing when to run as it is knowing when to fight. Timothy is warned to run from anything or anyone who produced evil thoughts. A wise person will realize that removing one's self from the scene of temptation is many times safer than trying to fight off the temptation. It is in these battles of temptation that our faith is severely tested.

We are to treasure our faith in Christ and respond, not to the temptation, but to the power of the presence of God in our lives. God will speak to us through our conscience in times of temptation. When we are walking with God, he will let us know the difference between right and wrong. We need to follow our conscience and do what is right in faith. Pilate knew the truth about Jesus. He knew he was innocent but he chose to reject the truth. Pilate violated his own conscience.

It is a tragedy when we fail to recognize the truth; but like Pilate, it is a greater tragedy when we recognize the truth but refuse to act on it. We are being told to fight the good fight today, just as Timothy was told by Paul. The day will come when all the believers who have fought the good fight will be with Christ in his Kingdom.

Paul describes to Timothy the type of God who will be with us at the end of the good fight. We are told that he is ageless and that all who have gone before us and all who come after us, believing in him, will be alive with him forever. He is a God who will never die. He is a God infinitely powerful, having dominion over everything; yet he wants to share all with us. Paul's message to Timothy is a message to you and me, and that is: Let us not put our trust in anything or anyone else but JESUS, because only he alone is permanent.

LUKE 16:19-31

Wealth was considered by the Pharisees to be a proof of righteousness. Today many people yield to the wealthy because they appear to be right on so many issues. Jesus tells us about a rich man who was punished and also about a poor man who was rewarded. We need to be very careful in the realization that the rich man was not punished because of his wealth; rather he was punished because of his selfishness.

He allowed Lazarus to eat the scraps at his table and take home whatever he wanted that was to be thrown away. The rich man was in hell, not for what he did, but rather for what he did not do. The rich man feasted in luxury every day in a country where the people were fortunate if they ate meat once a week. Lazarus was waiting for the crumbs that fell from the rich man's table. We need to remember that in those days, there were no knives, forks or napkins. Food was eaten with the hands. The hands were cleansed by wiping them on chunks of bread, which were then thrown away. This is what Lazarus waited to eat.

We need also to remember that Lazarus was a beggar with terrible running sores all over his body and even the dogs feasted on him. Can you picture the incredible contrast between the two men? Judgment day brought justice to both men and the rich man suffers forever in eternity while Lazarus rests in the arms of Abraham (Hebrew concept of heaven).

The rich man never ordered Lazarus removed from his gate. He did not kick him in passing. He was not deliberately cruel to him. The great sin of the rich man was that HE NEVER EVEN NOTICED HIM. He thought it perfectly natural that the beggar be accepted as part of the landscape. He also thought it acceptable that Lazarus should lie in pain and hunger while he wallowed in luxury. We need to reflect on our own status in today's world. The hungry, the homeless, the aborted, the abandoned, the mentally sick, and the poor are all around us. Do we think ourselves generous if the unfortunate people eat what we throw away? We need to make sure that our sin today is not the horrible sin of omission. What we fail to do to the least among us, we fail to do to Christ (Matthew 25:31-46).

Application

The first reading told us not to become insulated toward the people's needs. The second reading told us to listen to our conscience. The Gospel tells us not to ignore the suffering of others.

This week, as our conscience leads us, visit and comfort someone who is suffering, an old person, a relative, a friend, someone in a rest home, prison. Jesus tells us in scripture, "As often as you did it for one of my least brothers, you did it for me." (Matthew 25:40)

TWENTY-SEVENTH SUNDAY IN ORDINARY TIME - CYCLE C

BEFORE YOU BEGIN:

Pray and ask God to speak to you through His Holy Spirit. "THE PARACLETE, THE HOLY SPIRIT WHOM THE FATHER WILL SEND IN MY NAME, WILL INSTRUCT YOU IN EVERYTHING, AND REMIND YOU OF ALL THAT I TOLD YOU." (JOHN 14:26)

FIRST DAY   **Reread last week's readings.**

1.   What was a helpful or new thought from the readings or from the homily you heard on Sunday?

2.   From what you learned, what personal application did you choose to apply to your life this week?

SECOND DAY   **READ HABAKKUK 1:2-3; 2:2-4**   **FIRST READING**

(The just man, because of his faith, shall live.)

1.   Who is crying out for help? Habakkuk 1:1

2.   What is his complaint to God? Habakkuk 1:2

3.   What comes through hearing? Romans 10:17

4.   What did Habakkuk cry out to God and what does he say he does not do? Habakkuk 1:2

5.   What is he saying is before him? Habakkuk 1:3

6.   What was the Lord's answer? Habakkuk 2:2

7.   What does the vision (Habakkuk 1:2-3) still have and to what does it press? Habakkuk 2:3

8.   What will the vision not do and what are we to do if it delays? Habakkuk 2:3

9.   What does the rash man not have and what does the just man have and live by? Habakkuk 2:4

10.   What is wealth and the proud? Habakkuk 2:4

Personal – What do you do when you do not hear the Lord and are called to wait for the answer? What comes forth from your mouth?

THIRD DAY   **READ 2 TIMOTHY 1:6-8, 13-14**   **SECOND READING**

("The spirit God has given us is no cowardly spirit.")

1. What is the gift of God Paul reminds Timothy to stir into flame and when did he receive this gift? 2 Timothy 1:5-6

2. What is faith? Hebrews 11:1

3. The Spirit God has given us is not what, but it is one that makes us what three things? 2 Timothy 1:7

4. Because of this we are never to be ashamed of what to our Lord? 2 Timothy 1:8

5. Where does your strength come from and what are we to bear? 2 Timothy 1:8

6. What have you heard Paul say in faith and love in Christ Jesus? 2 Timothy 1:13

7. With whose help are you to guard this rich deposit of faith? 2 Timothy 1:14

8. How can you guard what has been committed to you? 1 Timothy 6:20

9. Where does the Holy Spirit dwell? 2 Timothy 1:14

10. How do we honor or glorify God? 1 Corinthians 6:19-20

11. Why should we take care of our body? Reread 2 Timothy 1:14 and 1 Corinthians 6:19-20

Personal - In what way have you testified to your faith in Jesus Christ to your family, friends, fellow workers or those you come in contact with every day? In what way can they see his Holy Spirit present in your body?

FOURTH DAY   **READ LUKE 17:5-10**   **GOSPEL**

("Increase our faith.")

1. What did the apostles say to the Lord? Luke 17:5

2. What did Jesus say would happen if you had faith the size of a mustard seed? Luke 17:6

3. What else will we do if we trust and do not falter, and what will we receive? Matthew 21:21-22

4. What did Peter and John do to the beggar and how did they do it? Acts 3:6-8, 16

Personal - How can you measure the amount of faith you have? How can you increase the faith you have?

5. Who plows or herds sheep? Luke 17:7

6. What would you say to him when he comes in from the fields? Luke 17:8

7. When are we not to expect gratitude for what we do? Luke 17:9

8. When we have done all that we have been commanded, what are we to say? Luke 17:10

9. In order to become great, what are we to do? Matthew 20:26-27

10. What did the Son of Man come to do? Matthew 20:28

11. What did Mary call herself when the angel came to her? Luke 1:38

Personal - In what way have you taken on the serving attitude of Jesus and Mary? In what way are you willing to serve those in your family, your friends and strangers?

FIFTH DAY   **READ PSALM 95:1-2, 6-9**

("Let us acclaim the Rock of our salvation.")

Read and meditate on Psalm 95:1-2, 6-9.

What is the Lord saying to you personally through the Psalm?

How can you apply this to your life?

SIXTH DAY   **READ ALL OF THE COMMENTARY**

HABAKKUK 1:2-3, 2:2-4

Habakkuk was extremely troubled with not only what was happening to his country, but why God seemed to show such indifference to the wickedness that was so common around him. He was a prophet during the reign of Jehoiakim (2 Kings 23:36-24:5). He was very active between the fall of Nineveh in 612 B.C. and the invasion of Judah in 589 B.C.

Babylon was becoming a world power and Judah was certain to be her next victim. This passage shows us a dialogue between a prophet and his God. The other prophetic books bring God's word to men; but this book brings man's questions to God. Habakkuk was crushed by all the corruption he saw around him and he poured out his heart telling God what he thought.

We can really empathize with Habakkuk when we look at the corruption going on around us. We have abortion, pornography, prostitution, drugs, homosexuality, alcoholism, child abuse that matches anything that Habakkuk saw. In short, today's injustice is still overwhelming. We, like Habakkuk, say today, "Why does God seem to ignore the evil that is going around?" We may be asking, "Why are so many people doing evil things and not being punished for them?"

In the second part of the passage we see God telling Habakkuk to write his response down and bring it to the people. God answers Habakkuk's questions just like he will ours, when like Habakkuk we pour out our hearts to him. God told Habakkuk that Judah was going to be punished by being destroyed by Babylon. God also tells Habakkuk, as well as us, that judgment, though slow to come, will certainly come.

Today, we hear that in regard to our civil courts of law. We are told justice may be slow, but it will be served. Many Christians, like Habakkuk, feel very angry as they see evil enjoying what seems to be the upper hand in the world. Habakkuk had a personal relationship with God and complained vigorously, and God responded to him personally. God's message to us is the same as the one he gave to Habakkuk: Be patient, trust in God, keep God in your thoughts and actions, stay close to his Holy Word. It isn't easy to be patient, but it helps to remember that God hates sin even more than we do. God told Habakkuk, "Do not despair."

Trusting God means to trust him even when we do not understand why things happen like they do. We need to remember, the just man shall live by faith. (Romans 1:17)

2 Timothy 1:6-8, 13-14

Paul is encouraging his young protege to be faithful in his role as a leader in the Christian community. Timothy was experiencing great opposition to his message and to himself as the leader of his community. Timothy's youth was his biggest disadvantage and Paul was encouraging him to persevere. Timothy had received special gifts of the Holy Spirit at his ordination, and Paul was telling him to call upon the Spirit for these gifts and use them regularly.

Timothy didn't need new gifts, he needed the courage and discipline to hang on to the truth and use the gifts he had already received (1:13-14). Paul is encouraging him to step out boldly in faith and proclaim God's Holy Word, and the Holy Spirit would be with him and give him power. We suffer the same as Timothy when we let people intimidate us, and it neutralizes our effectiveness for God. The same Holy Spirit that empowered Paul, Timothy and other heroes of the bible will empower us.

We can overcome our fear of what some might say or do to us and get on with doing God's work. Timothy may have been afraid to preach as he began experiencing rejection in the community. Today, we need to accept the fact that we will be persecuted too, when we proclaim and live God's Holy Word. Like Timothy, we too will enjoy the power of the Holy Spirit and his gifts of boldness and courage, when we yield ourselves in faith to Jesus Christ as our Lord and Savior.

Timothy was a leader in transition. He had moved from being Paul's helper to Paul's replacement. He called upon the Holy Spirit to give him courage to make the transition. We too can follow Paul's advice to Timothy when we are in our transitions. Like Paul who, knew even while in prison, that God was still in control, we need to reflect and then act on this powerful fact. No matter where we are in life, no matter what is happening to us, God is still in control.

Luke 17:5-10

How many times do we say the same thing to our Lord? "I need more faith, tell me how to get it." Jesus casts doubt on the possession of any faith of the apostles. Maybe because they were one of the selected few, they put too much emphasis on who they were. They may have been too self-assured because he was with them. (Jesus describes the power that comes through faith using the similarity between their faith and a tiny mustard seed.) The disciples' question was a valid one because they wanted the faith necessary to do what Jesus had been telling them to do.

Jesus implied that faith is not something you "get." What is Faith? Faith is described best with two words: confidence and certainty (Hebrews 11:1). You have to reach out and take hold of faith. Picture someone tossing a book at you. If you respond properly, you will catch it. If you do nothing, the book will fall at your feet. Knowing how to catch it will be of no value if you do not reach out and respond.

Jesus wasn't condemning the apostles for having substandard faith, he was trying to show them how important it would be in their ministry. We can only rise to the occasion if we know that within us is the solution (1 John 4:4). Our faith grows just like a mustard seed as we respond more and more to the power of the presence of God in our life. When we face a problem as big as a mountain, we need to take our eyes off that mountain and put them only on Christ. We need only remember Peter, when in faith he stepped out of the boat to go to the Lord in the raging sea; but when he took his eyes off the Lord and placed it on the enormous waves, he began to sink (Matthew 14:28-30).

Today, we need to continuously keep in prayer and let our faith grow in Christian fellowship. We also need to partake in the sacraments of our church. We must remember that there is great power in even a little faith when God is with us. When we feel weak or powerless we need to re-examine our faith and make sure that we are responding to the presence of God's power and not ours. In faith, we can all be like a mustard seed that begins very small and soon casts a shadow of comfort and healing over the entire world. In faith, we can see with the vision of God himself.

Application

In the first reading, we are told to persevere, be patient and to trust in God. In the second reading, we hear the call to courage and discipline. The Gospel calls us to step out boldly and live our life in faith.

This week let us, in faith, step out in boldness, discipline and practice being a Christian leader wherever we are. This will mean being a servant for the Lord by serving someone else in our family, job, community, etc.

TWENTY-EIGHTH SUNDAY IN ORDINARY TIME - CYCLE C

BEFORE YOU BEGIN:

Pray and ask God to speak to you through His Holy Spirit. "THE PARACLETE, THE HOLY SPIRIT WHOM THE FATHER WILL SEND IN MY NAME, WILL INSTRUCT YOU IN EVERYTHING, AND REMIND YOU OF ALL THAT I TOLD YOU." (JOHN 14:26)

FIRST DAY   **Reread last week's readings.**

1.   What was a helpful or new thought from the readings or from the homily you heard on Sunday?

2.   From what you learned, what personal application did you choose to apply to your life this week?

SECOND DAY   **READ 2 KINGS 5:14-17**   **FIRST READING**

("So Naaman went down and plunged into the Jordan seven times at the word of the man of God.")

1.   Who went down and plunged into the Jordan seven times, what made him do it and who was the man of God? 2 Kings 5:14, 2 Kings 5:8

2.   Who was Naaman and what was wrong with him? 2 Kings 5:1

3.   What happened to his flesh when he plunged into the Jordan seven times? 2 Kings 5:14

4.   What does Jesus say will happen to us through his word? John 15:3

5.   After being cleansed where did he go, and with whom did he go? 2 Kings 5:15

6.   As he stood before Elisha, what did he say about God and what did he offer the prophet? 2 Kings 5:15

7.   Where did he say that there is no God in all the world but there? 2 Kings 5:15

8.   What did Elisha say about the gift? 2 Kings 5:16

9.   For what did Naaman ask, and for what reason? 2 Kings 5:17

Personal - In what way have you been cleansed or healed through your obedience to the Word of God? Be specific.

THIRD DAY   **READ 2 TIMOTHY 2:8-13**   **SECOND READING**

("There is no chaining the Word of God.")

1.   Of whom is Jesus Christ a descendant and what was the gospel being preached? 2 Timothy 2:8

2. Who was preaching this gospel and in so doing, how does he suffer? 2 Timothy 1:1 and 2 Timothy 2:8-9

3. As he suffers, even to the point of being thrown into chains, of what does he say there is no chaining? 2 Timothy 2:9

4. Why does he bear all of this and for what reason? 2 Tim 2:10

5. On what can you depend? 2 Timothy 2:11

6. What does it mean to die with him? Romans 6:1-11

7. What will happen if we persevere to the end? 2 Timothy 2:12

8. What will happen if we deny him? 2 Timothy 2:12

9. If we are unfaithful, what will he do and for what reason? 2 Timothy 2:13

10. What does 1 Corinthians 1:9 say that God is?

Personal – In what way have you died with Jesus? How have you faced a hardship among your family, work, or circle of friends because of your witnessing to the power of Christ in your life?

FOURTH DAY   **READ LUKE 17:11-19**   **GOSPEL**

("Stand up and go your way;
your faith has been your salvation.")

1. On Jesus journey to Jerusalem what borders did he pass along? See if you can find this on your bible map. Luke 17:11

2. As he was entering a village who met him and what did they keep? Luke 17:12

3. As they raised their voices, what did they say to him and how did they address him? Luke 17:13

4. When Jesus saw them, what was his response to them? Luke 17:14

5. What happened to them when they went on their way as he told them? Luke 17:14

6. What did one of them do realizing he had been cured? Luke 17:15

7. What did he do at the feet of Jesus and of what did he speak? Luke 17:16

8. What was the man and what did Jesus take the occasion to say? Luke 17:16-17

9. What did they not return to do and what did he call the one man who did? Luke 17:18

10. What did he tell the one man to do? Luke 17:19

11. What did Jesus say it was that saved the man? Luke 17:19

12. What did Jesus say to the woman who was bleeding? Matthew 9:22

Personal- In what way have you thanked God this week and for what have you thanked him? Have you received healing in any way? What do you believe healed you, or what may be blocking you from being healed?

FIFTH DAY   **READ PSALM 98:1-4**

("The Lord has made his salvation known".)

Read and meditate on Psalm 98:1-4.

What is the Lord saying to you personally through the Psalm?

How can you apply this to your life?

SIXTH DAY   **READ ALL OF THE COMMENTARY**

2 KINGS 5:14-17

This is a great passage that deals with the sin of pride and the core of faith. Naaman was the commander-in-chief of the Syrian army and also a national hero. He was stricken with the dreaded disease of leprosy and would consider anything or anyone who could heal him. Leprosy, much like AIDS today, was one of the most feared diseases of that time. There was no cure and if it was determined to be bad enough, a person would be removed from the community and sent into exile.

Naaman's disease was probably still in its early stages. Naaman's wife was told by her servant that a prophet of God in Israel could cure him. He went to the prophet's home and Elisha told him to go and bathe himself in the Jordan river and he would be cured. Naaman was insulted at being told to do such a trivial thing in such a common, dirty river like the Jordan. He was advised by his counselor to follow the prophet's command and he was then healed of his leprosy.

Naaman was a great hero and he was used to getting respect and he was outraged when Elisha treated him like an average person. We need to learn the same lesson that Naaman learned, that obedience to God begins with humility. We too must believe that his way is much better than our own. We must always remember that God's ways are best and God can use anything to accomplish his purposes. Naaman then was so impressed with the Lord of Israel that he wanted to take two quantities of earth and make an earth altar and give worship to the God of Elisha, who is our Lord and Savior Jesus Christ. Like Naaman, obedience to God will also bring us healing and blessings.

2 TIMOTHY 2:8-13

Paul is really exhorting us to be courageous in our Christian walk and not to be afraid of suffering. He tells Timothy that he must teach others so that they may pass on the Good News. We are called to do that today, and we also need to know that suffering, persecution and, possibly, even death will be the hardship that goes with being an ambassador for Christ. False teachers were a problem in those days as they are in ours. The incarnation of Jesus Christ was the act of God voluntarily assuming a human body and soul, a human nature. He became a man without ceasing to be God, a human being, and his name was Jesus. He did not give up his divinity to become human. He became subject to place, time and many other human limitations. He was, however, not subject to sin and he was able to show us everything about God's character in human terms. Paul very clearly states that Jesus is fully God and fully man. Any other view than this is not biblical. The truth about Jesus then was no more popular than it is today in our time. Today, Jesus is Lord only to a receptive heart, as it was in Paul's time. Paul's declaration to the Jews that Jesus was God was an insult, and they condemned him for blasphemy. The Romans were outraged because they worshipped the emperor as God (Philippians 4:22). The

Greeks were disgusted because humanity soiled divine status (Acts 11:20-21). Many of these different cultures converted to Christianity only when, in faith, they believed in his being God and fully human.

Today we are free to choose to have a receptive heart. We see in scripture that God has chosen us first. It is in being obedient to his choice that we can really ever be totally free. This is a mystery that our humanity cannot fully understand, but we can be very grateful that he has chosen us. God is totally faithful to us; even in the middle of our present hardships he is with us, and he gives us the strength to persevere (1 Cor. 10:13). He tells us that someday we will live eternally with him and share in the administration of the kingdom (Matthew 16:24-27). We may be faith less in our times of trial and hardship but Jesus remains faithful to his promise to be with us, even to the end of the world (Matthew 28:20).

LUKE 17:11-19

We have learned that leprosy was a disease that was contagious and many times fatal, and the person was banned from his community. His life was one of suffering, horror, rejection, and finally death alone and unwanted. A leper had to announce his presence if he came into contact with a non-leper. If a leper thought he was cured, he had to present himself to the priest and be declared clean (Leviticus 14). Jesus sends the ten lepers to the priest before they were healed. Their obedience in faith resulted in their being healed. We need to reflect on our own level of faith. Do we act upon our being told by Jesus that we, too, have been healed (Matthew 8:17)? We see only one healed leper return to give thanks and to realize that because he believed, his cure became possible. God does not demand that we thank him for healing us, but in our spirit of thankfulness our faith grows more and more to his delight. It is significant that Jesus mentioned that the only thankful leper was a Samaritan, who because of his race was despised by the Jews as idolatrous riff-raff. We see that the grace of God is for everyone and yet not everyone is grateful.

Jesus shows us in these verses that his healing power is just waiting to be released, that all we have to do is have faith, and step out and act upon that faith. Jesus changed a situation for those lepers that probably had been going on for several years. He was immediately responsive to the plea of these untouchables. They were not able to live a normal life and be with their families but Jesus changed that and restored them to good health. Jesus never gives up on us no matter how incurable, or untouchable, we may be. Sometimes we are tempted to give up on people or situations which have not changed for many years.

God can change the unchangeable and we need to let the change begin with ourselves. We need to believe that he can cure us physically, emotionally, and spiritually. We then need to come and kneel before Jesus and say, "Thank you for dying for me even while I was still sinning" (Romans 5:8). Our faith will grow; and the "unclean" in our families, in our churches, in our country, and on our planet earth will see in us that healing light of Christ, the Morning Star (2 Peter 1:19). They too will become healed and run through the countryside joyfully singing out the praises of a loving God who will some day cleanse the earth from sin, and there will be no more sickness and death (Matthew 8:17).

Application

In the first reading, we saw pride prevent a cure; then we saw obedience bring the cure. In the second reading, we were encouraged to endure suffering for the sake of preaching the Good News. In the Gospel, we saw the joy of the Lord over the thankful, unclean one being cured.

This week, let us show our thanks to the Lord for healing us by doing something specific for the "unclean," like a day of fasting or a week of daily prayer for a specific person at a specific time. Maybe spend some time at a soup kitchen or help with the homeless, etc. Let the unwanted see that they are wanted by Christ through you this week.

TWENTY-NINTH SUNDAY IN ORDINARY TIME - CYCLE C

BEFORE YOU BEGIN:

Pray and ask God to speak to you through His Holy Spirit. "THE PARACLETE, THE HOLY SPIRIT WHOM THE FATHER WILL SEND IN MY NAME, WILL INSTRUCT YOU IN EVERYTHING, AND REMIND YOU OF ALL THAT I TOLD YOU." (JOHN 14:26)

FIRST DAY   **Reread last week's readings.**

1. What was a helpful or new thought from the readings or from the homily you heard on Sunday?

2. From what you learned, what personal application did you choose to apply to your life this week?

SECOND DAY   **READ EXODUS 17:8-13**   **FIRST READING**

*("As long as Moses kept his hands raised up,
Israel had the better of the fight.")*

1. What did Amalek do at Rephidim? Exodus 17:8

2. Who was Joshua and what tribe was he from? Numbers 13:8,16

3. What did Moses tell Joshua to do the following day? Exodus 17:9

4. What did Moses say he would be doing and what would he have in his hand? Exodus 17:9

5. What did Joshua do and who climbed to the top of the hill with Moses? Exodus 17:10

6. What happened when Moses had his hands raised up and what happened when he let his hands rest? Exodus 17:11

7. When Moses' hands got tired, what two things did Hur and Aaron do for him? Exodus 17:12

8. How long did they do this? Exodus 17:12

9. What happened on another occasion when Moses extended his hands to the Lord? Exodus 9:29

10. What did Joshua do with Amalek? Exodus 17:13

Personal – In what way have you been fighting a spiritual battle and had a family member or a friend support you, or in what way have you supported or held their hands up to the Lord in their battle? Where have your hands been lifted during physical, spiritual, or emotional battles?

THIRD DAY   READ 2 TIMOTHY 3:14-4:2   SECOND READING

("I charge you to preach the Word.")

1.   Who is speaking and to whom is he speaking in 2 Timothy 3:14? Timothy 1:1-2

2.   What two things have we done that for our part we must remain faithful?
      2 Timothy 3:14

3.   Who is our teacher? Matthew 23:10

4.   How does he teach us today? John 14:26

5.   What did Timothy know since infancy and how was it passed on to him?
      2 Timothy 3:15, 2 Timothy 1:5

6.   Of what is the sacred Scripture the source, and what does it lead to through faith in
      Jesus Christ? 2 Timothy 3:15

7.   What is all Scripture, and for what is it useful? 2 Timothy 3:16

8.   What makes the man of God fully competent and equipped for every good work?
      2 Timothy 3:16-17

9.   In the presence of God and of Christ Jesus, who is coming to do what? What does
      he charge us to do? 2 Timothy 4:1-2

10.   With what are we to stay whether convenient or inconvenient, what three things are
      we to do, and what are we to never lose? 2 Timothy 4:2

11.   What are we to teach? Matthew 28:20

Personal – What have you been teaching your children, grandchildren, friends, co-workers, etc? Have you personally been called to teach? What do you see as the difference between worldly teaching and spiritual teaching? John 14:18-26

FOURTH DAY   READ LUKE 18:1-8 GOSPEL

*("Will not God then do justice to his
chosen who call out to him day and night?")*

1.   Of what did Jesus tell his disciples the necessity, how did he tell them, and what did
      he tell them not to lose? Luke 18:1

2.   To what did his disciples, the women in their company, and Mary (the mother of
      Jesus) devote themselves? Acts 1:13-14

3.   What did Jesus say about a judge? Luke 18:2

4.   Who came to the judge, and what did she say? Luke 18:3

5.   What was she doing to him, and why did he settle in her favor? Luke 18:5,
      Luke 11:8

6.   What did the Lord say in Luke 18:6-7?

8.   What did he say about justice and about delaying over them? Luke 18:7

9.   What did Jesus say God would do? Luke 18:8

10.   About what did Jesus ask his disciple when the Son of Man comes? Luke 18:8

11.   When the Son of Man comes with what will he come, who will accompany him,
      and how will he repay each man? Matthew 16:27

Personal - How do you combat the evil that is around you? How is God speaking to you personally in this passage regarding your own prayer life?

FIFTH DAY   **READ PSALM 121:1-8**

("He is beside you at your right hand.")

Read and meditate on Psalm 121:1-8

What is the Lord saying to you personally through the Psalm?

How can you apply this to your life?

SIXTH DAY READ ALL OF THE COMMENTARY

EXODUS 17:8-13

This passage clearly shows how tenacity and steadfastness win the day for Israel. The Amalekites were descendants of Amalek, a grandson of Esau. They were a fierce nomadic nation or tribe who lived and controlled the caravan routes between Egypt and Arabia in the southeast desert region of the Dead Sea. They conducted frequent raids on other settlements and many times they killed simply for pleasure. No insult to an Israelite could be greater than calling him "a friend of Amalek."

The Amalekites saw Moses and his rag tag band of followers and thought this would be a chance for some fun and profit. They did not know that these people were being led by God, and the wrath of God was about to be spent upon them. Moses commissions Joshua to make the battle preparations and tells him that he, Aaron, and Hur will be positioned on top of a nearby hill. Joshua was the great leader who brought God's people into the promised land after Moses died. He gained tremendous experience for future battles especially against the Canaanites.

The incredible stamina and persistence displayed by Moses in keeping his hands raised, with the support of Aaron and Hur, resulted in turning the tide of the battle. It is the courage and example of this one man that inspired a tired band of followers in the hot barren desert to turn certain defeat into a stunning upset of a victory. We need to look at our spiritual leaders in our churches and help them by supporting them too. We can be like Aaron and Hur and hold them up as they lead us in battle. We can really be warriors of the Lord by taking on some of the responsibilities of the parish community.

We can become strong, committed prayer warriors; and finally, we can offer some life-giving words of encouragement when the battle seems to rage in full fury. Our spiritual leaders need us to be like Aaron and Hur and in faith we need to call forth the spiritual giants like Moses from among our midst. The God of Moses is also our God, too. Let us persevere in battle and, like Moses, we too shall be lifted up in victory.

2 TIMOTHY 3:14-4:2

Timothy was faced with "watering" down his doctrine of faith. False teachers were trying to put pressure on him and the pressures of a growing ministry were heavy upon his spirit. Timothy's hometown of Lystra was where Paul was stoned and left for dead (Acts 14:19). Timothy was undergoing pressure, not only for being young and inexperienced, but also because Paul was his principal teacher.

Paul exhorts him to hold on, look to his past and hold to the basic teaching about Jesus that are eternally true. Today we are caught up with many false teachers who are trying to "waterdown" the Gospel and many of us are so busy, we don't even protest. We need to spend time every day thinking about the foundations of our faith and the great truths on which we build our lives.

Timothy was a second generation Christian and it was not because an evangelist preached a great sermon; it was because he was taught the holy scriptures when he was a child. The parents' work to teach the child should never be replaced by an evangelist or religious teacher. The teaching of the child by the parent is a sacred duty and we, as parents, should look to the church to help us fulfill this tremendous privilege.

We need to realize the Bible is not a collection of stories, fables, or myths or merely human ideas about God. It is not just a human book. God revealed his plan to godly men through the power of the Holy Spirit—men who then wrote down his message for his people (2 Peter 1:20,21). We believe that even though they used their own minds, talents, language, and style, they wrote what God inspired them to write.
Scripture is God's inspired Word, and we should read it and apply it to our lives. We can clearly see God speaking to us through his church which speaks in accordance with his holy Scripture. Jesus told us when he was tempted in the desert that he began his defense with "Scripture." God's Word will set us free today as it did yesterday and will forever and ever.

LUKE 18:1-8

Jesus began this passage by telling his disciples a story to bring home the power of persevering in their prayer life. He really wanted them to realize that all prayer is answered and they must not get discouraged and quit. The judge in this story was not a Jewish judge. Most ordinary Jewish problems were taken before the elders, not into public courts unless a special situation arose. A Jewish court had three judges, one for the defendant, one for the court, and one that was neutral. The judge in this story was probably appointed by Herod or the Romans, and they were well known as the "Robber Judges." He kept this woman coming back so many times because he expected her to pay a bribe. A widow symbolized the poor and defenseless, and the only weapon she had was persistence. In the end, fearing his loss of reputation, the judge was worn down; and the persistent widow won her case.

To be persistent in prayer does not mean endless repetition of long prayer sessions. Constant prayer means keeping our requests before him as we live for him day by day, always believing he will answer us. God may delay, but he always has a reason for his delay; and we must not confuse delay with neglect. As we, like the widow, persist in our prayer we grow in faith and hope. Our character and our faith are direct indication of the intensity of our prayer life.

We need to reflect on today's story and realize that if an evil judge can be worn down by the persistence of a defenseless widow, how much more will a person who persists in prayer be heard and rewarded by such a loving God as ours. We are told in scripture to call out to Jesus and he will never turn us away (John 6:37). The prayers of a righteous man have great power (James 5:16). Praying is talking to God, and meditating is listening to God, so be persistent in your praying and be persistent in your listening and you will grow tremendously in faith, hope, and love.

Application

In the first reading, we see the courage of Moses change defeat into victory over the Amalekites. Then we hear Timothy being challenged to draw on his childhood family training and Scripture when a crisis threatens. In the Gospel, we see the widow persevere and finally wear the judge down and win.

This week, let us read God's Word to someone who cannot read. This could be a small child, a handicapped person, or an elderly person in a rest home. Share with that person how God has protected you when you thought the battle was lost; and because of God, you also won.

THIRTIETH SUNDAY IN ORDINARY TIME - CYCLE C

BEFORE YOU BEGIN:

Pray and ask God to speak to you through His Holy Spirit. "THE PARACLETE, THE HOLY SPIRIT WHOM THE FATHER WILL SEND IN MY NAME, WILL INSTRUCT YOU IN EVERYTHING, AND REMIND YOU OF ALL THAT I TOLD YOU." (JOHN 14:26)

FIRST DAY   **Reread last week's readings.**

1. What was a helpful or new thought from the readings or from the homily you heard on Sunday?

2. From what you learned, what personal application did you choose to apply to your life this week?

SECOND DAY   **READ SIRACH 35:12-14, 16-18**   **FIRST READING**

("He who serves God willingly is heard.")

1. Of what is our God a God, and of what does he not know? Sirach 35:12.

2. What does he not accept? Deuteronomy 10:17, 2 Chronicles 19:7

3. Why does God have no favorites? Job 34:19.

Personal - How do you treat those in your family, at church, or at work without showing favoritism? Why do you think you should do this?

4. Whose cry does God hear? Sirach 35:13

5. Toward what two people is God not deaf? Sirach 35:14

6. Whose cry does the Lord hear and who should we not wrong? Exodus 22:21-22.

7. Whom does the Lord hear and what reaches the heavens? Sirach 35:16

8. What does the prayer of the lowly pierce and what does it not do till it reaches its goal? Sirach 35:17

9. What does the prayer of the lowly not do till the Most High responds? Sirach 35:18

10. What does the Most High judge do and who does he affirm? Sirach 35:18

Personal - In what way has God answered your prayer with justice, and in what way were you affirmed by it?

THIRD DAY   **READ 2 TIMOTHY 4:6-8, 16-18**   **SECOND READING**

("The Lord stood by my side and gave me strength.")

1.   Who is speaking, and to whom is he speaking in 2 Timothy 4:6-8, 16-18? 2 Timothy 1:1-2?

2.   What did he say was happening to him and was near him? 2 Timothy 4:6

3.   What has he fought, what has he finished, and what has he kept? 2 Timothy 4:7

4.   To what is Paul to bear witness? Acts 20:24

5.   From now on what awaits Paul, how does he refer to the Lord, and what will happen to him and all who have looked for the Lord's appearing with eager longing? 2 Timothy 4:8

6.   What happened to Paul at his first hearing of his case in court and what did he not do? 2 Timothy 4:16

7.   Who stood by his side and what did he give him? 2 Timothy 4:17

8.   What are we not to do and for what reason? Matthew 10:19-20.

9.   How was Paul saved from the lion's jaws? 2 Timothy 4:17

10.   What will the Lord continue to do and where will he bring him? 2 Timothy 4:18

11.   Who is to get all the glory? 2 Timothy 4:18, Romans 16:27

Personal - What is your reaction when friends or family abandon you when you stand up for your faith? Where do you look for your strength in a crisis? Hebrews 13:6.

FOURTH DAY   **READ LUKE 18:9-14**   **GOSPEL**

("O God, be merciful to me, a sinner.")

1.   To whom did the Lord address this parable? Luke 18:9

2.   What do the self-righteous do and what does God know? Luke 16:15

3.   What two men went up to the temple to pray and how was the Pharisee's head when he prayed? Luke 18:10-11

4.   For what did the Pharisee say he was thankful, who did he say he was not like, and what did he say he did? Luke 18:11-12

5.   What three things are important in the eyes of the Lord without neglecting the other? Matthew 23:23

6.   What did the tax collector do, and what did he say to the Lord? Luke 18:13

7.   What did Jesus say about the self-righteous and the sinner? Matthew 9:13.

8.   How did the tax collector go home and how did the Pharisee go home? Luke 18:14

9.   How do we become justified? Romans 5:8-11

10.   What will happen to everyone who exalts himself and what will happen to everyone who humbles himself? Luke 18:14

11.   Who is the greatest among you? Matthew 23:11-12

Personal – In what way do you approach the Lord? Examine your prayer life. What do you say to the Lord? In what way do you compare yourself with others? How do you really see yourself? Remember, God reads the heart. (Luke 16:15)

FIFTH DAY   **READ PSALM 34:2-3, 17-19, 23**

("*When the just cry out, the Lord hears them.*")

Read and meditate on Psalm 34:2-3, 17-19, 23.

What is the Lord saying to you personally through the Psalm?

How can you apply this to your life?

SIXTH DAY   **READ ALL OF THE COMMENTARY**

SIRACH 35:12-14, 16-18

This passage stresses that our God does not have favorites. His love for the rich is the same as it is for the poor. It is the same for the young and old, the healthy ones or the sickly ones. His love falls equally on the righteous and the unrighteous. Our God will not, under any circumstances, take a bribe (Deuteronomy 10:17). A just God is one who loves us because of who we are, not because of what we do. He loves the weak, yet he hears the cry of the oppressed. He always responds to our call for support.

Our calls of help do not fall on deaf ears (John 6:37). We are to be persistent, like the widow, in our prayers to our loving God. The petitions of all who call out to God are heard. He knows each one of us by name and knew us when we were formed in our mother's womb (Psalm 139). We are to respond to his answer with a contrite heart and humble spirit (Psalm 51). Many times we are tempted to give up and forget our petitions and become angry. We must remember that we have a God whose ways are not our ways.

Our God is a just God and he will answer us in his time and we must not become anxious (Philippians 4:6,7), rather we must become joyful and give him thanks and praise. A just God loves to bring freedom, and his justice brings love and peace. We need to reflect on this Scripture and remember that the God of Justice is the God of Love and the God of Love is Jesus Christ, our Lord and Savior.

2 TIMOTHY 4:6-8, 16-18

Paul is exhorting Timothy to keep his faith active and to be ready to take over as a leader rather than as an assistant. Paul tells Timothy that his time is running out and it won't be long before he, Paul, is in heaven. Paul was going to face death just like he was facing living in this world and that was with courage in the Lord. We need to ask ourselves some of these questions that Paul probably did. Is your life preparing you for death? Do you have a deep expectation of meeting Christ when you die?

We can all breathe a little easier because the "good news" is that salvation is not just for spiritual giants like "Paul," "Moses," or even Timothy. Rather it is for those who confess with their lips and believe in their heart that Jesus is Lord (Romans 10:10). Paul gave us these words to encourage us to go on, to keep up the good fight. He wanted us to train and become even better. No matter what the difficulty, we must always remember that the Spirit within us is greater than he that is in the world (1 John 4:4), and we must keep fighting and continue in the race.

We will realize completely, when we are finally at home in heaven with our wonderful Lord Jesus, that the fight and the race were well worth it. Timothy probably did not feel all that strong, with his leader in prison and his church still reeling from exhaustion and expansion. We need to trust in Jesus, as Paul did, and our Lord will use our repentant hearts in a powerful way. We need to remember that God always gives us the strength to do whatever he has commanded, and he has commanded us to go forth and preach his Word. He has called us and commissioned us to evangelize the world (Matthew 28:19).

LUKE 18:9-14

This passage deals with the quality of our prayer life and not the quantity of it. When we come to pray before God, the question is not, "Am I as good as my fellow-men?" The question is, "Am I as good as God?" True prayer can only come from setting our lives beside the life of God. We may do well to remember that we are one of a great legion of sinning, suffering, sorrowing humanity, that comes occasionally to kneel before the throne of God's mercy. Before we can say, "I am glad I am not like that pompous Pharisee," let us all remember that no man who is proud can pray. It is told that the gate of heaven is so low that no one can enter it unless one is on one's knees.

In today's Gospel we see the men in the temple praying. The devout religious people were always in the temple about 9:00 a.m., noon, and 3:00 p.m. These were the times when most of the community went up to the temple. The story deals with only two of them, one a highly respected church-goer called a Pharisee; the other man was called a tax collector, someone of poor social standing. The tax collector was a symbol of dishonesty, lying, and cheating. The Pharisee began telling God how much he was doing for him. The Pharisee did not really go to pray; he went to inform God how good he was. The tax collector, on the other hand, stood in back of the temple and wouldn't even lift his eyes up to God because he knew that he was a sinner. His prayer was very simple and very direct: "O God be merciful to me, the sinner."

Let us not pray like the Pharisee, because self-righteousness is dangerous Pride leads to sin, and the wages of sin are death (Romans 6:23). The tax collector's prayer should be our prayer, because Jesus hears our cry of unworthiness and repentance (Psalm 51:10). Let us call out to him to cleanse our heart and to give us a repentant spirit, and he will do that. Prayer is two persons – God and man – telling each other how much they love each other. God loves you and wants you to be a prayerful person.

Application

The first reading tells us that God does not have any favorites. The second reading reveals that we should update our spiritual inventory on a regular basis. The Gospel shows that the quality of a prayer life is far more important than its quantity.

Let us spend some quiet time alone with the Lord everyday this week and listen very carefully to his plan for our life (John 10:10). God wants each one of us to have an abundant grace-filled life. He wants us to call out to him in deep sincerity, and he will heal us. Let your family see you as one in prayerful communion with God.

THIRTY-FIRST SUNDAY IN ORDINARY TIME - CYCLE C

BEFORE YOU BEGIN:

Pray and ask God to speak to you through His Holy Spirit. "THE PARACLETE, THE HOLY SPIRIT WHOM THE FATHER WILL SEND IN MY NAME, WILL INSTRUCT YOU IN EVERYTHING, AND REMIND YOU OF ALL THAT I TOLD YOU." (JOHN 14:26)

FIRST DAY   **Reread last week's readings.**

1.   What was a helpful or new thought from the readings or from the homily you heard on Sunday?

2.   From what you learned, what personal application did you choose to apply to your life this week?

SECOND DAY READ WISDOM 11:22-12:1 FIRST READING

("For you love all things that are.")

1.   What two things is the whole universe like? Wisdom 11:22

2.   What does God have on all and what can he do? Wisdom 11:23

3.   What does God overlook and for what reason? Wisdom 11:23

4.   Of what is God not unaware and for what does he give man space? Wisdom 12:10

5.   What does God call men everywhere to do? Acts 17:30

6.   What does God do to all things that are, what does he loathe, and for what reason? Wisdom 11:24

7.   What is the Lord to all people and toward all his works? Psalm 145:9

8.   Unless God does what, how can anything remain or be preserved? Wisdom 11:25

9.   What does God do to all things, for what reason and of what is he a lover? Wisdom 11:26

10.   What is in all things? Wisdom 12:1

11.   What does the spirit of the Lord fill and what does he know? Wisdom 1:7

Personal – How have I accepted God's love for me? In what way have I overlooked the sins of a family member, friend, or co-worker and given them an opportunity to repent and thus show my love for them?

THIRD DAY   READ 2 THESSALONIANS 1:11-2:2   SECOND READING

("We pray for you always.")

1. Who is speaking and to whom is he speaking in 2 Thessalonians 1:11-2:2?
    2 Thessalonians 1:1

2. What do they do always for the church and for what reason? 2 Thessalonians 1:11

3. How does God fulfill every honest intention and work of faith? 2 Thessalonians 1:11

4. Who begets (brings forth) in you any measure of desire or achievement?
    Philippians 2:13

5. Who may be glorified in you and you in him and how is this done?
    2 Thessalonians 1:12

6. On the question of whose coming, and of who is being gathered with him, how is
    Paul addressing the brothers? 2 Thessalonians 2:1

7. What two things is he begging them not to let happen so easily? 2 Thessalonians 2:2

8. What three ways is he saying not to be swayed into believing that the day of the
    Lord is here? 2 Thessalonians 2:2

9. How is the Lord going to come again and what will happen to those who have died
    in Christ? 1 Thessalonians 4:13-16

10. What will happen to those who are living, the survivors and what are we to do with
    this message? 1 Thessalonians 4:17

Personal - In what way have you been preparing for the Lord's second coming?

FOURTH DAY   READ LUKE 19:1-10   GOSPEL

("The Son of Man has come to search out and save what is lost")

1. As Jesus entered Jericho who was there, what was his name, what position did he
    hold, and what economic status did he hold? Luke 19:1-2

2. Who came to be baptized by John the Baptist and what did he tell them?
    Luke 3:12-14

3. Which one of Jesus' disciples was a tax collector? Matthew 9:9

4. What was Zacchaeus doing, why did he want to do this and what prevented him
    from doing this? Luke 19:3

5. What did he first do and when that did not work, what did he then do? Luke 19:4

6. What did Jesus do when he came to the spot where Zacchaeus was and what did he
    say to him? Luke 19:5

7. How did Zacchaeus descend and how did he welcome Jesus? Luke 19:6

8. When this was observed what did everyone begin to murmur? Luke 19:7

9.   What did Zacchaeus do and what did he say to the Lord? Luke 19:8

10.   What did Jesus say to him? Luke 19:9

11.   Why did the Son of Man come? Luke 19:10

Personal - In what way have you repaid anyone you may have defrauded? In what way has Jesus come to search you out and save you personally? Share with someone in your family or with a friend.

FIFTH DAY   **READ PSALM 145:1-2, 8-11, 13-14**

("The Lord is good to all.")

Read and meditate on Psalm 145:1-2, 8-11, 13-14.

What is the Lord saying to you personally through the Psalm?

How can you apply this to your life?

SIXTH DAY   **READ ALL OF THE COMMENTARY**

WISDOM 11:22-12:1

This passage forces us to reflect on how much we are loved and protected by God. We are being told that this awesome universe is like being compared to a small particle used for weighing on sensitive scales. In God there is so much more and yet our universe is as precious to him as early morning dew. We hear about a God who is so majestic that even though he can do all things, he loves being merciful. Wisdom is so precious because it helps us to understand God's incredible love for us.

God doesn't miss anything, he sees our failures and yet he constantly encourages us to go forward. He gives us so much room to repent and to enjoy his kingdom (Mark 1:15). It is so hard for man to understand God's love, because God loves everything that he has created. God does not make junk, we are not junk, and God will never make junk. That is why he loves us always. God loves us so much he gave us his only Son, so that all who believe in him will not perish but have eternal life (John 3:16). Do you really believe that he loved you so much he died knowing that you would be sinning (Romans 5:8)? He did.

Wisdom is fear of the Lord, not a fear of punishment but fear of offending his love and goodness, because true love drives out fear (1 John 4:18). God's love for us is complete in Jesus. He gives us his command, love one another as I have loved you (John 15:12). Wisdom is knowing that the Spirit of the Lord is given for all men and that the Spirit will instruct us in everything (John 14:26). The Holy Spirit is all embracing and this means that the arms of Christ were stretched out wide on the cross of Calvary so that you and I can have the incredible privilege of choosing life or death. The wise person will choose life; the fool will choose death.

2 THESSALONIANS 1:11-2:2

Paul is now encouraging the people because they had been going through a time of turmoil and confusion about the "last days." The thought of the world coming to an end and Jesus coming back led many to give up the responsibilities of daily life. Some of the people did not want to go back to work, some did not want to continue to meet their financial obligations. Paul is telling them in this passage that their life and the way that they live is a reflection of our Lord and Savior Jesus Christ. Paul also tells them that God calls us to live in honor and have faith in his promise. His promise is that all who believe in him will not perish but instead have eternal life with him.

Paul goes on to tell them that the day which the Lord is to come back is not yet known, but his Spirit will be within us until then (John 14:26). We hear today many new ways to "talk the talk" and "walk the walk." We hear and see quite a bit of the "new age" theology which calls us to become gods unto ourselves. We really need to reflect on the seduction of the age that Paul spoke about in verse three. When the Church marries the age or times, the church quickly becomes a widow.

Paul is telling them, as he is telling us, that there is only one way to eternal life, and that is through Jesus; and that only God knows when the end days are near. Our faith depends only on the living presence of the power of God in our lives. We are to live our lives as if this is the day that Jesus comes to take us home to the Father.

LUKE 19:1-10

Once again we see Jesus being the classic minister. Jesus knew full well what the local townspeople thought about tax collectors and knew that his actions would provoke a tremendous amount of controversy. He wanted them to love the sinner and hate the sin, but not hate the sinner as well as the sin. He chose to show them that by having dinner with Zacchaeus he was open to healing a person's heart no matter what his station in life.

Zacchaeus knew that the people thought that he was a crook as most tax collectors were in those days (Luke 5:27-32). Zacchaeus was wealthy but not happy. He probably was very lonely because he had chosen a way that made him an outcast. He no doubt had heard of Jesus and his love for outcasts like tax collectors and sinners like himself, and wondered if he had any "good news" for him. Despised and hated by the local town people, Zacchaeus was reaching out for the love and acceptance of God. One has to remember that Zacchaeus was small in stature and he took a great risk to be seen alone in public. He could not see over the crowd so he finally found a tree that he could climb and see Jesus as he walked by.

Can you imagine the thrill that went through Zacchaeus when he heard Jesus' invitation. He literally jumped out of the tree in joy and shock and proclaimed to the community that he was a changed man. He knew that Jesus was risking the rejection of the crowd by saying that he wanted to stay at the home of a known sinner. Jesus does that today with you and me. He tells us that he wants to stay in our house, which means in our hearts. Zacchaeus then made a decision; he decided to love, because he had experienced the incredible gift of God's love. Because of this love he then decided to give half of his goods to the poor. In his restitution he went far beyond what the law required. Only if robbery was a pre-meditated violent act of destruction was a fourfold giving back necessary (Exodus 22:1).

Zacchaeus showed that he was a changed man by his actions not just his words. Zacchaeus was a man who had repented because of love not force. A man or woman who repents, changes completely. Repentance is not only saying "I am sorry." Zacchaeus' testimony would have been completely worthless if it was not backed up by deeds. We should reflect on today's story and see where, in our lives, repentance is needed.

Like Zacchaeus, we need to have Jesus reside in our hearts in order to love and be loved (John 15:12). This passage ends with Jesus telling us that he came to search out and save the lost. Zacchaeus was a Jew, a child of Abraham, and the Lord came to him and brought him back into the kingdom. We have that same loving God who is always ready to come to our "house" and bring us home, too.

Application

The first reading tells us how much we are loved and protected by God in spite of our selfishness. The second reading shows that the way we live is a reflection of what we believe. The Gospel demonstrates through the story about Zacchaeus that actions speak louder than words. Repentance means change.
Pick one specific bad habit and in prayer and faith work on it for this week. Testimony of words without action is worthless, so share with someone special your progress. The way that you talk to your children tells that they are either special or a burden. Let your family know that you are submitting yourself to the Lord and are giving him permission to change you. It works. He changed Zacchaeus and he wants to change you.

THIRTY-SECOND SUNDAY IN ORDINARY TIME - CYCLE C

BEFORE YOU BEGIN:

Pray and ask God to speak to you through His Holy Spirit. "THE PARACLETE, THE HOLY SPIRIT WHOM THE FATHER WILL SEND IN MY NAME, WILL INSTRUCT YOU IN EVERYTHING, AND REMIND YOU OF ALL THAT I TOLD YOU." (JOHN 14:26)

FIRST DAY   **Reread last week's readings.**

1.   What was a helpful or new thought from the readings or from the homily you heard on Sunday?

2.   From what you learned, what personal application did you choose to apply to your life this week?

SECOND DAY   **READ 2 MACCABEES 7:1-2, 9-14**   **FIRST READING**

("We are ready to die rather than transgress
the laws of our ancestors.")

1.   How many brothers were arrested and who was with them? 2 Maccabees 7:1

2.   What did the king do to them? Why did he do this and of what was this in violation? 2 Maccabees 7:1

3.   What did one of the brothers say in speaking for the other brothers? 2 Maccabees 7:2

4.   What would they rather do than transgress the laws of whom? 2 Maccabees 7:2

5.   After killing the first brother what did they do to the second brother and what did he say? 2 Maccabees 7:7-9

6.   Who is the King of the world and for what will he raise us up? 1 Timothy 6:14-15, 2 Maccabees 7:9

7.   What happened to the third brother and what did he say? 2 Maccabees 7:10-11

8.   At what did the king and his attendants marvel, and for what reason? 2 Maccabees 7:12

9.   What happened to the fourth brother and what did he choose to do at the hands of men? 2 Maccabees 7:13-14

10.   What was the fourth brother's God-given hope and what did he say there would not be for the torturers? 2 Maccabees 7:14

11.   When we die who gives back both breath and life and for what reason? 2 Maccabees 7:23

12.   What does the Son, Jesus, do? John 5:19-30.

Personal - In what way have you been willing to suffer for your belief in Jesus? What have you said lately to those around you that took courage to say to them? Pray and ask God to give you the courage to stand up for what you believe in.

THIRD DAY   **READ 2 THESSALONIANS 2:16-3:5**   **SECOND READING**

*("...console your hearts and strengthen them for
every good work and word.")*

1.   What did God our Father in his mercy give us? 2 Thessalonians 2:16

2.   What does God do for your heart and for what reason does he do this? 2 Thessalonians 2:17

3.   For what reason did Paul and the others ask the brothers to pray for them? 2 Thessalonians 3:1

4.   What is another reason that Paul asks others to pray for them? Colossians 4:3-4

5.   Paul asks them to pray that they be delivered from whom? 2 Thessalonians 3:2

6.   What is it that not every man has and that the Lord always keeps? 2 Thessalonians 3:2-3

7.   What two things does the Lord do for you against the evil one? 2 Thessalonians 3:3

8.   How does God strengthen us? Psalm 119:28, Ephesians 3:16

9.   How do we receive this strength? Acts 3:16

10.   About what are Paul and the others confident in the Lord? 2 Thessalonians 3:4

11.   In what are they asking the Lord to rule their hearts? 2 Thessalonians 3:5

12.   How do we speak and of what is God the tester? 1 Thessalonians 2:4

Personal - In what way has God strengthened you for every good work and word through his Word and the teaching of the Holy Spirit this past week? Be specific.

FOURTH DAY   **READ LUKE 20:27-38**   **GOSPEL**

*("God is not the God of the dead but of the living.
All are alive for him.")*

1.   Who came forward to pose a problem to Jesus and what did they claim? Luke 20:27-28

2.   What was the problem they proposed to Jesus? Luke 20:28-33

3. What did Jesus say children of this age do? Luke 20:34

4. What do those judged worthy of a place in the age to come and of resurrection from the dead do in regard to marriage? Luke 20:35

5. What do those judged worthy become like and what will not happen to them? Luke 20:36

6. Who are the ones that will rise? Luke 20:36

7. What did Moses in the passage about the bush show? Luke 20:37

8. Who does not have God and who does have God? Luke 20:38

9. For what are we alive? Luke 20:38

10. What does Corinthians say about being raised up from the dead? 1 Corinthians 15:12-19

11. What does it take to believe in Christ's resurrection? Acts 20:21.

Personal – In what way have you already been resurrected and to what do you look forward? In what way do others see the resurrected Christ living in you?

FIFTH DAY   READ PSALM 17:1, 5-6, 8, 15

("Keep me as the apple of your eye; hide me in
the shadow of your wings...")

Read and meditate on Psalm 17:1, 5-6, 8, 15.

What is the Lord saying to you personally through the Psalm?

How can you apply this to your life?

SIXTH DAY   READ ALL OF THE COMMENTARY

2 MACCABEES 7:1-2, 9-14

This passage has a powerful message of justice and resurrection. Can you imagine how horrible it must have been for that mother to watch each one of her seven sons being tortured and then being executed? Can you just imagine the pain in her heart as she leans closely to her last remaining son and encouraging him to save his life by giving it up for God (Matthew 16:25)? What tremendous courage this mother, who is herself later tortured and murdered, and her sons had. We need to reflect on this story.

The fear of pain and death was not in their responses because the hunger and thirst to be at one with God was greater. We must not dismiss this passage as an exaggerated story told to make a point. These young men loved life as much as you or I do. They dreamed about their futures just like you and I do. They knew that to refuse this command meant torture and death. Could we do the same? Today, here in our society, we are being threatened with such a barrage of filth in our movies, television, magazines and now even in our home video tape recordings. The level of filth and profit is so high that like Habakkuk (1:2), we cry out, how long will I call for help, and you do not hear?

The degree of brutality has never been equalled as it has here in the United States when we look at the 25 million unborn babies we have murdered. Our nation is being savagely attacked, and our throats are being slashed by the incredibly overwhelming use of drugs. The primary motive for this plague of evil is greed and profit. Where are men like these brothers who will stand up and protest against these outrages? Where are these men who will die if they have to? The questions upon us today are: Do we really believe in the Resurrection? Do we really believe that Jesus died to make all men free and live forever with him? I pray that our nation will come forth and give us men and women like the spiritual giants in today's passage. I pray with confidence because he tells us that he will never turn away anyone who calls out to him (John 6:37).

2 THESSALONIANS 2:16-3:5

Paul knew that the pressures of persecutions, apathy among the people, worldliness of the people and false teachers would cause a wavering of the faith and a looseness with the truth. He exhorted them to stand firm in the teachings of the Lord Jesus Christ passed on to us through scripture and the teachings of the church. We, too, are being confronted with these temptations that try to turn us away from God. We need to more than ever hold onto the truth. This is found in the teachings of Jesus, simply because our lives depend on it.

We must never forget the reality of his life and love. Paul is not only exhorting the people, but he is also warning them about the dangers of evil men in their midst. He is telling them that beneath the surface calm of daily living is the struggle that goes on among invisible spiritual powers. The question we need to ask ourselves is, do we really believe that? Our battle is not against human forces but against the principalities and powers, the rulers of this world of darkness, the evil spirits in regions above (Ephesians 6:12). These evil rulers, satanic beings and evil princes of darkness are not people, but fallen angels over whom Satan has control. They are not fantasies; they are very real. We need only to look around and see how the drugs are tearing Americans' throats open.

The pornography industry is colossal and it is in every city in the United States. Abortion or murder is accepted and legally protected in all parts of this great nation. Is there any doubt that these demons of Satan are active in these abominations that are crippling our nation? When we accept Jesus as our Lord and Savior and follow the teachings of our Catholic Church, Satan becomes our arch-enemy. He is out to kill us, and we must remember that the Spirit within us is greater than he that is in the world (1 John 4:4). Jesus is the only answer to our problems and he has won the victory over Satan for us. He is the one who will strengthen us and guard us against the evil one (2 Thess. 3:3). Let us in the Lord follow the teachings of the church with the same obedience and confidence that Paul had in the Thessalonians.

LUKE 20:27-38

The Sadducees were a group of conservative religious leaders who honored only the Pentateuch (Genesis to Deuteronomy). They did not believe in the resurrection of the dead because they could not find any mention of it in their first five books of the Old Testament. They tried to trick Jesus with a question that always bothered the Pharisees. Jesus answered their real question about resurrection after he addressed their other question on marriage. Jesus based his response on the writings of Moses. The Sadducees respected Moses so much that they honored only the books that dealt with him and his ancestors.

Jesus knew that they respected Moses and his answers upheld belief in the resurrection. Jesus' answer on marriage didn't mean that people will not recognize their spouses when they get to heaven; he meant that heaven is not an extension of life as we know it here on earth. Jesus talks about those who are counted worthy of being raised from the dead to heavenly life. We might ask ourselves: What does it mean to be worthy of being raised to heavenly life? We are told that if we believe in Jesus Christ, we shall not perish, rather we shall have eternal life (John 3:16).

Jesus told them that they can't compare what we have on earth with what we will have in heaven. He answered their question about "the resurrection" by showing that the writings of Moses proved that there is a resurrection. Moses' God is the God of Abraham, Isaac, and Jacob. This means that the Lord is some person's God, which means that person is alive, not dead. God sees all men who believe in him as living children of him.

We need to ask ourselves this question: Do we believe in the resurrection? Will we rise from the dead like Jesus did? Will we some day be reunited in heaven with all of our loved ones who died before us? We are told in Scripture to confess with our lips and believe in our hearts that Jesus is Lord and then we are his children and we will be with him forever. The real question for the Sadducees was: "Is the Resurrection real?" God said "YES" when he said that all who believe in his Son will not die but live forever in heaven (John 3:16).

Application

The first reading shows that hunger and thirst for God was much stronger than the fear of pain and death. The second reading calls us to stand firm in the teaching of scripture and the teachings of our beloved church. The gospel tells us that heaven is not an extension of life as we know it here on earth.

This week, let all who come in contact with you see that the message of justice and resurrection is alive in you. Let your prayers be heard in your home. Do not be afraid to give thanks and praise to God for something that happens to you in public. Look around and see where opportunities to witness are present. Your family will see and experience this courage and follow your example.

THIRTY-THIRD SUNDAY IN ORDINARY TIME - CYCLE C

BEFORE YOU BEGIN:

Pray and ask God to speak to you through His Holy Spirit. "THE PARACLETE, THE HOLY SPIRIT WHOM THE FATHER WILL SEND IN MY NAME, WILL INSTRUCT YOU IN EVERYTHING, AND REMIND YOU OF ALL THAT I TOLD YOU." (JOHN 14:26)

FIRST DAY   **Reread last week's readings.**

1. What was a helpful or new thought from the readings or from the homily you heard on Sunday?

2. From what you learned, what personal application did you choose to apply to your life this week?

SECOND DAY   **READ MALACHI 3:19-20**   **FIRST READING**

("...There will arise the sun of justice with its healing rays...")

1. What will the day be like that is coming? Malachi 3:19

2. What will happen to all the proud and evildoers? Malachi 3:19

3. How will that day leave them? Malachi 3:19

4. Who says this will happen? Malachi 3:19

5. What do the proud and evildoers do? Malachi 3:5, 13-14

6. For those who fear the name of the Lord, what will arise and with what kind of rays? Malachi 3:20

7. What will you do? Malachi 3:20

8. What do those who fear the Lord do? Malachi 3:16

9. What is the difference between the proud, the evildoer and the one who fears the Lord? Malachi 3:18

10. To fear the Lord brings what and what does it avoid? Proverbs 14:27

Personal - Examine your conscience over this past week. What ways have you served the Lord and what ways have you not served him? Do you have one foot in the kingdom and one outside? Read Revelation 3:15-16.

THIRD DAY   **READ 2 THESSALONIANS 3:7-12**   **SECOND READING**

("...That we might present ourselves as an example for you to imitate.")

1. Who is speaking? To whom are they speaking? What are they asking them to do in 2 Thessalonians 3:7? 2 Thessalonians 1:1

2. Why were they asking the Thessalonians to imitate them? 2 Thessalonians 3:6–8

3. What is the workman worth? Matthew 10:10

4. How did they want to present themselves and for what reason? 2 Thessalonians 3:9

5. What was the rule that they laid down while they were with them? 2 Thessalonians 3:10

6. With what did they tell them to work, and for what reason? 1 Thessalonians 4:11–12

7. What did Paul and the others hear that some of them were not doing and how were they acting? 2 Thessalonians 3:11

8. What happens when you don't keep busy but waste time? 1 Timothy 5:13

9. What did Paul and the others urge them strongly in the Lord Jesus Christ to do and how were they to do it? 2 Thessalonians 3:12

10. What should we remember when working? Colossians 3:23

Personal – If you are a student, if you are a homemaker or working on a job, or if you are retired, what has your attitude been towards the work you are doing? What kind of example are you to outsiders? Reflect on this.

FOURTH DAY   **READ LUKE 21:5–19 GOSPEL**

("All will hate you because of me,…")

1. About what were some people speaking? Luke 21:5

2. What did Jesus say to them about the things they were contemplating? Luke 21:6

3. What two things did they ask Jesus? Luke 21:7

4. Who did Jesus say not to follow and what would they be saying? Luke 21:8

5. What is bound to happen first about which we are not to become perturbed? Does the end immediately follow this? Luke 21:9

6. What did Jesus continue to say to them? Luke 21:10–11

7. What did he say would happen to them before all this took place? Luke 21:12

8. What action concerning his name would result in persecution and trial? Acts 5:28

9. What will we be brought to do? What are we not to do and for what reason? Luke 21:13–15

10. With what did Stephen speak when engaged in debate? Acts 6:9–10

11. Who will deliver us up and what will happen to some of us? Luke 21:16

12. What will all do to us because of Jesus and, yet, what will happen to the hair on our heads? Luke 21:17–18

13. How will we save our lives? Luke 21:19

14. Read the following scriptures and write out what they say about patient endurance: Hebrews 3:14 Hebrews 6:11-12 Hebrews 10:36

Personal - In what way do you see yourself being persecuted because of the name of Jesus? In what way are you persecuting others for their obedience to God? Where do you stand?

FIFTH DAY   **READ PSALM 98:5-9**

("He will rule the world with justice and the peoples with equity.")

Read and meditate on Psalm 98:5-9.

What is the Lord saying to you personally through the Psalm?

How can you apply this to your life?

SIXTH DAY   **READ ALL OF THE COMMENTARY**

MALACHI 3:19-20

We read in this passage that the day of judgment is coming like a blazing furnace for those who have turned their backs on God. Malachi exhorted and warned the people about being obedient to the Lord or facing terrible consequences. A blazing furnace is white hot and its function is to burn impurities out of precious metal. It require a hot, dangerous and all consuming fire. Malachi compared judgment day to this.

Many people were disobedient to God's will and dishonored his name (Mal.1:6). They offered false worship (Mal.1:7-14), and they led others into sin (Mal.2:7-9). Many became arrogant and proud, and they called "evil" good (Mal.2:17). These were the people who Malachi promised would be reduced to stubble on Judgment Day. We need to reflect on our own lifestyle in these troubled times and see if this warning applies to us also. The name of God is mocked and profaned on television and in the movies with great regularity. Idolatry is as common today in this country as it ever was in the time of Abraham. Today many pay homage to the god of sports, television, pornography, abortion, money, and power. That blazing furnace is as real today as it was in the time of Malachi.

Malachi was not a prophet of doom, and he left them with a strong message of hope and forgiveness. He gave us the image of a loving God who will be like a healing warmth of the sun to those that repent and come back to love and obey him. God wills that no man perish. John the Baptist told about the coming of Jesus and said he was like the dawn about to break with light for those in sin and darkness (Luke 1:76-79). Jesus is the light of the world, and we are called to bring that light everywhere.

2 THESSALONIANS 3:7-12

Paul takes a strong stand against laziness in the church leaders and in the people themselves. He strongly exhorts them to be responsible and hard working Christians. Paul certainly did not think that working or insisting that people who should work was an attack on their integrity or dignity. Paul thought that a person should make the most of his time and talents. Paul exhorted them to provide for themselves and for others as well. Paul stresses very strongly how important example is to a community.

We need to stress that today more than ever to our young people and especially our children. What kind of example are you setting? Do people see you as a hard working, kind and patient Christian? Do you spend too much time watching television? Do you spend time alone every day with the Lord in quiet prayer? Do you read and study Scripture every day? These are the type of examples we need to set for others.

Paul really admonishes the people about wasting time gossiping, a sin against the fifth commandment: "Thou shalt not kill." You kill a person socially, emotionally, and even spiritually inch by inch when you are gossiping about him. Gossips breed distrust, division, discouragement and, finally, despair in the body of Christ. Gossip, in some cases, is exciting to hear; and it means those who are hearing it feel like insiders. Instead of building up, gossiping tears down. Jesus calls us to love others as he has loved us (John 15:12). We cannot be tearing someone down through gossip and think we are loving, obedient Christians. We need to pray to the Lord so that he will heal us of this miserable, bad habit. Our prayers are powerful because our Lord listens and heals (James 5:16).

LUKE 21:5-19

The temple the disciples were admiring was not Solomon's temple. Solomon's temple was destroyed by the Babylonians in the sixth century B.C. The temple in Jesus' day was the one built by Herod the Great, begun in 20 B.C. It was much larger than the earlier temples. This temple, after many restorations, was destroyed completely in 70 A.D. by the Roman army. The disciples were commenting on the beauty and durability of the temple. Jesus tells them the temple will be knocked down and it will become a pile of rubble. They wanted to know when this terrible event would happen. Jesus warned them about false Messiahs and natural disasters. He told them that he would never leave them and that he would be with them even unto the end of time (Matthew 28:16-20). he warned them about persecution and being dragged into court because of being associated with him. We see that happening today to those involved in a movement to stop abortion by blocking the entrance into the abortion clinics. Many of the protestors have been arrested and hauled into court. A tremendous witness is taking place in our country, so many people have come forward and are being imprisoned for the sake of Christ. Jesus' warning and his promises still apply to us as we look forward to his return. In response to their question of "knowing when the end of the age will come," Jesus stated that they should be less concerned about the date and more concerned about being prepared. We are called to live God's way constantly so that no matter when he comes, we will be prepared. The early church thrived despite incredible persecution. In the early second century the blood of the Christians was considered the seeds of future believers. We need to remember that Jesus' words are as true today as they were yesterday. Today we have many families who have turned against each other and suffer great persecution at the hands of their own loved ones. We can be assured that no matter how rough the times may get, he is with us, and his Spirit even teaches us what to say in time of trial.

Jesus tells us, "Not a hair of your head will be harmed." He means that none of his followers will suffer spiritual or eternal loss. You may lose all of your possessions here on earth, you may be beaten, robbed and even put to death, but you will be saved forever and ever.

Application

In the first reading we are choosing to be either hot or cold. In the second reading we are called to be a role model. In the Gospel we heard that we need to take a stand with God or against him. Let us choose Christ in every situation we encounter in our homes, church, and jobs. Before we take action in any situation this week let us ask ourselves, "Am I compromising what I believe in by doing this?"

THIRTY-FOURTH SUNDAY IN ORDINARY TIME - CYCLE C

BEFORE YOU BEGIN:

Pray and ask God to speak to you through His Holy Spirit. "THE PARACLETE, THE HOLY SPIRIT WHOM THE FATHER WILL SEND IN MY NAME, WILL INSTRUCT YOU IN EVERYTHING, AND REMIND YOU OF ALL THAT I TOLD YOU." (JOHN 14:26)

FIRST DAY   **Reread last week's readings.**

1. What was a helpful or new thought from the readings or from the homily you heard on Sunday?

2. From what you learned, what personal application did you choose to apply to your life this week?

SECOND DAY   **READ 2 SAMUEL 5:1-3**   **FIRST READING**

("You shall shepherd my people Israel...")

1. Who came to David and what did they say to him? 2 Samuel 5:1

2. Where was David? If you can locate this place on a bible map, give location. 2 Samuel 5:1

3. Who led the Israelites out and brought them back? 2 Samuel 5:2

4. Who did the tribes of Israel say spoke to David and what did he say to him? 2 Samuel 5:2, Ezekiel 34:23-24

Personal – Who, then, do you think appoints those to shepherd the people? Are you following the One whom God has appointed King of kings for all times?

5. To whom was David speaking? 2 Samuel 24:17

Personal – How does God speak to you and how do you speak to him as David did?

6. What will happen to the shepherd God has appointed that does not listen and submit to the words of God? Zechariah 11:17 and Jeremiah 25:34-36

7. Who is our Great Shepherd? Read and write out the following scriptures: Genesis 48:15 Psalm 23:1 John 10:6-7, 11 John 10:16

8. Who was made king of Israel? With whom did the king make an agreement before and who anointed him? 2 Samuel 5:3

Personal – What do you see as the difference between a good shepherd, a good king, and a bad king? What are you?

THIRD DAY   **READ COLOSSIANS 1:12-20**   **SECOND READING**

("Through him we have redemption, the forgiveness for our sins.")

1. For what are we to give thanks to the Father? Colossians 1:12

2. What does it mean "the saints in light" and who is the light? John 8:12

3. Who rescued us and from whom did he rescue us? Colossians 1:13

4. Who is the power of darkness? Acts 26:18

5. When he rescued us, where did he bring us? Colossians 1:13

6. What do we receive through Jesus? Colossians 1:14, 1 Peter 2:9

Personal - Have you been redeemed? Have you asked the Lord to cleanse you and make you whole? Reread verse 14. This is a promise from God. Write out this verse and meditate on it.

7. Who is the image of our God we cannot see and who is the first-born of all creatures? Colossians 1:15

8. Read and write out: Psalm 89:28 John 1:3 John 1:18

Personal - How do you see God the Father? How has Jesus revealed him to you personally? Is he holding a rod ready to punish you or is he gentle, kind and forgiving? As you see Jesus, you see the Father.

10. What was created in him and where was it created? Colossians 1:16, 1 Corinthians 8:6

11. For what reason was all created? Colossians 1:16

12. How does everything continue its being? Colossians 1:17

13. Who began the church and who is the head of it? Ephesians 1:22, Revelation 1:5, Colossians 1:18

14. Onto whom did Christ pass this headship? Matthew 16:18

15. How have we been reconciled with the Father? Colossians 1:19-20

Personal - Have you allowed Jesus to wash you with his blood and bring you to peace with the Father? What changes can you see in your life since you have done this?

FOURTH DAY   **READ LUKE 23:35-43 GOSPEL**

("This is the King of the Jews")

1. Who stood there watching? Who was jeering at Jesus, and what were they saying? Luke 23:35

2. Was there anyone else making fun of Jesus? What did they offer him, and what were they telling him to do? Luke 23:36-37

Personal - Why do you think Jesus did not come down off the cross and save himself from this agonizing death? Luke 22:42

3. Was it the Father's will that Jesus, his only begotten Son, die on the cross and why? Read and write out: 1 Timothy 2:4 John 12:47 John 3:16 John 10:10

4. If Jesus was obedient to the Father and hung on the cross and suffered from the weight of our sins in order to save us, what must we do? John 1:12, Revelation 3:20

5. How are we to follow Jesus' example? Matthew 16:24-25, Mark 8:35, Luke 9:24

6. Was it through any effort of our own that we have been saved? Titus 3:4-5

7. What was the inscription written over Jesus' head? Luke 23:38

Personal - How have you made Jesus your King of Kings and Lord of Lords? 1 Timothy 1:17, Revelation 17:14, Revelation 19:16

8. What did the one criminal say to Jesus in Luke 23:39?

9. About whom was he concerned? Luke 23:39

10. What did the other criminal do and say? Luke 23:40-41

Personal - In what way are you like either one of the criminals? Who was denying himself and how do you deny yourself?

11. What did he say to Jesus in verse 42 of Luke 23 and what was Jesus' reply?

12. Read Matthew 25:33-34, 41. How can this be compared to Luke 23:39-40?

Personal - Are you the one on the left or the right? In what ways have you denied yourself this week for your spouse, children, friends, neighbor, business associates, or school friends?

FIFTH DAY   **READ PSALM 122:1-5**

("Give thanks to the name of the Lord.")

Read and meditate on Psalm 122:1-5.

What is the Lord saying to you personally through the Psalm?

How can you apply this to your life?

SIXTH DAY   **READ ALL OF THE COMMENTARY**

2 SAMUEL 5:1-3

David was finally anointed king over all Israel, and this was a fulfillment of God's promise. He first was anointed king in private by Samuel (1 Samuel 16:13). David was just a teenager then and spent many years in the service of King Saul. David was thirty years old when he was crowned King of Judah, which was the southern half of the Promised Land (2 Samuel 2:4). He was crowned king of the whole country at the age of thirty-seven and reigned for forty years.

When David was young and an outlaw, his future looked very bleak, but God's promise to make him king was now fulfilled. David had to wait very patiently for God's promise to be fulfilled, even though he had been promised the kingship many years earlier. We need to reflect on the patience and humility that David practiced in his long wait. He went on to become a great king, warrior, poet, singer, musician, writer and spiritual leader of his people. David was anointed by God and he knew that in time, God's time, the plan would come into being.

David's time of waiting prepared him for the very important task of being the good shepherd that his country needed. We too need to wait on the Lord and trust that he will direct us in our walk through the kingdom. David was a leader because he was a follower of God. Later David took his eyes off of God and he fell into great sin. David repented and saw how puny his kingdom was next to God's and he came back and received God's gift of grace and forgiveness. We too can be like David; we can all come back to God's holy light by repenting and realizing that God is our only good shepherd and he will never fail to go out and save the lost sheep. Let us follow David's example and let our baptismal anointing be the beginning of our eternal life with the "Good Shepherd," Jesus, who will set us all free forever (John 8:32).

COLOSSIANS 1:12-20

Paul was bringing to light a heresy in the Colossian church that was the beginning of Gnosticism. The word "Gnosticism" means knowledge and the word "heresy" means a teaching contrary to true doctrine. The Gnostic heresy attacked Christianity in several ways. It held that important secret knowledge was to be kept from most believers, and it taught that the body is evil. Paul responded to this heresy by stating that Jesus chose to dwell in a human body. This heresy denied the humanity of Christ and Paul insisted that in Jesus we see one who is fully alive, human and good.

Gnosticism was beginning to get known and it could easily sway believers' minds that did not know God's will through the teachings of the church. We see many signs of this heresy still lingering on in our church. Today, as in the times of Paul, the best way a church can remain true to the teachings of the Lord is through personal study and church teachings. Paul lists five benefits that Jesus gave us through his death on the cross. He made us to be part of his kingdom. He rescued us from Satan and made us his children. He brought us into his eternal kingdom (Eph 2:5-6).

The Colossian church was caught up in believing that all matter is basically evil. They believed that God, being a spirit which is all good, would never come to earth as a true human being (being human is part of matter). They believed that Christ did not make the world, because they believed God would not create anything that was evil. They believed that special and secret knowledge was the only way people could find God. Paul told them that only Christ has the power to save. Paul told them that Jesus is not only equal to God (Phil 2:6), he is God (John 10:30).

We need to understand that Paul is combatting a heresy that tries to put knowledge above the saving aspects of God. We, like the Colossians, must believe that Jesus Christ is God and not simply some great prophet. Our faith will be hollow, misdirected, and meaningless if we see Jesus as anything less than God.

LUKE 23:35-43

In this passage, Jesus is placed on the cross; and even in his own incredible pain, he seeks to comfort and to forgive others. The place where Jesus was led to be crucified was called "Golgotha" which means "the skull." This was a small hill just outside of the city walls, alongside a main road. The Romans made the execution a public display as an example of what happens to those who defy Roman law. It is ironic that Jesus was asked by James and John for the places of honor next to him in his Kingdom (Mark 10:35-39). Now that Jesus was preparing to enter his Kingdom through his crucifixion, the places on his left and right were to be taken by dying, convicted criminals. This is an incredible example for all of us that Jesus' death was for all men, not just a selected few. We must take Jesus' words to his two power-hungry disciples, to our own hearts and remember that anyone who wants to be close to Jesus must be prepared to suffer and die as he did. The only way to paradise is through the cross. Even as he hung there dying in agony, Jesus was asking his Father to "forgive them for they do not know what they are doing." We need to reflect on those words, especially with what is going on in today's world.

Do we really understand how horrible sin is to God? Do we really understand how horrible it is when we let others starve, go homeless, or we fail to clothe the naked? Do we really understand when we turn our backs on the old, the lonely, the imprisoned, the mentally ill? Do we really understand how horrible it is when we cause others to live in fear, and when we fail to love? Jesus understands that we don't really understand our own cruelty and he shows us the real reason why he died for all of us. He freed us from the deathhold that Satan had on us and now, in faith, we can choose to love, choose to make all men free, and choose to forgive. God tells us that if we accept his son, we will live forever (John 3:16).

Jesus died for us and forgave us our sins. We must also forgive others as he has forgiven us (Matt 6:15). Let us be like the good thief (Dismas) on Jesus' right, and say, "Lord, will you remember me in your Kingdom?" He will say to us as surely as he said to Dismas, "Believe in me and you too shall be with me in Paradise." Jesus is the dawn that breaks into the darkness of sin and gives us the light eternal.

Application

In the first reading, we saw David being patient and humbly waiting to be crowned King in God's time. In the second reading, Paul is telling the Colossians that salvation is a person named Jesus, not some intellectual doctrine. The Gospel shows us that even as he was dying, Jesus was forgiving those who hurt him.

Let us look at the people and situations around us and specifically say, "Father, forgive so and so for what he or she is doing to me." Apply this to family, friends, boss, fellow workers, etc.

IMMACULATE CONCEPTION CYCLE A-B-C

BEFORE YOU BEGIN:

Pray and ask God to speak to you through His Holy Spirit. "THE PARACLETE, THE HOLY SPIRIT WHOM THE FATHER WILL SEND IN MY NAME, WILL INSTRUCT YOU IN EVERYTHING, AND REMIND YOU OF ALL THAT I TOLD YOU." (JOHN 14:26)

FIRST DAY **Reread last week's readings.**

1. What was a helpful or new thought from the readings or from the homily you heard on Sunday?

2. From what you learned, what personal application did you choose to apply to your life this week?

SECOND DAY **GENESIS 3:9-15, 20** **FIRST READING**

("He will strike at your head, while you strike at his heel.")

1. Who called to the man, and what did he ask him? Genesis 3:9

2. Whom did Jesus come to call? Mark 2:17

3. Why did the man hide himself? Genesis 3:10

4. With what are we longing to be clothed? 2 Corinthians 5:1-3

5. What did God ask the man? Genesis 3:11

6. What did the man say about the woman, and what did he do? Genesis 3:12

7. What did the Lord ask the woman, and who did she say tricked her? Genesis 3:13

8. What was Paul's fear that the serpent may corrupt in the people of Corinth? 2 Corinthians 11:3

Personal - When you lose the peace of God within you, whom do you blame? Who is responsible?

9. What did the Lord say to the serpent, what did he say he would put between the serpent and the woman, and at what would he strike? Genesis 3:14-15

10. To what are we to be wise, and what will crush Satan under our feet? Romans 16:19-20

11. What did the man call his wife, and for what reason? Genesis 3:20

Personal - In what way can you protect your mind and thoughts from the evil one?

("...so that we might exist for the praise of his glory.")

1. Who is blessed, and with what has he blessed us? Ephesians 1:3

2. What two things does the Father show toward us? 2 Corinthians 1:3

3. How did God choose us to be before him, and when did he choose us? Ephesians 1:4

4. How do you become holy and without blemish? Ephesians 5:25-27

5. How did God destine us for adoption, and with what was it in accord? Ephesians 1:4-5

6. To whom did he give power to become children of God? John 1:12

7. What are we to praise? Ephesians 1:6

8. How were we chosen, and how does God plan and guide all things? Ephesians 1:11

9. What happens to those who are called according to his purpose, and how are we predestined? Romans 8:28-29

10. For what purpose do we exist? Ephesians 1:12

Personal - When things work out for your good, to whom do you give the glory? In what way do your actions show that you have been chosen by God?

FOURTH DAY   **LUKE 1:26-38**   GOSPEL

("May it be done to me according to your word.")

1. Who was sent by God to a town of Galilee named Nazareth, and when was he sent? Luke 1:26

2. To whom was he sent, and what was her name? Luke 1:27

3. What did the angel say to Mary, and what was her reaction to this greeting? Luke 1:28-29

4. What did the angel tell her not to do, and what did he say would happen to her? Luke 1:30-33

5. What did Jesus say to his disciples, and what cast out fear? Matthew 14:27, 1 John 4:18

6. What was Mary's response to the angel telling her she would conceive and bear a son? Luke 1:34

7. Who did the angel say would come upon Mary, who would over- shadow her, and what would the child be called? Luke 1:35

8. What did the angel tell Joseph not to be, and how did he tell him the child was conceived in Mary? Matthew 1:20

9. What did the angel tell Mary about Elizabeth, and what did he say about God? Luke 1:36-37

10. What was Mary's response, and what did the angel do? Luke 1:38

Personal – What specific plan does God have for your life? Have you responded as Mary did, "May it be done to me according to your word?" Think and pray about this.

FIFTH DAY   **READ PSALM 98:1-4**

("The Lord has made his salvation known,")

Read and meditate on Psalm 98:1-4.

What is the Lord saying to you personally through the Psalm?

How can you apply this to your life?

SIXTH DAY   **READ ALL OF THE COMMENTARY**

GENESIS 3:9-15, 20

Nothing really prepares us for the presence of the devil serpent in the garden. The ancient word "Nahash" brought fear into the hearts of the Israelites because they were forbidden to attend any type of liturgy that involved snake worship upon pain of violating the covenant. The mention of a serpent would identify something evil in the minds of the pious Israelites. The word Nahash and evil were synonymous and the serpent's entrance into the garden brought sinful pollution.

This reading shows us how the serpent was cleverly working his way into new territory, and it shows the existence of evil forces outside the sphere of mankind. We see that God does not crash-in at people with death and punishment. In fact, God places himself on the side of people in the ongoing battle against the serpent.

The message of hope in this passage is that God always remains on man's side. Sin, evil, and Satan are always the enemy of God and man. God states that Satan will be crushed by our Lord and Savior Jesus Christ. The good news is that Jesus has won for us the victory of eternal life. He defeated Satan on the cross at Calvary. We are assured of this because scripture tells us that it is so. God is with us, on our side, to save us from sin. If God is with us, who can be against us? In today's passage the Messianic promise of ultimate salvation has been announced.

EPHESIANS 1:3-6, 11-12

Paul wrote this passage from inside the walls of a Roman prison. He had been a Christian for nearly thirty years, and he had taken three missionary trips and established churches all around the Mediterranean Sea. Ephesus was a commercial, political and religious center for all Asia Minor. The temple of the pagan Greek goddess Diana was located there. It is in this environment that we hear about blessings and heaven.

What is heaven? Heaven is where God is, and blessings mean all the good things that God has given to us, such as salvation, the gifts of the Holy Spirit, and the power to do God's will. We can enjoy these blessings now if we live in an intimate relationship with Jesus Christ.

Paul tells us that God chose us to emphasize that salvation depends totally on God. We are not saved because we deserve it, but because God is gracious and freely gives it. There is no way to take credit for our salvation, or to find room for pride. God chose us, and when we belong to him through Jesus Christ, we are transformed from sinner to a life of grace. God has adopted us as his own children through the sacrifice of Jesus Christ (Romans 8:17). When you feel that your life is not worth much to anyone, remember that you are special in God's eyes, a precious present that brings him great joy. God has offered salvation to you, and when your life seems chaotic, rest in this truth: Jesus is Lord, and God is in control.

LUKE 1:26-38

In the old covenant, Jerusalem was the center and symbol of God's union with his people. In the new covenant, the symbol is no longer a city, but a person, and she is Mary, the Mother of God. She seals the covenant's beginning with the free gift of herself in love.

Mary was young and poor, all characteristics that, to the people of her day, would make her seem very unlikely to be chosen as the Mother of the long-awaited Messiah. But God chose her for one of the most important acts of obedience he has ever demanded of anyone. You might feel that your situation in life today makes you an unlikely candidate for God's service. Do not limit God's choices, He can use you if you, like Mary, trust in Him. Mary's honor of being blessed to become the Mother of God brought her much pain and ridicule. Her peers would gossip about her; her fiance would come close to leaving her; her Son would be tortured and murdered on a cross as a convicted criminal. But through Mary, her Son would become the world's only hope, and this is why Mary has been called by countless generations "Blessed among women." Her submission led to our salvation.

If your blessings lead to sorrows, think of Mary, and wait patiently for God to finish working at his plan. Think of a small young teen-age girl who understood little and trusted much, and said humbly, and yet courageously, that she was a humble servant of the Lord, and he could do with her whatever was in accordance with his Holy Word (Luke 1:38).

Application

The first reading shows us that God is always on man's side, and Satan and sin are always the enemy. The second reading reveals that a blessing is something that God has given you: life, salvation, family, friends, etc. The Gospel shows courage is made up of obedience and trust.

This week let yourself, like Mary, experience being in accordance with God's Word. Take time every day this week to pray alone as she did throughout her life, to study God's holy word, and to do what is necessary in work and school for you. Remember each day to take time to relax and enjoy yourself for a few moments. Develop each day a discipline of prayer, study, work, and leisure. God has chosen you, and you, like Mary, can say, "Yes, Lord, do with me whatever is in accordance with your Holy Word."

CHRISTMAS CYCLE A-B-C

BEFORE YOU BEGIN:

Pray and ask God to speak to you through His Holy Spirit. "THE PARACLETE, THE HOLY SPIRIT WHOM THE FATHER WILL SEND IN MY NAME, WILL INSTRUCT YOU IN EVERYTHING, AND REMIND YOU OF ALL THAT I TOLD YOU." (JOHN 14:26)

FIRST DAY	**Reread last week's readings.**

1. What was a helpful or new thought from the readings or from the homily you heard on Sunday?

2. From what you learned, what personal application did you choose to apply to your life this week?

SECOND DAY	**READ ISAIAH 52:7-10**	**FIRST READING**

("Your God is King")

1. Whose feet are beautiful and what does he announce? Isaiah 52:7, Romans 10:15

2. What are we not to be afraid to cry out? Isaiah 40:9

3. Why do the watchmen shout for joy? Isaiah 52:8

4. What are the watchmen never to do? Isaiah 62:6

5. What are we to do together and for what reason? Isaiah 52:9

6. Why does God comfort and encourage us? 2 Corinthians 1:3-4

7. Whom does the Lord redeem? Psalm 34:23

8. What has the Lord done with his holy arm and in the sight of whom? Isaiah 52:10

9. What will all the ends of the earth see? Isaiah 52:10

10. What is to be known upon the earth, among all nations? Psalm 67:3

Personal - To whom have you been announcing peace and good news? How do people see the joy and salvation of the Lord upon you?

THE BREAD OF LIFE CATHOLIC BIBLE STUDY

("Let all the angels of God worship him.")

1. How did God speak in times past? Hebrews 1:1

2. How does God speak to us now, what did he make him, and what did he do through him? Hebrews 1:2

3. What came to be through him (Jesus)? John 1:3-4

4. Of whom is Jesus the reflection and perfect copy, and by what are all things sustained? Hebrews 1:3

5. When Jesus accomplished purifications from sins what did he do? Hebrews 1:3

6. How did Jesus accomplish this purification? Colossian 1:15-20

7. What has Jesus inherited, and to what is he far superior? Hebrews 1:4

8. Because Jesus humbled himself becoming obedient to death, what did God do to him? Philippians 2:8-9

9. What are the questions asked about angels, and what does he say about his first born? Hebrews 1:5

10. Who is ruler of the kings of the earth and who loves us? Revelations 1:5

Personal – How have you been sustained by God's mighty Word and how have you worshipped his son Jesus this past week ?

FOURTH DAY   **READ JOHN 1:1-18**   **GOSPEL**

("And the Word became flesh and made his dwelling among us,")

1. Who was in the beginning? John 1:1,14

2. Who did Jesus say he was to the Father? John 10:30

3. Who was in the beginning with God and what was this life that came to be through him? John 1:2-4

4. What has the darkness not overcome? John 1:5

5. Who came for testimony, to what did he testify and what did he say about himself? John 1:6-8

6. What does the true light do, how did the world come to be, and who did not accept him? John 1:9-11

7. To those who did accept Jesus what did he give them power to become, in what did they believe, and how were they born? John 1:12-13

8. Who can enter the kingdom of God? John 3:5

9. What has not been revealed and what will happen to us when it is revealed? 1 John 3:2

10. When the Word became flesh of what was he full? John 1:14

11. What did John say about Jesus, what came through Moses, and what came through Jesus? John 1:15-17

12. Who has revealed the Father to us? John 1:18

Personal – What has Jesus revealed to you about the Father?

FIFTH DAY   READ PSALM 98:1-6

("The Lord has made his salvation known.")

Read and meditate on Psalm 98:1-6

What is the Lord saying to you personally through the Psalm?

How can you apply this to your life?

SIXTH DAY   READ ALL OF THE COMMENTARY

ISAIAH 52:7-10

In today's passage God urges his people to draw comfort from past history and to look forward to a greater exodus. He is telling them that it is time to shake off the grief and lethargy that has overtaken them. There is the sound of Good News that God is about to escort his people home to Jerusalem, God's holy city, the city with God's temple. But the people experienced desolation instead of prosperity, and destruction instead of liberty. The people suffered terribly because of their sins, but God promised to restore Jerusalem as a holy city. God reigns, and today he still is very much in control. Today's verse states how beautiful are the feet of those who bring good news of peace and salvation (v.7). How beautiful are the feet of those who go forth and preach the Gospel of Jesus Christ (Romans 10:15). How welcome are those who bring the message of hope to a broken, hopeless, segment of our world.

God's great message of salvation must be through us to others so they can have the chance to respond to the "Good News". How will our loved ones hear it unless we take it to them? How will the nations hear it unless someone takes it to them? God is calling you to take a part in making his message known in your family and your community. Think of one person who needs to hear the good news, and think of something you can do to help him or her hear it. Then you go out and do that act, in Jesus' name, as soon as possible.

HEBREWS 1:1-6

The letter to the Hebrews was written to a group of Jewish Christians who appeared to be having second thoughts about Jesus Christ being their long-awaited Messiah. They should have been a community of mature christians by this time; instead, they seemed to be sort of withdrawn and inward-looking in their spiritual walk. They needed a strong reminder that what they now possess in Christ is far better than what they had before they became Christians.

This passage begins with a tremendous affirmation of Jesus' divinity. Through Jesus, God has made his supreme and final revelation of himself to man. Jesus is the living embodiment of the character and majesty of God. Jesus has dealt with the problem of human sin by sacrificing himself on the cross and paying the ransom for all mankind with his blood. He is now at God's side in the position of supreme power. The angels, whom the Jews came very close to worshipping themselves, worship Jesus Christ. They are spiritual beings and they are to serve and glorify God himself.

The people were well versed in scripture and whether through doubt, persecution, or false teaching, they seemed to be in danger of falling away from their Christian faith. This danger is very much present in today's world. There is much false teaching today and many so-called "Shepherds" are just wolves in sheep's clothing. We need to stay in fellowship, pray, and study God's Holy Word, and follow the teachings of our church. Take the time this Christmas season to thank the Lord for bringing his light into your heart and bringing about a better relationship with him. Remember, it is Jesus birthday, and the present he wants most is YOU!

JOHN 1:1-18

This passage clearly shows that what Jesus taught and what he did are tied inseparably to who he is. In today's reading John shows Jesus as fully human and fully God. Although Jesus took upon himself full humanity and lived as a man experiencing all the emotions that all of us have, he never ceased to be God who has always existed. This is the truth about Jesus, and the foundation of all truth. If we cannot or do not believe this basic truth, we will not have enough faith to trust our eternal destiny to him. This is the reason John writes this gospel, to build faith and confidence in Jesus Christ, so that we may believe he truly was and is God in the flesh (John 20:30-31).

Jesus' life brings light to mankind, in his light we see ourselves as we really are: sinners in need of a savior. We fall on our knees, and like the shepherds at the little cave in Bethlehem, we too give praise and glory to the light of the world, our Lord and Savior Jesus Christ. The wise men followed the light of a star to see the light of the world. When we follow Jesus, the light of the world, we can avoid walking blindly and falling into sin. He lights the path ahead of us so we can see how to live. He removes the darkness of sin from our lives, and if we have allowed the light of Christ to shine in our lives this Christmas season, then we will never stumble in the darkness.

As the world celebrates the birth of Christ, let yourself be reborn spiritually. Through faith in Christ this new birth changes us from the inside out - rearranging our attitudes, desires and motives. Have you asked Christ to make you a new person on Christmas day? This fresh start is available to all who believe in him. Merry Christmas.

Application

The first reading tells us how beautiful are the feet of those who go forth and proclaim God's Word. The second reading shows that encouragement and discipline lead to a stronger commitment to God. The gospel reveals Christmas as a time of new birth, a time of giving your life over to God.

This week, give those you love the greatest present you could give them for Christmas. How beautiful are your feet as you go forth and gift them with the gift of your presence, of your love, of salvation by bringing them to Christ. Remember, it is Christ's birthday, and the presents should all be for him, and he only wants you!

OCTAVE OF CHRISTMAS CYCLE A-B-C

FEAST OF MARY, MOTHER OF GOD

BEFORE YOU BEGIN:

Pray and ask God to speak to you through His Holy Spirit. "THE PARACLETE, THE HOLY SPIRIT WHOM THE FATHER WILL SEND IN MY NAME, WILL INSTRUCT YOU IN EVERYTHING, AND REMIND YOU OF ALL THAT I TOLD YOU." (JOHN 14:26)

FIRST DAY   **Reread last week's readings.**

1. What was a helpful or new thought from the readings or from the homily you heard on Sunday?

2. From what you learned, what personal application did you choose to apply to your life this week?

SECOND DAY   READ NUMBERS 6:22-27   **FIRST READING**

("The Lord bless you and keep you!")

1. To whom was the Lord speaking, and to whom did he tell him to speak? Numbers 6:22-23

2. Who was Aaron, and what did the Lord say to Moses about him? Exodus 4:14-16

3. About what was Moses to speak to them? Numbers 6:23

4. What six things were included in the blessing? Numbers 6:24-26

5. Who will be blessed? Proverbs 28:20

6. What brings wealth? Proverbs 10:22

7. Who was blessed by the Lord, what did he do for her, and what was her response? Luke 1:46-55

8. What has the Lord given us? Psalm 118:27

9. Who did Jesus say he was? John 8:12

10. What shall be invoked upon the Israelites, and what will the Lord do? Numbers 6:27

Personal – In what way have you blessed a family member or a friend? What do others see shining forth from your face?

("...God sent the spirit of his Son into our hearts,
crying out, 'Abba, Father!'")

1. Under what was God's Son born? Galatians 4:4

2. What did God's Son do? Galatians 4:5

3. What happens to everyone who believes in Jesus? John 3:16

4. Who did the law come through, and what did Jesus bring? John 1:17

5. Who are the children of God, and who bears witness that we are? Romans 8:14-16

6. What proof do we have that we are His children? Galatians 4:6

7. To whom did he give the power to become children of God? John 1:12-13

8. Why are the children of God not known to the world? 1 John 3:1

9. What are we no longer, and what has he made us? Galatians 4:7

10. With whom are the children of God joint heirs? Romans 8:17

Personal – In what way have you cried out to "Abba," Daddy, this week? What have you inherited from God? What are your parents leaving you as an inheritance, or what are you leaving your children as an inheritance?

("And Mary kept all these things, reflecting on them in her heart.")

1. When the shepherds went off in haste, who did they find? Luke 2:16

2. Why did Mary lay her firstborn Son in a manger? Luke 2:7

3. What did the shepherds do when they saw the child? Luke 2:17

4. What was the reaction of those who were told the message? Luke 2:18

5. What amazed or astonished the people listening to Jesus? Matthew 7:28-29

Personal – What have you seen and made known to others since you have been studying God's Word?

6. What did Mary do? Luke 2:19

7. What did Mary do when Jesus became lost and then told her he was about his Father's business? Luke 2:49-51

Personal – What have you personally pondered in your heart that God revealed to you, and how have you followed Mary's example?

8.   How did the shepherds return? Luke 2:20

9.   What was the reaction of the paralytic and the people upon the healing? Luke 5:25-26

10.   What happened on the eighth day, and to whom had the name been given? Luke 1:31, 2:21

11.   What has his name done for us? Acts 4:12

12.   To what is the name Jesus inherited far superior? Hebrews 1:3-4

Personal – What name has been given to you, and of what is it a reflection?

FIFTH DAY   **READ PSALM 67:2-6, 8**

("...may he let his face shine upon us.")

Read and meditate on Psalm 67:2-6, 8.

What is the Lord saying to you personally through the Psalm?

How can you apply this to your life?

SIXTH DAY   **READ ALL OF THE COMMENTARY**

NUMBERS 6:22-27

When Mary said, "Generation after generation shall call me blessed of God," she was recognizing and accepting the gift God had given her (Luke 1:48). If Mary had denied her incredible position, she would have been throwing God's blessing back at him.

In today's reading we are being shown that a blessing was one way of asking God's divine favor to rest upon others. All of God's blessings had their fulfillment in the coming of Christ on earth. Mary received the fullness of these promises and blessings when she said, "Be it done unto me according to thy word." At that very moment she conceived Jesus Christ in her womb. As proof of this blessing we have the angel Gabriel's words as he salutes her as "full of grace." She has the full friendship of God, and no man or woman had ever received the fullness of God's blessing until then. A blessing conveys that God will (1) bless and protect, (2) be pleased because of us, (3) be gracious, merciful, and compassionate to us, (4) show favor to us, and (5) give us peace. When we ask God to bless us and others, we are asking him to do these five things. We will have the full friendship of God as we ask him to bless others as well as ourselves.

Today, on this special feast, let us thank God for all the blessings that he has given Mary, the Mother of God. We have all profited through her blessings; and the title, Mother of God, that the church confirmed in her regard at the Council of Ephesus in 431 AD, demonstrates all this.

GALATIANS 4:4-7

In today's reading Paul uses the example of slavery to show that before Christ came and died for our sins, people were in bondage to the law. By becoming enslaved to the law, people thought they could be saved. At just the right time, God sent Jesus to earth to die for our sins, and we who were once slaves are now God's very own children with an intimate relationship with Him. For centuries the Jews were wondering when their Messiah would come, but God's timing was perfect.

We may sometimes wonder if God will ever respond to our prayers, but we must never stop trusting or give up hope. At the right time, he will respond to us. Jesus was born of a woman and was subject to God's law and fulfilled it. His death brought freedom for us who were enslaved to sin so we could be adopted into God's family. Under the Roman law, an adopted child was guaranteed all legal rights to his father's property. As adopted children of God, we share with Jesus all rights to God's resources.

As God's heirs, we can claim what he has provided for us; which is our full identity as his children. The Old Testament was based on the law, but was only a shadow of things to come. Christianity is the fulfillment of the Old Testament. Christianity is the reality, and the reality is God has become man, and man is now free and has been adopted into God's family as rightful heirs to the kingdom.

LUKE 2:16-21

What a tremendous sign of comfort and hope it is when we read that the first visitors to lay eyes on the long-awaited Messiah were simple, hard-working, uneducated, common folks called shepherds. Even in birth Jesus has shown us the ultimate in humility, and his choice of those who were part of his birth experience were of humble origins themselves.

Can you imagine the thoughts that flowed through Mary's head as she observed the shepherds coming to pay homage to her Son? She certainly was aware of the power and beauty of the angels singing praises of glory to God to their new born king. The Jewish custom was when a new child was born the local musicians would come by and sing some congratulatory songs. Mary had, not earthly musicians to sing to her son, but she had a choir of angels to fill the air with heavenly sounds.

On this very special day, we can honor Mary in her blessed role as Mother of God. God himself honored her by making her the mother of his Son. Jesus, in one of his last acts on this earth before dying on the cross, made his mother our mother. It was through no merit of her own that she earned this dignity. This honor was given as a sheer gift of God. When we honor her, we are in fact thanking God for his gift of her to us.

Application

The first reading explains that a blessing is God giving someone his protection and direction. The second reading tells how the Old Testament was a time of preparation, and the New Testament was a time of the reality of God entering into human history as a human being named Jesus. The Gospel reveals Jesus beginning his life on earth humbly, and in humility he went to his death on a cross for us.

This week, let the humility of the shepherds be your model of conduct during the Christmas holidays. Bring to your family, friends, and co-workers, the gift of listening, the gift of gentleness, and the gift of humility. Mary was a role model for the whole world, for both male and female.

ASSUMPTION CYCLE A-B-C

BEFORE YOU BEGIN:

Pray and ask God to speak to you through His Holy Spirit. "THE PARACLETE, THE HOLY SPIRIT WHOM THE FATHER WILL SEND IN MY NAME, WILL INSTRUCT YOU IN EVERYTHING, AND REMIND YOU OF ALL THAT I TOLD YOU." (JOHN 14:26)

FIRST DAY   **Reread last week's readings.**

1. What was a helpful or new thought from the readings or from the homily you heard on Sunday?

2. From what you learned, what personal application did you choose to apply to your life this week?

SECOND DAY   **READ REVELATION 11:19; 12:1-6, 10**   **FIRST READING**

("Her child was caught up to God and his throne.")

1. When God's temple in heaven was opened, what could be seen, and what was happening? Revelation 11:19

2. What was in the ark of the covenant? Hebrews 9:4

3. What did Jesus say would happen before the persecution? Luke 21:5-12

4. What appeared in the sky, who was clothed with the sun, the moon under her feet, and twelve stars as a crown on her head? Revelation 12:1

5. What was happening to the woman? Revelation 12:2

6. What did God say to the woman after she sinned? Genesis 3:16

7. What was another sign that appeared in the sky? Revelation 12:3

8. What did the tail of the dragon do, who did it stand before, and what was it about to do? Revelation 12:4

9. To what did the woman give birth, what was he destined to do, and what happened to him? Revelation 12:5

10. Where did the woman go, and what happened to her? Revelation 12:6

11. What did a loud voice in heaven say, and who was cast out? Revelation 12:10

Personal – How has Satan been accusing you, and how has God protected you from him?

THIRD DAY   **READ 1 CORINTHIANS 15:20-26**   **SECOND READING**

("The last enemy to be destroyed is death.")

1. What has Christ done, and what is he to those who have fallen asleep?
    1 Corinthians 15:20

2. What did God the Father give us in his great mercy? 1 Peter 1:3-4

3. What will happen to our mortal bodies, and how does it happen? Romans 8:11

4. How did death come, and how did the resurrection of the dead come?
    1 Corinthians 15:21

5. How did death come to man? Genesis 3:17-19, Romans 5:12-18

6. Just as in Adam who dies, so too in Christ who is brought to life?
    1 Corinthians 15:22

7. In what order are they brought to life, and then what happens?
    1 Corinthians 15:23-24

8. How long must he reign? 1 Corinthians 15:25

9. What is the last enemy to be destroyed? 1 Corinthians 15:26

10. What did Jesus Christ do? 2 Timothy 1:10

Personal - When you have faced the fear of death in your life, have you been able to overcome that fear through Christ's resurrection?

FOURTH DAY   **READ LUKE 1:39-56**   **GOSPEL**

("He has thrown down rulers from their thrones,
but lifted up the lowly.")

1. Who traveled to the hill country to a town of Judah, whose house did she enter, and who did she greet? Luke 1:39-40

2. What did the baby do that was in Elizabeth's womb, with what was she filled, and with what did she cry out? Luke 1:41-42

3. What was Elizabeth's response? Luke 1:43-44

Personal - What is your response to the presence of God in your life?

4. What did Elizabeth say for what was Mary blessed? Luke 1:45

5. What did Mary say her soul proclaimed, and in what did her spirit rejoice?
    Luke 1:46-47

6. Who and what is the joy of my soul? Isaiah 61:10

7. What has the Lord looked upon, and what would all ages call her? Luke 1:48

8. What does God do for the lowly? Psalm 113:7

9.   What has the mighty one done for Mary, what does she say about his name, and to whom is his mercy? Luke 1:49-50

10.   What has he shown, what has he done with the arrogant of mind and heart, and the rulers? Luke 1:51-52

11.   What has he done with the lowly, the hungry and the rich? Luke 1:52-53

12.   What has he done to Israel, and to what was it according? Luke 1:54-55

13.   How long did Mary remain with Elizabeth, and then where did she go? Luke 1:56

Personal - How can you identify with Mary's lowliness? In what way has God lifted you up, or in what way has he brought you down?

FIFTH DAY   **READ PSALM 45:10-12, 16**

("They are borne in with gladness and joy;")

Read and meditate on Psalm 45:10-12, 16.

What is the Lord saying to you personally through the Psalm?

How can you apply this to your life?

SIXTH DAY   **READ ALL OF THE COMMENTARY**

REVELATION 11:19; 12:1-6, 10

John was writing this passage for a persecuted church to take heart. The woman stands for God's faithful people (the church) and Mary, the Mother of Christ, the Messiah. The pain of childbirth refers to the sufferings of the early church, the flight into the desert is also a description of pain. The sun covering the woman is an image of the glory of Mary, the mother of the Messiah. The powers of evil are represented by a dragon who fights bitterly to kill the Messiah at birth but fails.

Jesus ultimately fulfills his mission by dying on the cross for the sins of the world and triumphantly returns to the throne of God. Mary also has triumphed in her role of obedience and humility. The dragon bent on destruction is Satan, and we are reminded that the struggle of Christians today is part of a much greater conflict. The message of today's reading is that although Satan is strong and powerful and his attack is fierce, his time is short. He has been overpowered by Christ. God's people at all times and everywhere are under his sovereign protection. This reading brings out the closeness between Christ our Messiah and his Blessed Mother. Mary was chosen from all eternity to be the Mother of God. She was intimately connected with her Son in the completion of this divine plan. Satan directed much opposition to Mary, but she was triumphant in her mission here on earth. We celebrate Mary's assumption into heaven because we believe that, after Christ, she occupies the next highest place of glory.

1 CORINTHIANS 15:20-26

In today's reading Paul is proving that we shall all rise from the dead one day. The Christian converts of Corinth were not denying the resurrection of Jesus Christ, but the resurrection of the body. Paul was very strong and clear in his reply that if you denied the resurrection of the body, then you have denied the resurrection of Jesus Christ. In fact, you have emptied the Christian message of its truth and the Christian life of its reality.

Paul goes on to tell them that one of the basic doctrines of the Christian faith which they have accepted was Christ's resurrection. Paul tells them that if it is for this life only that we hope, we of all people are most to be pitied. This means that if there was no resurrection for us then Christianity can gain us nothing but the grave.

It is very important today that the center of Christian teaching, which is Christ died, was buried, was raised from the dead, and appeared again on earth, be believed. Christ's burial emphasized the reality of his dying. Christ then was raised from the dead by God and left an empty tomb. Christ then appeared to many leaders of the church. Jesus' resurrection is a promise of the future to all those who die. The final enemy is death, and Christ defeated death on the cross at Calvary.

The Good News is a message of hope, and Paul tells the Corinthians and us that, like Christ, we too will rise one day and be with him in a new incorruptible body. The foundation of the church is being the bearer and the repository of the Good News. We are told that no man can have God for his Father unless he has the church for his mother. Mary is the mother of all of us who are "church," and we celebrate her being raised up to be with her Son and Messiah, Jesus Christ.

LUKE 1:39-56

Today's Gospel shows us something about the kind of woman through whom God chose to fulfill his purpose. Mary, upon hearing the incredible news about her aged relative, Elizabeth, becoming pregnant, sets out on a four or five day journey south. The meeting becomes a meeting of special joy and significance because they both had so much to share.

The power of their thoughts and feelings emerge very strongly in Elizabeth's benediction and Mary's hymn of praise. The gift of blessedness makes a powerful impact on Mary. To her was granted the blessedness of being the Mother of the Son of God. Her heart must have been bursting with joy at so great a privilege. Yet, that very blessedness was to be a sword to pierce her heart. It meant that one day she would see her only Son hanging on a cross.

Many times, to be blessed and chosen by God means a crown of joy and a cross of sorrow. We must come to know that God does not choose a person for ease and comfort and selfish joy. He chooses one to do a task that will take all one's head, heart and hands. God chooses a person in order to use him or her. It is the mystery of blessedness that it confers on a person both the greatest joy and the greatest task in all the world. We will do well to remember that Jesus Christ came, not to make life easy, but to make men great.

We celebrate today that "all ages have come to call her blessed." She saw nothing in herself but a maid-servant who understood little, but trusted and obeyed completely. Let us all assume her holy attributes of gentleness, humility and obedience, and we too will be blessed.

Application

The first reading reveals the Spirit within us is stronger than he that is in the world (1 John 4:4). The second reading showed that a Christian is born to live forever. The Gospel reveals that a blessing is a gift from God to you, and for others.

This week can be a time of great joy and possibly even a time of great pain for you. You can ask God to bless you with a spirit that hungers and longs for him. You will be opposed by many distractions when you decide to submit yourself to Christ.

Each day, make time alone to pray to Jesus. Read a passage of scripture and meditate on it, and then, like Mary, be submissive to someone who is near you. That means, putting that person first. It might mean ridicule or even rejection. Remember, blessedness is loving others, not yourself. Jesus died for you and this makes you blessed too.

ALL SAINTS DAY CYCLE A-B-C

BEFORE YOU BEGIN:

Pray and ask God to speak to you through His Holy Spirit. "THE PARACLETE, THE HOLY SPIRIT WHOM THE FATHER WILL SEND IN MY NAME, WILL INSTRUCT YOU IN EVERYTHING, AND REMIND YOU OF ALL THAT I TOLD YOU." (JOHN 14:26)

FIRST DAY   **Reread last week's readings.**

1. What was a helpful or new thought from the readings or from the homily you heard on Sunday?

2. From what you learned, what personal application did you choose to apply to your life this week?

SECOND DAY   **READ REVELATION 7:2-4, 9-14**   **FIRST READING**

("They prostrated themselves before the throne,")

1. What was seen coming up from the east, what was he holding, and to whom did he cry out in a loud voice? Revelation 7:2

2. On whom has God the Father set his seal? John 6:27

3. With what were you sealed as the first installment of your inheritance towards redemption? Ephesians 1:13-14

4. What were the angels told not to damage until the seal was put upon whose foreheads? Revelation 7:3

5. How many had been marked, and from where were they? Revelation 7:4

6. Who were standing with the lamb, and what were they doing? Revelation 14:1, 3

7. What was John's vision, before whom did they stand, and what were they wearing? Revelation 7:9

8. From whom did they say salvation comes, and where is he seated? Revelation 7:10

9. What did the angels standing around the throne do? Revelation 7:11

10. As the angels worshipped God, what did they exclaim? Revelation 7:12

11. What did one of the elders speak up and say, and who were the ones wearing the white robes? Revelation 7:13-14

12.   What did the blood of Jesus do for us? Hebrews 9:14, 1 John 1:7

Personal – How often do you worship the Lord during the day in practice for the time you will spend in eternity worshipping him?

THIRD DAY   **READ 1 John 3:1-3**   **SECOND READING**

("What we shall be has not yet been revealed.")

1.   What has the Father bestowed on us, what might we be called, and why does the world not know us? 1 John 3:1

2.   How do we become a child of God? John 1:12, John 3:16

3.   What did Jesus make known to us, and for what reason? John 17:25-26

4.   What are we now, what has not been revealed, and what will happen when it is revealed? 1 John 3:2

5.   What does Jesus do to our bodies? Philippians 3:20-21

6.   Why should we remain in Jesus? 1 John 2:28

7.   What is happening to us, and how is the veil lifted? 2 Corinthians 3:14-18

8.   What does everyone do who has this hope based on him? 1 John 3:3

9.   How do we make ourselves pure? 1 John 2:5-6

10.   What is pure and true? Psalm 19:10

Personal – How have you become more like Jesus this past week? Be specific.

FOURTH DAY   **READ MATTHEW 5:1-12**   **GOSPEL**

("Blessed are you when they insult you and persecute you
and utter every kind of slander against you because of me.")

1.   Where did Jesus go when he saw the crowds, and who came to him? Matthew 5:1

2.   What did he do with the disciples, what did he say belongs to the poor in spirit and those who are persecuted for the sake of righteousness? Matthew 5:2-3, 10

3.   What will happen to those who mourn and to those who are meek? Matthew 5:4-5

4.   Where is God's dwelling, and what will he do? Revelation 21:3-4

5.   In what shall the meek delight? Psalm 37:11

6. What will happen to those who hunger and thirst for righteousness and to those who are merciful? Matthew 5:6-7

7. Over what does mercy triumph? James 2:13

8. Who will the clean of heart see, and who will be called the children of God? Matthew 5:8-9

9. Whose heart is clean? Psalm 24:4-5

10. Who is to rejoice and be glad, for what reason, and who was persecuted before them? Matthew 5:10-12

11. What happened to those who proclaimed the name of Jesus, and what was their reaction? Acts 5:40-42

Personal - In which of the beatitudes do you find yourself blessed? In what way have you been persecuted for your faith by your family, friends, work associates or school friends?

FIFTH DAY   **READ PSALM 24:1-6**

("The Lord's are the earth and its fullness;")

Read and meditate on Psalm 24:1-6.

What is the Lord saying to you personally through the Psalm?

How can you apply this to your life?

SIXTH DAY   **READ ALL OF THE COMMENTARY**

REVELATION 7:2-4, 9-14

This reading shows John is seeing a vision of the last terrible day and in particular the great tribulation which is to come. During the tribulation there will be a final assault by all the forces of evil and a final devastation of the earth. But before this time of horror and devastation comes, the faithful are to be sealed with the great seal of God so they may survive it. It is not that they escape from experiencing it, but that they may survive it.

A seal on a scroll identified and protected its contents. God places his great seal on his followers, identifying them as his own and guaranteeing his protection over their souls. This is why we have the Sacrament of Baptism, and it shows how valuable we are to him. Our physical bodies may be beaten or even destroyed, but nothing can harm the souls of those marked by God.

We see the seal of God that is placed on the forehead of the believers is the exact opposite of the mark of the beast (Revelation 13:6). These two marks place the people in two very distinct categories. There are those owned by God and those owned by Satan. Satan is always trying to imitate the great works of God.

The number of believers in today's passage symbolizes completeness. All God's followers will be brought safely to him. You will always be protected from spiritual harm when Jesus is Lord and master of your life and soul, and not even death can separate his love from you (Romans 8:39).

1 JOHN 3:1-3

As believers, our self-worth is based on God's love for us and that he calls us his children. To belong and to be loved is the deepest need there is in a human being. The numbers in the mental hospitals and prisons would be drastically reduced if the people in those places really had a good self-image.

We are God's children now, not just sometime in the distant future. We are children of the king, and we are heirs to his kingdom of heaven. We have been adopted into God's family through the sacrifice of our Lord Jesus. To be called a child of God is a great privilege, and yet, we are not just called children of God; we are the children of God. By nature a man is a creature of God, but it is by grace that he becomes a child of God.

The Old Testament tells us that the Israelites are the covenant people of God. In the New Testament, by a deliberate act of adoption on the part of God, the children enter into his family. We become his children in the intimate and loving sense of the term only by an act of God's initiating grace and the response of their own hearts in the Sacrament of Baptism. When we become children of God, our life has only just begun. We will continue to grow in the image and likeness of God by following the teachings and examples of Jesus Christ. We can do this through the power of the Holy Spirit and the loving guidance of the Catholic Church. One day you will be face to face with "ABBA," your heavenly Father and your Loving Savior Jesus Christ, and what a wonderful joy it will be when he says to you, "Welcome, my obedient, loving child."

MATTHEW 5:1-12

This passage reveals to us the Christian attitude of being. Jesus is not calling his disciples to live in such a way that they will be blessed. he is in fact saying that because they are living in accordance with God's will, they are already blessed. Blessed means being joyful, and this is a joy that no man or circumstance can take away.

This passage begins with Jesus sitting down as he began to preach. This was a signal that what he was saying was an official message, a message that was to be heard and responded to. When a Jewish rabbi was teaching officially, he sat to teach. We speak today of a professor's chair, and the Pope only speaks "Ex cathedra" from his seat.

We hear Jesus say blessed are the poor in spirit, for theirs is the kingdom of God. The Jews had four levels of being poor. The first was just being unable to make ends meet, second was having no power, third was having no influence, and finally, having no earthly resources whatsoever and putting their whole trust in God. The Jews described the word poor as the humble and hapless man who puts his whole trust in God. This really means blessed is someone who realized his own helplessness and put his whole trust in God. He will become completely detached from things and will become completely attached to God. The man who is poor in spirit is the one who has realized that things mean nothing and that God means everything.

Do not think that poverty is a good thing. Jesus would never call living in slums, not having enough to eat, and poor health as being blessed. The poverty which is blessed is the poverty of the spirit. The kingdom of heaven awaits the one who realizes that God is his real treasure. Are you that person?

Application

The first reading shows that God has placed his great seal on all of his believers through baptism. The second reading tells us that adoption means being selected and God chose you to be his child. The Gospel reveals that nothing can separate us from God's love, not even death (Romans 8:39).

This week, let yourself be completely poor in spirit. Let your attachment be only to people, not things. Look in your closet and see what clothes you do not really need and then give them to the poor. Look at your financial picture and see what you can cut out of your spending and give that expense to the poor.

Look at how you spend your time. Is it mostly for your benefit? Try to see where you can give more time to others in need. Mother Teresa says, "Unless life is lived for others, it is not worthwhile." Blessed are you because you are poor in spirit (Matthew 5:3).

NOTES:

NOTES:

NOTES:

NOTES:

NOTES:

NOTES: